W9-CUG-753

O
V]
Y
S

MANU LARCENET

ORDINARY
VICTORIES

colors by Patrice Larcenet

ComicsLit

ISBN-10: 1-56163-423-9
ISBN-13: 978-1-56163-423-1
© Dargaud 2004 by Larcenet
www.dargaud.com
© 2005 NBM for the English translation
Translation by Joe Johnson
Lettering by Ortho
Printed in China

3   2

Library of Congress Cataloging-in-Publication Data

Larcenet, Manu.
  [Combat ordinaire. English]
  Ordinary victories / Manu Larcenet ; [translation by Joe Johnson].
      p. cm.
  ISBN 1-56163-423-9 (pbk.)
  I. Title.
  PN6747.L37O7313 2005
  741.5'944--dc22

                              2005041463

Comicslit is an imprint
and trademark of

NANTIER · BEALL · MINOUSTCHINE
Publishing inc.
new york

Ordinary Victories

You could not say they were slaves
But from there to say they lived...
Jacques Brel

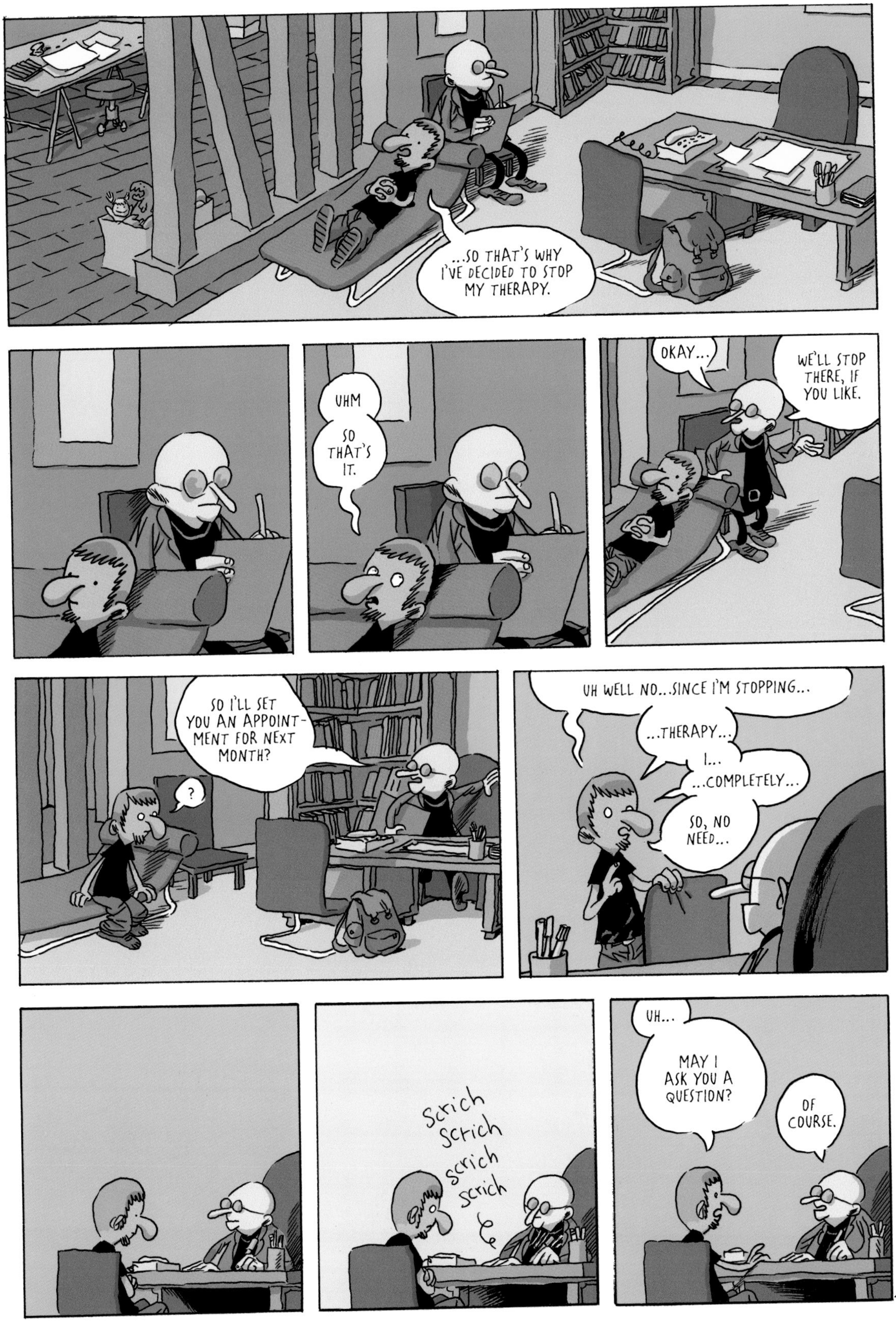
...SO THAT'S WHY I'VE DECIDED TO STOP MY THERAPY.
UHM
SO THAT'S IT.
OKAY...
WE'LL STOP THERE, IF YOU LIKE.
SO I'LL SET YOU AN APPOINT-MENT FOR NEXT MONTH?
?
UH WELL NO...SINCE I'M STOPPING...
...THERAPY...
I...
...COMPLETELY...
SO, NO NEED...
Scrich
Scrich
scrich
Scrich
UH...
MAY I ASK YOU A QUESTION?
OF COURSE.

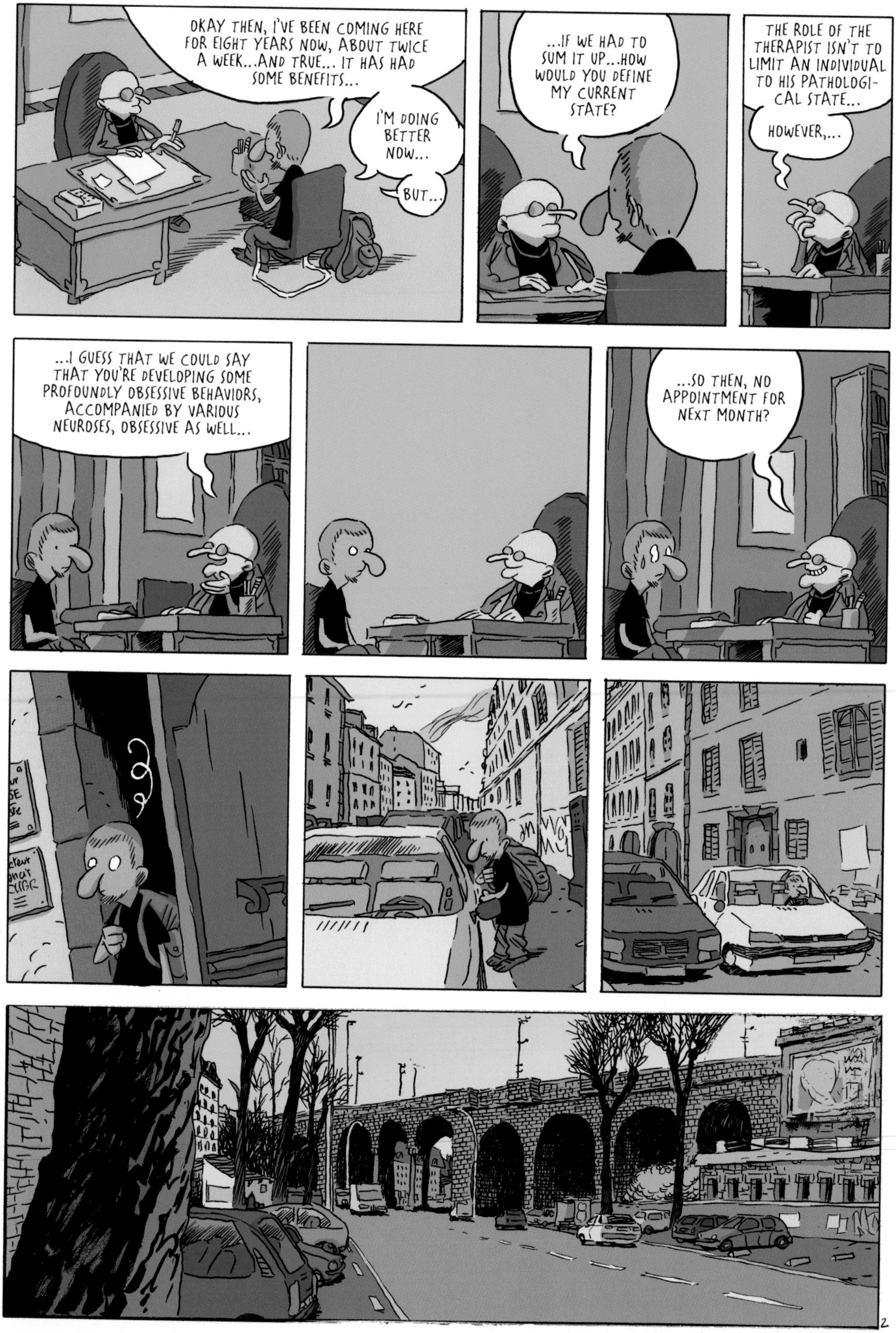
OKAY THEN, I'VE BEEN COMING HERE FOR EIGHT YEARS NOW, ABOUT TWICE A WEEK...AND TRUE... IT HAS HAD SOME BENEFITS...
I'M DOING BETTER NOW...
BUT...
...IF WE HAD TO SUM IT UP...HOW WOULD YOU DEFINE MY CURRENT STATE?
THE ROLE OF THE THERAPIST ISN'T TO LIMIT AN INDIVIDUAL TO HIS PATHOLOGICAL STATE...
HOWEVER,...
...I GUESS THAT WE COULD SAY THAT YOU'RE DEVELOPING SOME PROFOUNDLY OBSESSIVE BEHAVIORS, ACCOMPANIED BY VARIOUS NEUROSES, OBSESSIVE AS WELL...
...SO THEN, NO APPOINTMENT FOR NEXT MONTH?

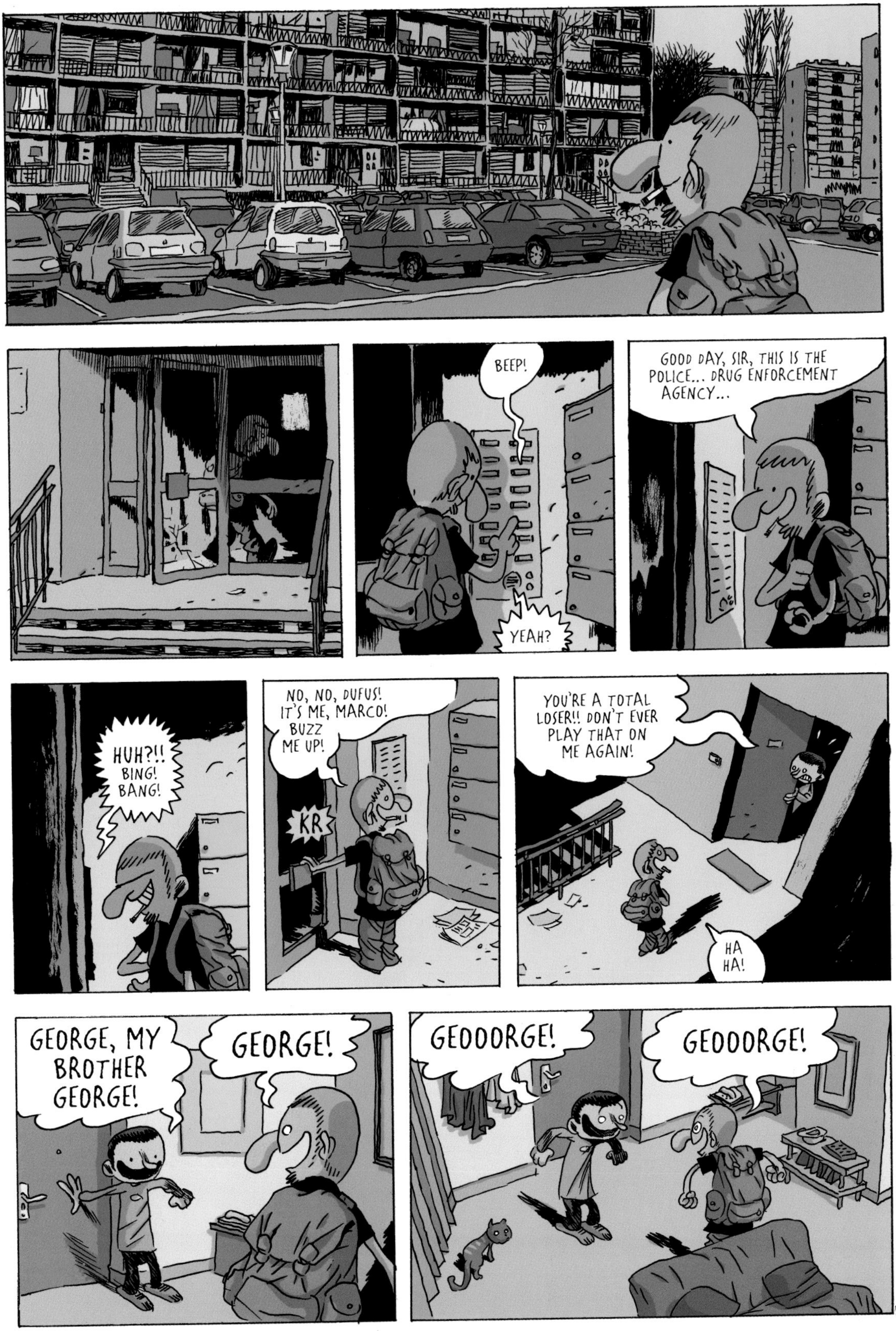
BEEP!
YEAH?
GOOD DAY, SIR, THIS IS THE POLICE... DRUG ENFORCEMENT AGENCY...
HUH?!! BING! BANG!
NO, NO, DUFUS! IT'S ME, MARCO! BUZZ ME UP!
KR
YOU'RE A TOTAL LOSER!! DON'T EVER PLAY THAT ON ME AGAIN!
HA HA!
GEORGE, MY BROTHER GEORGE!
GEORGE!
GEOOORGE!
GEOOORGE!

GEDOORGE...

WHAT?

I WAS JUST WONDERING WHY WE CALL EACH OTHER "GEORGE" EVERY TIME WE SEE ONE ANOTHER.

HA HA! YOU DON'T REMEMBER?

UH... NOPE.

WHEN WE WERE KIDS, MOM WOULD RENT THE VIDEO "OF MICE AND MEN" FOR US...

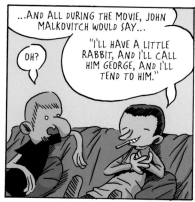

...AND ALL DURING THE MOVIE, JOHN MALKOVITCH WOULD SAY...

OH?

"I'LL HAVE A LITTLE RABBIT, AND I'LL CALL HIM GEORGE, AND I'LL TEND TO HIM."

EVER SINCE, WE'VE BEEN CALLING EACH OTHER "GEORGE."

OH? IT'S SORTA STUPID, WHEN YOU THINK ABOUT IT. YEAH.

GEDORGE!

GEDORGE!

I DIDN'T KNOW YOU WERE AROUND. YOU SHOULD HAVE CALLED ME.

NAHH

I CAME UP FOR ONE LAST THERAPY SESSION.

ARE YOU GONNA GO SEE THE FOLKS?

OH I DON'T KNOW. THE LAST TIME, POPS WASN'T DOING WELL AT ALL.

YOU OUGHT TO HEAD THERE FOR A DAY. IT'D MAKE MOM HAPPY.

4

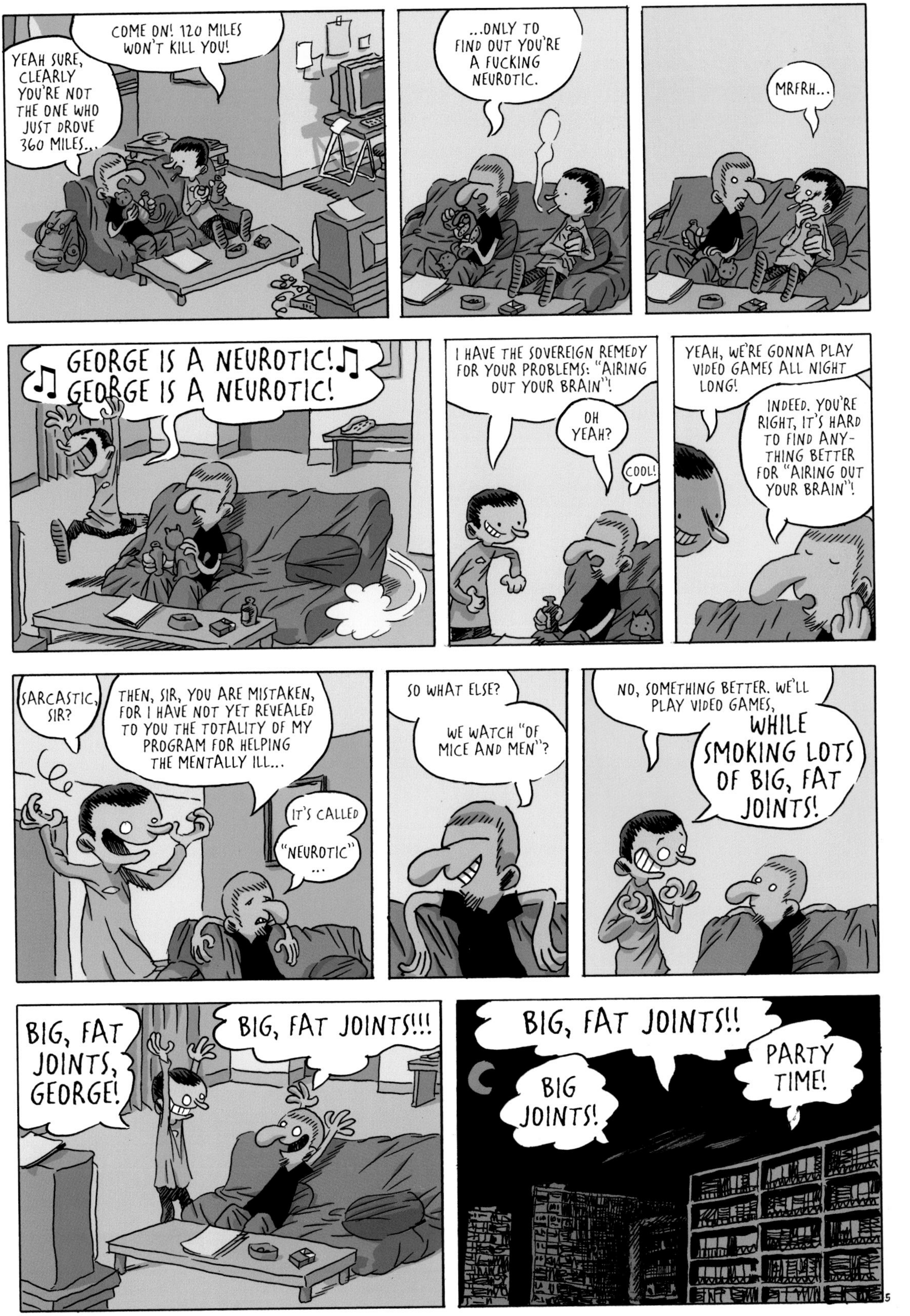

YEAH SURE, CLEARLY YOU'RE NOT THE ONE WHO JUST DROVE 360 MILES...
COME ON! 120 MILES WON'T KILL YOU!
...ONLY TO FIND OUT YOU'RE A FUCKING NEUROTIC.
MRFRH...
♫ GEORGE IS A NEUROTIC! ♫ GEORGE IS A NEUROTIC!
I HAVE THE SOVEREIGN REMEDY FOR YOUR PROBLEMS: "AIRING OUT YOUR BRAIN"!
OH YEAH?
COOL!
YEAH, WE'RE GONNA PLAY VIDEO GAMES ALL NIGHT LONG!
INDEED. YOU'RE RIGHT, IT'S HARD TO FIND ANY-THING BETTER FOR "AIRING OUT YOUR BRAIN"!
SARCASTIC, SIR?
THEN, SIR, YOU ARE MISTAKEN, FOR I HAVE NOT YET REVEALED TO YOU THE TOTALITY OF MY PROGRAM FOR HELPING THE MENTALLY ILL...
IT'S CALLED
"NEUROTIC"...
SO WHAT ELSE?
WE WATCH "OF MICE AND MEN"?
NO, SOMETHING BETTER. WE'LL PLAY VIDEO GAMES,
WHILE SMOKING LOTS OF BIG, FAT JOINTS!
BIG, FAT JOINTS, GEORGE!
BIG, FAT JOINTS!!!
BIG, FAT JOINTS!!
BIG JOINTS!
PARTY TIME!

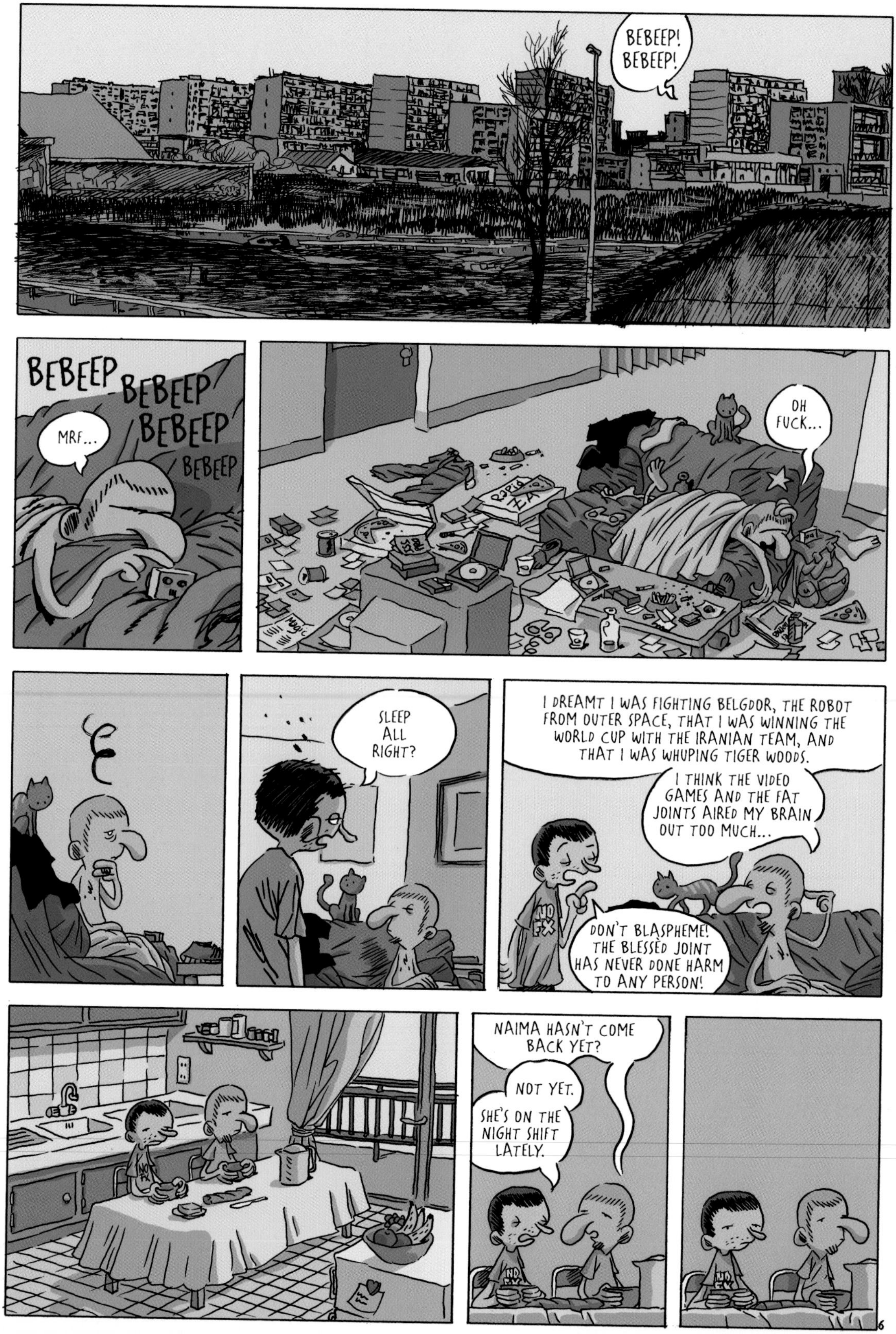
BEBEEP! BEBEEP!
BEBEEP BEBEEP BEBEEP BEBEEP
MRF...
OH FUCK...
SLEEP ALL RIGHT?
I DREAMT I WAS FIGHTING BELGDOR, THE ROBOT FROM OUTER SPACE, THAT I WAS WINNING THE WORLD CUP WITH THE IRANIAN TEAM, AND THAT I WAS WHUPING TIGER WOODS.
I THINK THE VIDEO GAMES AND THE FAT JOINTS AIRED MY BRAIN OUT TOO MUCH...
DON'T BLASPHEME! THE BLESSED JOINT HAS NEVER DONE HARM TO ANY PERSON!
NAIMA HASN'T COME BACK YET?
NOT YET.
SHE'S ON THE NIGHT SHIFT LATELY.

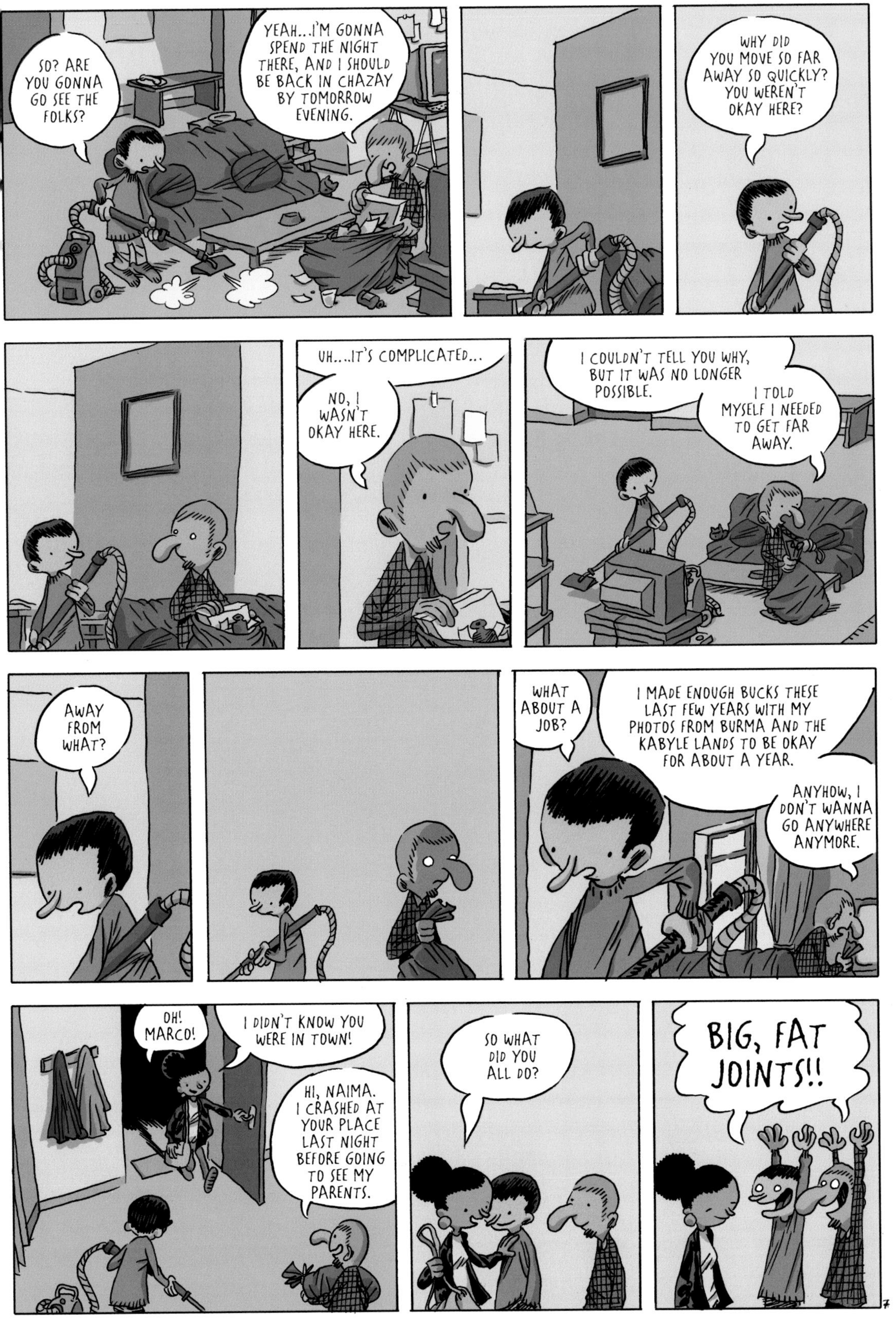
SO? ARE YOU GONNA GO SEE THE FOLKS?
YEAH...I'M GONNA SPEND THE NIGHT THERE, AND I SHOULD BE BACK IN CHAZAY BY TOMORROW EVENING.
WHY DID YOU MOVE SO FAR AWAY SO QUICKLY? YOU WEREN'T OKAY HERE?
UH....IT'S COMPLICATED...
NO, I WASN'T OKAY HERE.
I COULDN'T TELL YOU WHY, BUT IT WAS NO LONGER POSSIBLE.
I TOLD MYSELF I NEEDED TO GET FAR AWAY.
AWAY FROM WHAT?
WHAT ABOUT A JOB?
I MADE ENOUGH BUCKS THESE LAST FEW YEARS WITH MY PHOTOS FROM BURMA AND THE KABYLE LANDS TO BE OKAY FOR ABOUT A YEAR.
ANYHOW, I DON'T WANNA GO ANYWHERE ANYMORE.
OH! MARCO!
I DIDN'T KNOW YOU WERE IN TOWN!
HI, NAIMA. I CRASHED AT YOUR PLACE LAST NIGHT BEFORE GOING TO SEE MY PARENTS.
SO WHAT DID YOU ALL DO?
BIG, FAT JOINTS!!

DRIVING ON THE FREEWAY SCARED ME FOR A LONG TIME.

IN FACT, I WAS COMPLETELY INCAPABLE. I'D DRIVE ON THE MORE REGULAR ROADWAYS WHERE, CURIOUSLY, I WAS MORE AT EASE.

I TALKED A LOT ABOUT IT TO THE SHRINK BECAUSE I DIDN'T UNDERSTAND WHY I WAS SO AFRAID, AND ALSO BECAUSE IT WAS A REAL HANDICAP FOR WORK AND LIFE IN GENERAL.

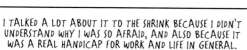

AND IT'S ONE OF THE FEW SUBJECTS UPON WHICH HE DEIGNED TO TELL ME HIS OPINION...

HE TOLD ME THAT, IF YOU REALLY THOUGHT ABOUT IT, A CAR HAD MANY POINTS IN COMMON WITH A COFFIN...

...THAT ACCELERATING TO UNNATURAL SPEEDS ON A ROAD WHERE YOU KNOW NOTHING OF THE PEOPLE PILOTING THE OTHER COFFINS MADE YOU THINK...

...AND THAT, UNDER THESE CONDITIONS, IT SEEMED TO HIM FAIRLY LEGITIMATE TO BE AFRAID.

SINCE THEN, I'VE NOT BEEN AFRAID ANYMORE. PSYCHOANALYSIS IS FUNNY.

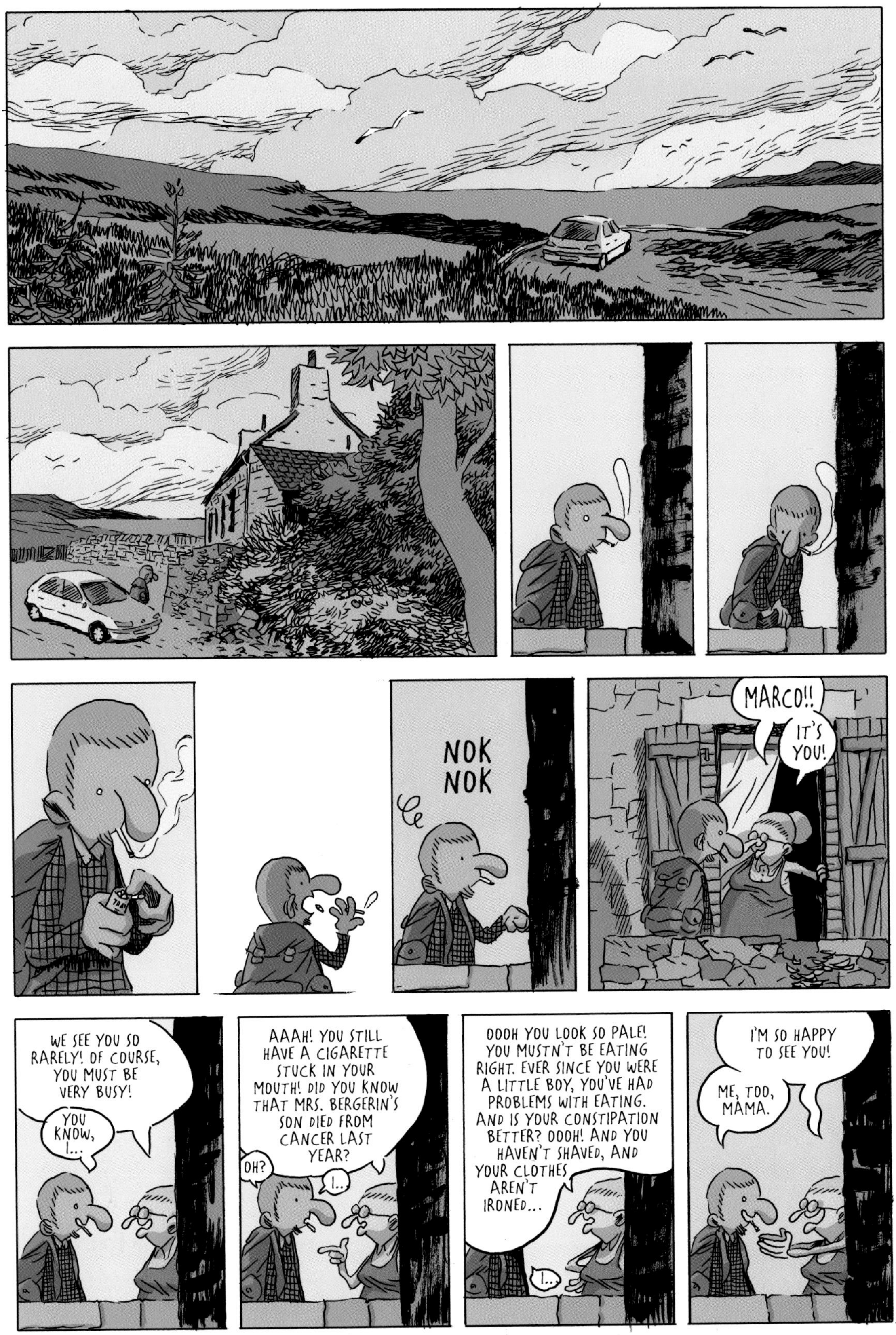
NOK
NOK
MARCO!!
IT'S YOU!
WE SEE YOU SO RARELY! OF COURSE, YOU MUST BE VERY BUSY!
YOU KNOW, I...
AAAH! YOU STILL HAVE A CIGARETTE STUCK IN YOUR MOUTH! DID YOU KNOW THAT MRS. BERGERIN'S SON DIED FROM CANCER LAST YEAR?
OH?
I...
OOOH YOU LOOK SO PALE! YOU MUSTN'T BE EATING RIGHT. EVER SINCE YOU WERE A LITTLE BOY, YOU'VE HAD PROBLEMS WITH EATING. AND IS YOUR CONSTIPATION BETTER? OOOH! AND YOU HAVEN'T SHAVED, AND YOUR CLOTHES AREN'T IRONED...
I...
I'M SO HAPPY TO SEE YOU!
ME, TOO, MAMA.

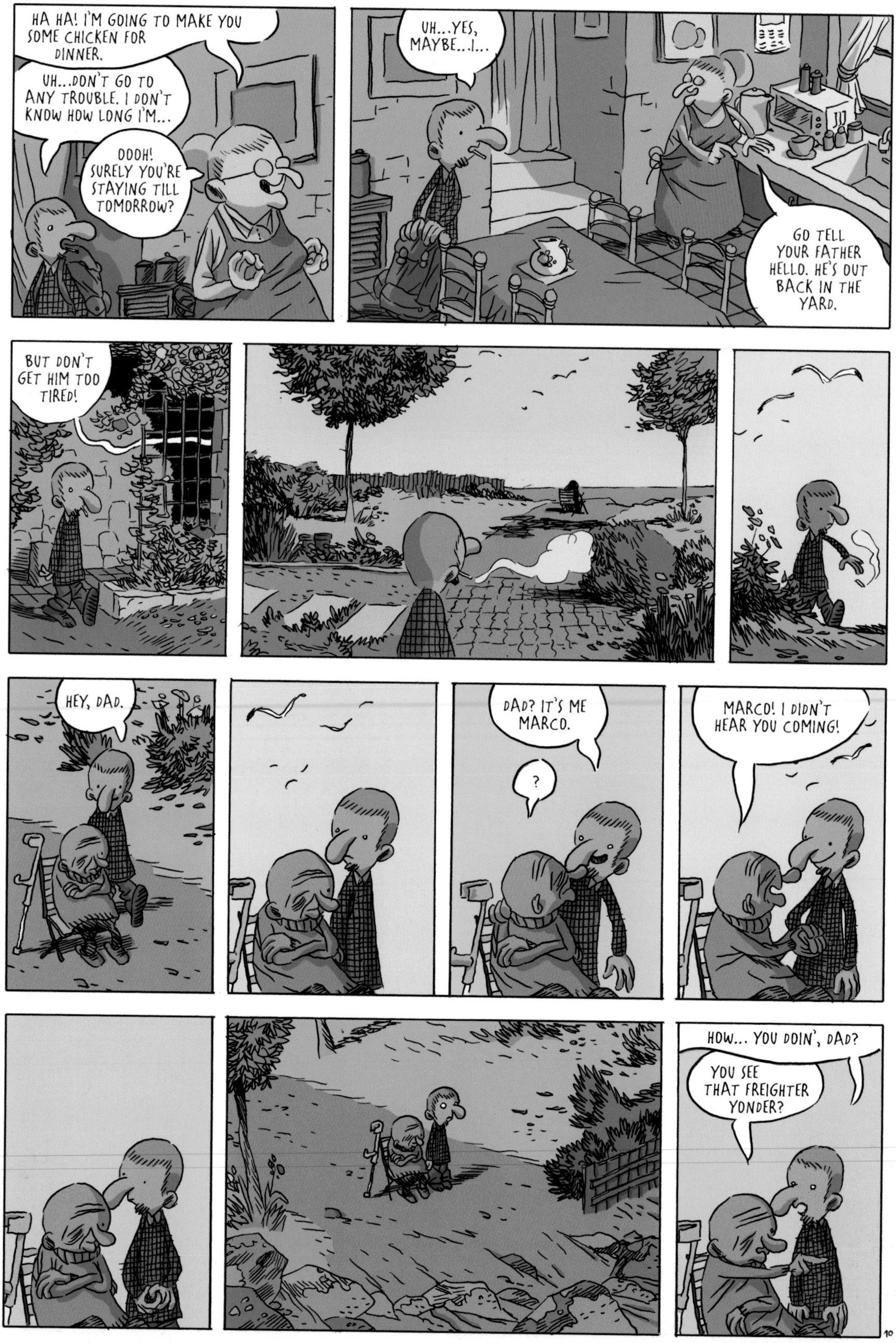
HA HA! I'M GOING TO MAKE YOU SOME CHICKEN FOR DINNER.
UH...DON'T GO TO ANY TROUBLE. I DON'T KNOW HOW LONG I'M...
OOOH! SURELY YOU'RE STAYING TILL TOMORROW?
UH...YES, MAYBE...I...
GO TELL YOUR FATHER HELLO. HE'S OUT BACK IN THE YARD.
BUT DON'T GET HIM TOO TIRED!
HEY, DAD.
DAD? IT'S ME MARCO.
?
MARCO! I DIDN'T HEAR YOU COMING!
HOW... YOU DOIN', DAD?
YOU SEE THAT FREIGHTER YONDER?
10

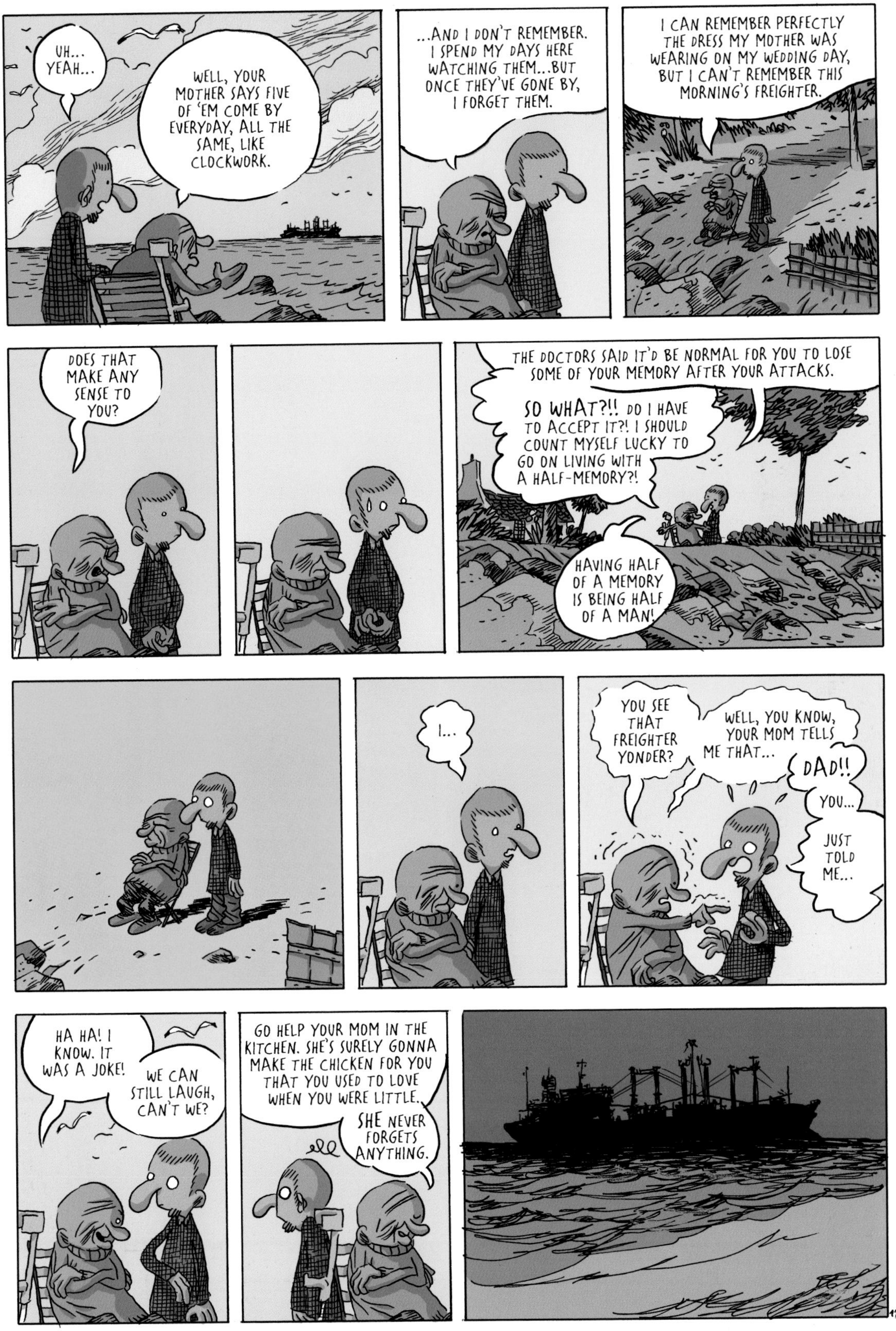
UH... YEAH...
WELL, YOUR MOTHER SAYS FIVE OF 'EM COME BY EVERYDAY, ALL THE SAME, LIKE CLOCKWORK.
...AND I DON'T REMEMBER. I SPEND MY DAYS HERE WATCHING THEM...BUT ONCE THEY'VE GONE BY, I FORGET THEM.
I CAN REMEMBER PERFECTLY THE DRESS MY MOTHER WAS WEARING ON MY WEDDING DAY, BUT I CAN'T REMEMBER THIS MORNING'S FREIGHTER.
DOES THAT MAKE ANY SENSE TO YOU?
THE DOCTORS SAID IT'D BE NORMAL FOR YOU TO LOSE SOME OF YOUR MEMORY AFTER YOUR ATTACKS.
SO WHAT?!! DO I HAVE TO ACCEPT IT?! I SHOULD COUNT MYSELF LUCKY TO GO ON LIVING WITH A HALF-MEMORY?!
HAVING HALF OF A MEMORY IS BEING HALF OF A MAN!
I...
YOU SEE THAT FREIGHTER YONDER?
WELL, YOU KNOW, YOUR MOM TELLS ME THAT...
DAD!!
YOU...
JUST TOLD ME...
HA HA! I KNOW. IT WAS A JOKE!
WE CAN STILL LAUGH, CAN'T WE?
GO HELP YOUR MOM IN THE KITCHEN. SHE'S SURELY GONNA MAKE THE CHICKEN FOR YOU THAT YOU USED TO LOVE WHEN YOU WERE LITTLE.
SHE NEVER FORGETS ANYTHING.

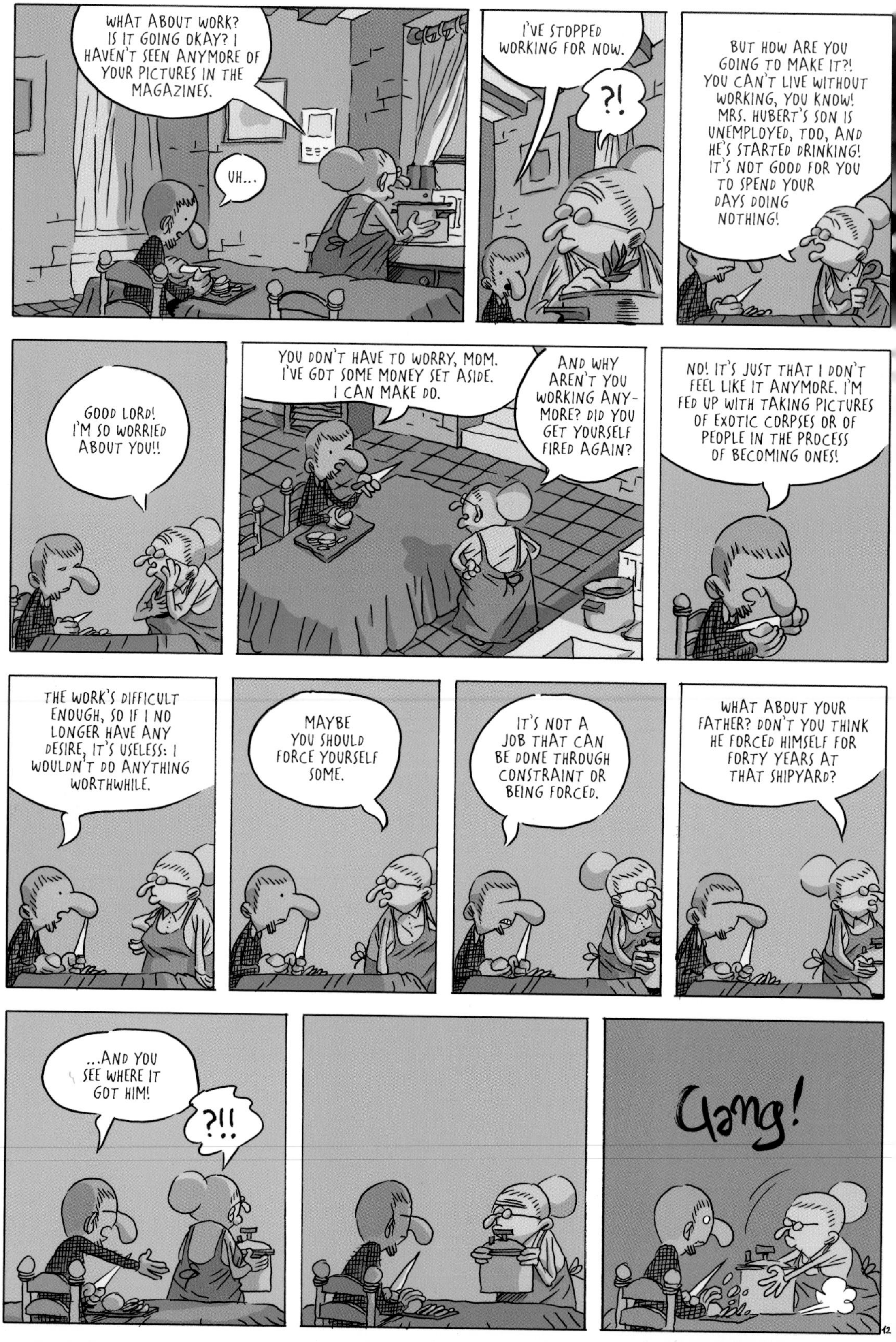
WHAT ABOUT WORK? IS IT GOING OKAY? I HAVEN'T SEEN ANYMORE OF YOUR PICTURES IN THE MAGAZINES.
UH...
I'VE STOPPED WORKING FOR NOW.
?!
BUT HOW ARE YOU GOING TO MAKE IT?! YOU CAN'T LIVE WITHOUT WORKING, YOU KNOW! MRS. HUBERT'S SON IS UNEMPLOYED, TOO, AND HE'S STARTED DRINKING! IT'S NOT GOOD FOR YOU TO SPEND YOUR DAYS DOING NOTHING!
GOOD LORD! I'M SO WORRIED ABOUT YOU!!
YOU DON'T HAVE TO WORRY, MOM. I'VE GOT SOME MONEY SET ASIDE. I CAN MAKE DO.
AND WHY AREN'T YOU WORKING ANY-MORE? DID YOU GET YOURSELF FIRED AGAIN?
NO! IT'S JUST THAT I DON'T FEEL LIKE IT ANYMORE. I'M FED UP WITH TAKING PICTURES OF EXOTIC CORPSES OR OF PEOPLE IN THE PROCESS OF BECOMING ONES!
THE WORK'S DIFFICULT ENOUGH, SO IF I NO LONGER HAVE ANY DESIRE, IT'S USELESS: I WOULDN'T DO ANYTHING WORTHWHILE.
MAYBE YOU SHOULD FORCE YOURSELF SOME.
IT'S NOT A JOB THAT CAN BE DONE THROUGH CONSTRAINT OR BEING FORCED.
WHAT ABOUT YOUR FATHER? DON'T YOU THINK HE FORCED HIMSELF FOR FORTY YEARS AT THAT SHIPYARD?
...AND YOU SEE WHERE IT GOT HIM!
?!!
Clang!

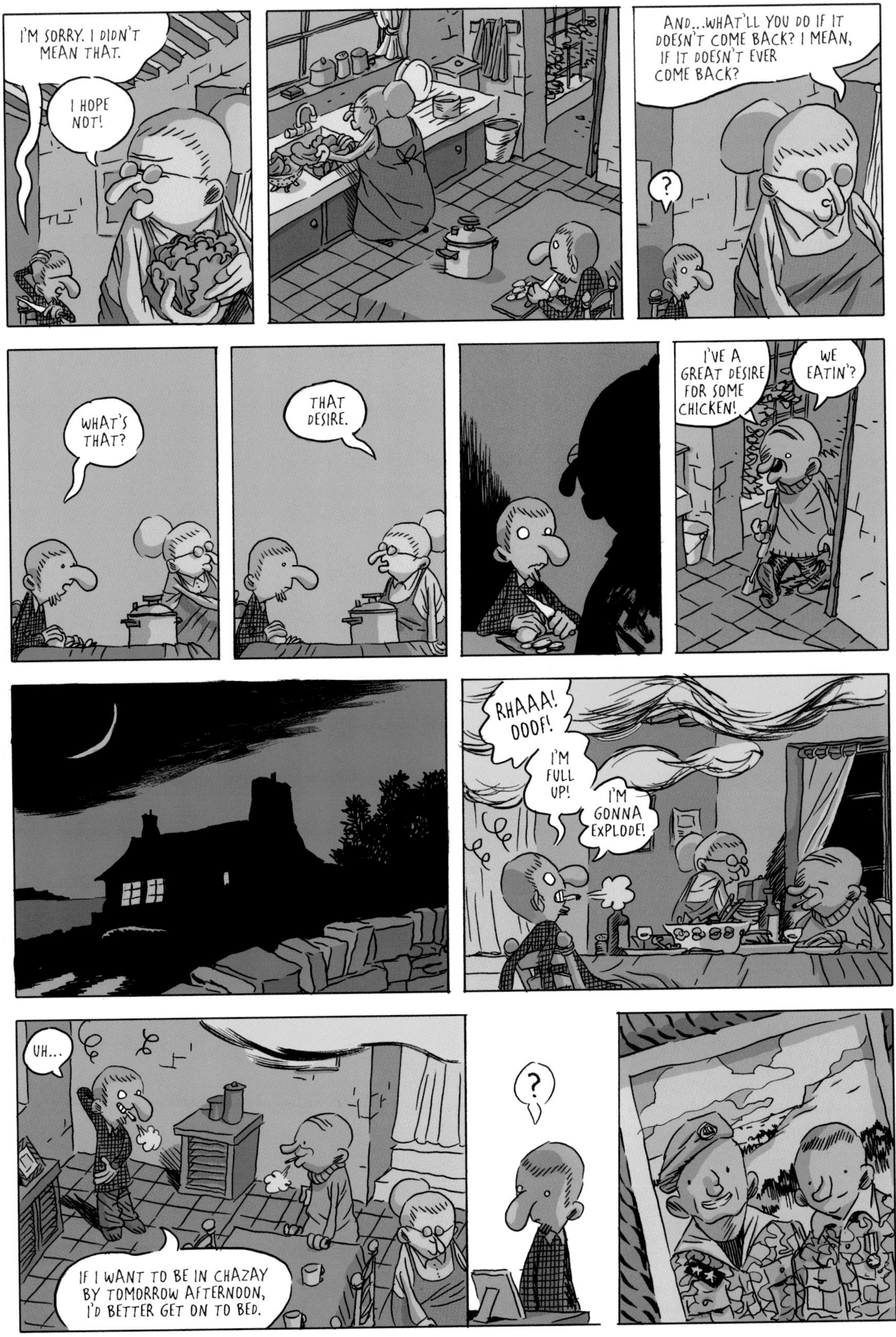
I'M SORRY. I DIDN'T MEAN THAT.
I HOPE NOT!
AND...WHAT'LL YOU DO IF IT DOESN'T COME BACK? I MEAN, IF IT DOESN'T EVER COME BACK?
?
WHAT'S THAT?
THAT DESIRE.
I'VE A GREAT DESIRE FOR SOME CHICKEN!
WE EATIN'?
RHAAA! DOOF!
I'M FULL UP!
I'M GONNA EXPLODE!
UH...
IF I WANT TO BE IN CHAZAY BY TOMORROW AFTERNOON, I'D BETTER GET ON TO BED.
?

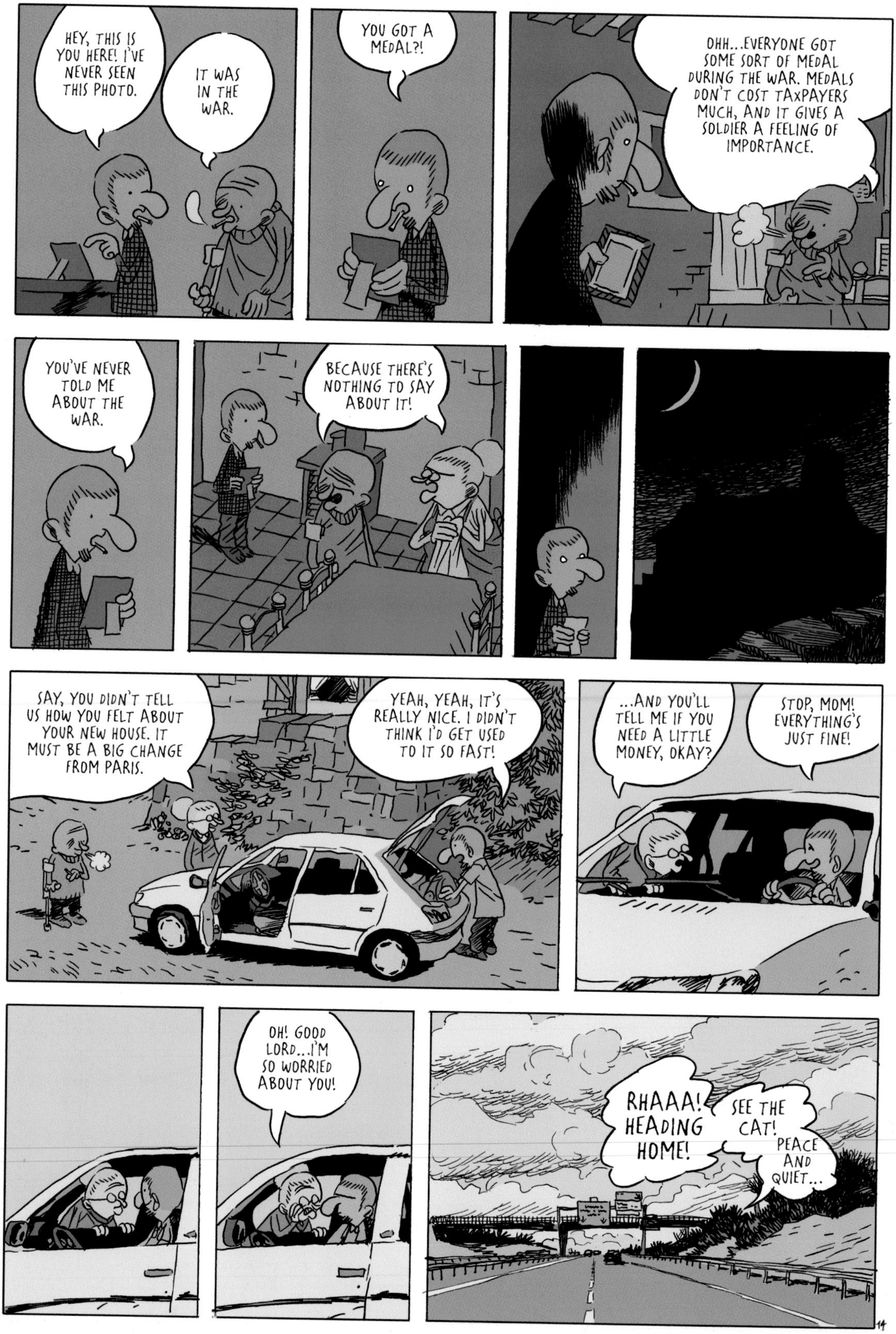
HEY, THIS IS YOU HERE! I'VE NEVER SEEN THIS PHOTO.
IT WAS IN THE WAR.
YOU GOT A MEDAL?!
OHH...EVERYONE GOT SOME SORT OF MEDAL DURING THE WAR. MEDALS DON'T COST TAXPAYERS MUCH, AND IT GIVES A SOLDIER A FEELING OF IMPORTANCE.
YOU'VE NEVER TOLD ME ABOUT THE WAR.
BECAUSE THERE'S NOTHING TO SAY ABOUT IT!
SAY, YOU DIDN'T TELL US HOW YOU FELT ABOUT YOUR NEW HOUSE. IT MUST BE A BIG CHANGE FROM PARIS.
YEAH, YEAH, IT'S REALLY NICE. I DIDN'T THINK I'D GET USED TO IT SO FAST!
...AND YOU'LL TELL ME IF YOU NEED A LITTLE MONEY, OKAY?
STOP, MOM! EVERYTHING'S JUST FINE!
OH! GOOD LORD...I'M SO WORRIED ABOUT YOU!
RHAAA! HEADING HOME!
SEE THE CAT!
PEACE AND QUIET...

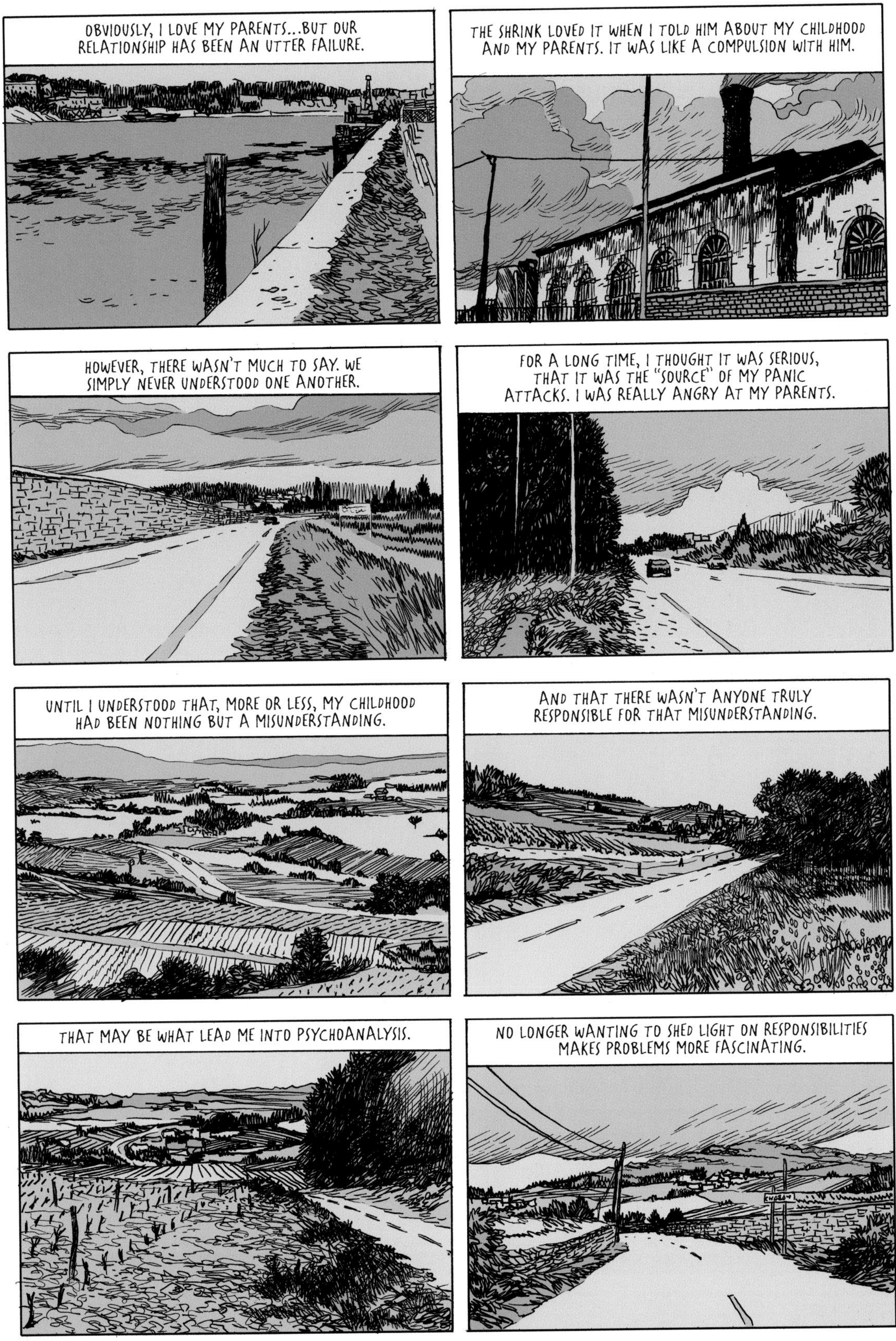
OBVIOUSLY, I LOVE MY PARENTS...BUT OUR RELATIONSHIP HAS BEEN AN UTTER FAILURE.
THE SHRINK LOVED IT WHEN I TOLD HIM ABOUT MY CHILDHOOD AND MY PARENTS. IT WAS LIKE A COMPULSION WITH HIM.
HOWEVER, THERE WASN'T MUCH TO SAY. WE SIMPLY NEVER UNDERSTOOD ONE ANOTHER.
FOR A LONG TIME, I THOUGHT IT WAS SERIOUS, THAT IT WAS THE "SOURCE" OF MY PANIC ATTACKS. I WAS REALLY ANGRY AT MY PARENTS.
UNTIL I UNDERSTOOD THAT, MORE OR LESS, MY CHILDHOOD HAD BEEN NOTHING BUT A MISUNDERSTANDING.
AND THAT THERE WASN'T ANYONE TRULY RESPONSIBLE FOR THAT MISUNDERSTANDING.
THAT MAY BE WHAT LEAD ME INTO PSYCHOANALYSIS.
NO LONGER WANTING TO SHED LIGHT ON RESPONSIBILITIES MAKES PROBLEMS MORE FASCINATING.

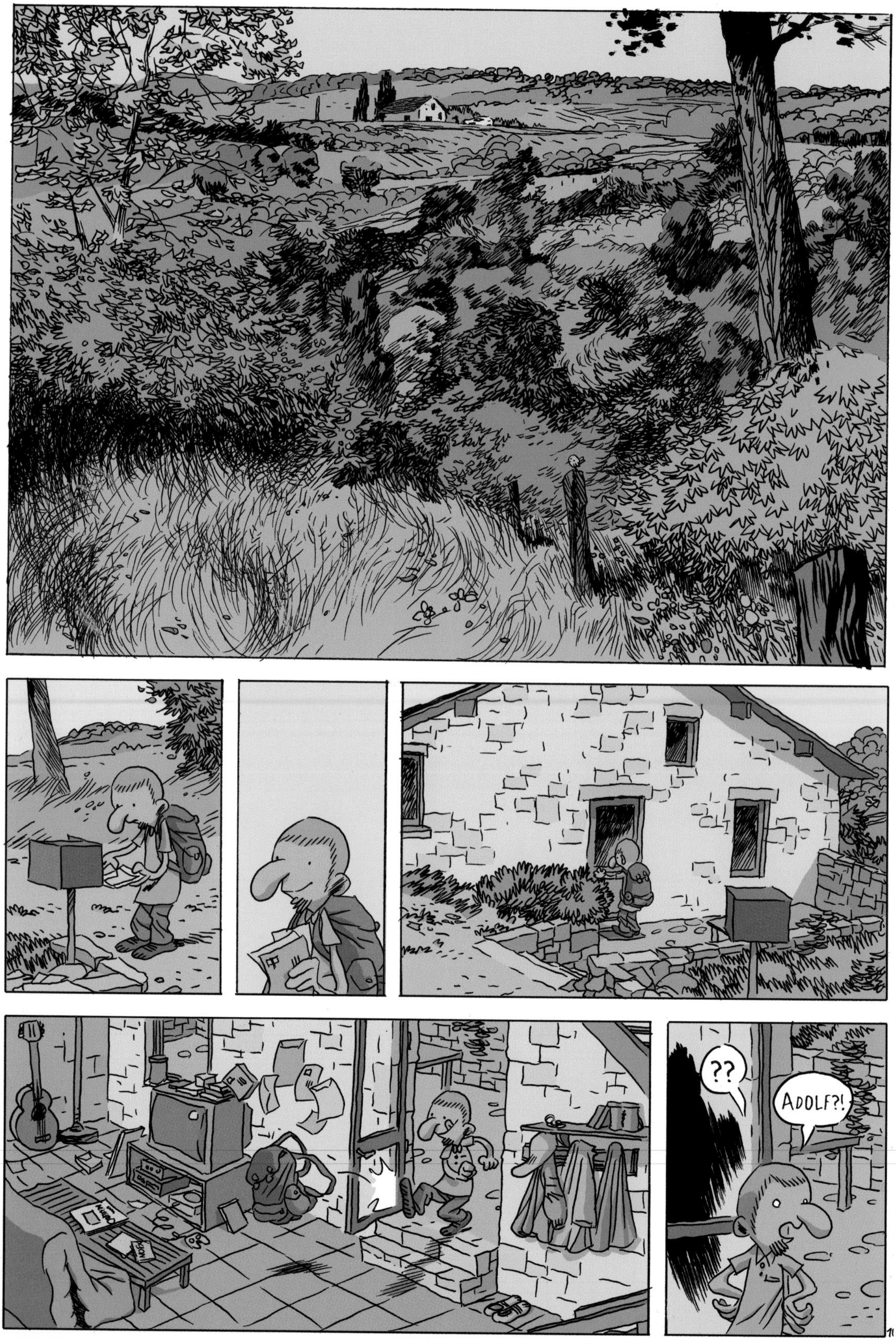
??
ADOLF?!

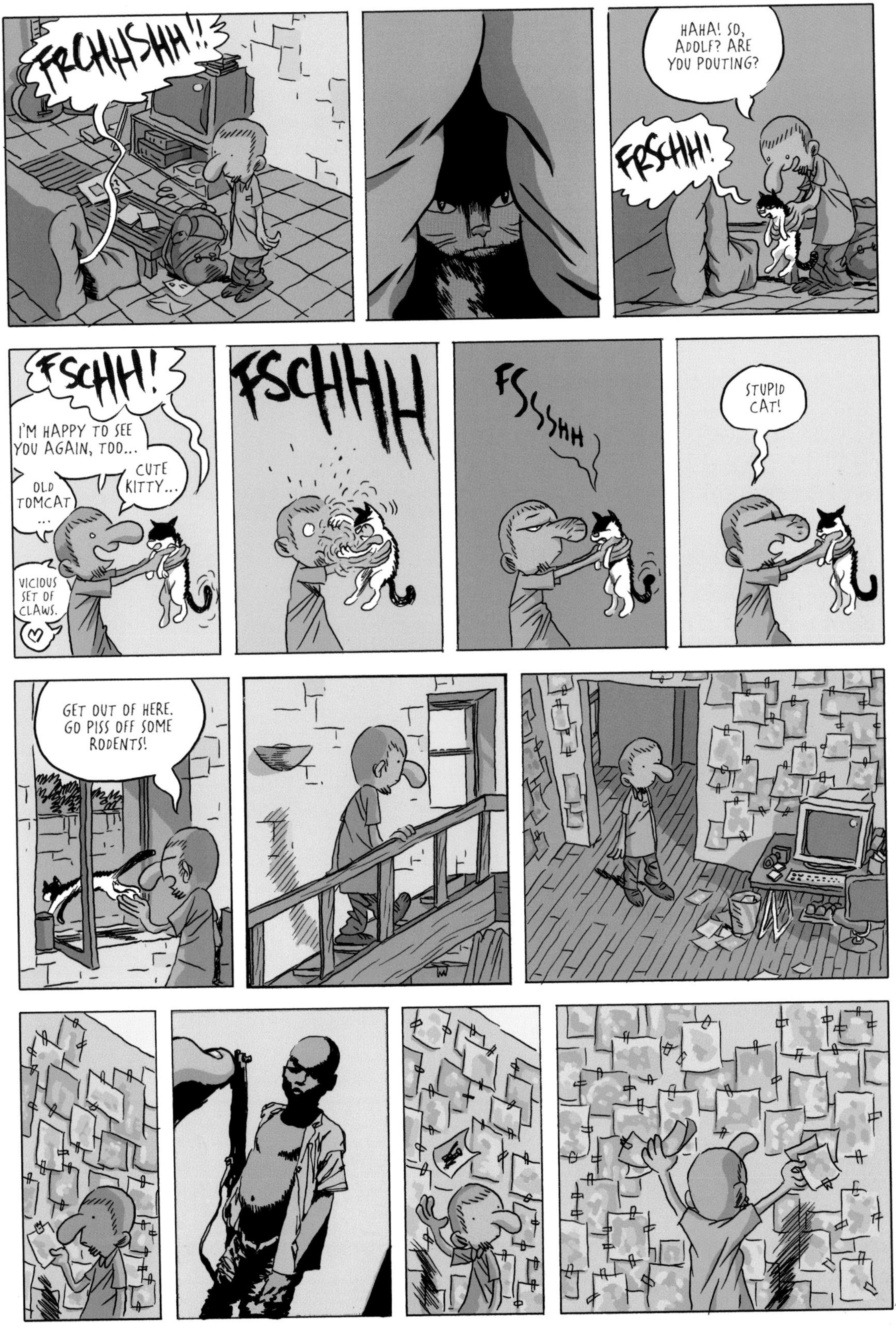
FRCHHSHH!!
HAHA! SO, ADOLF? ARE YOU POUTING?
FRSCHH!
FSCHH!
I'M HAPPY TO SEE YOU AGAIN, TOO...
OLD TOMCAT ...
CUTE KITTY...
VICIOUS SET OF CLAWS.
FSCHHH
FSSSSHH
STUPID CAT!
GET OUT OF HERE. GO PISS OFF SOME RODENTS!

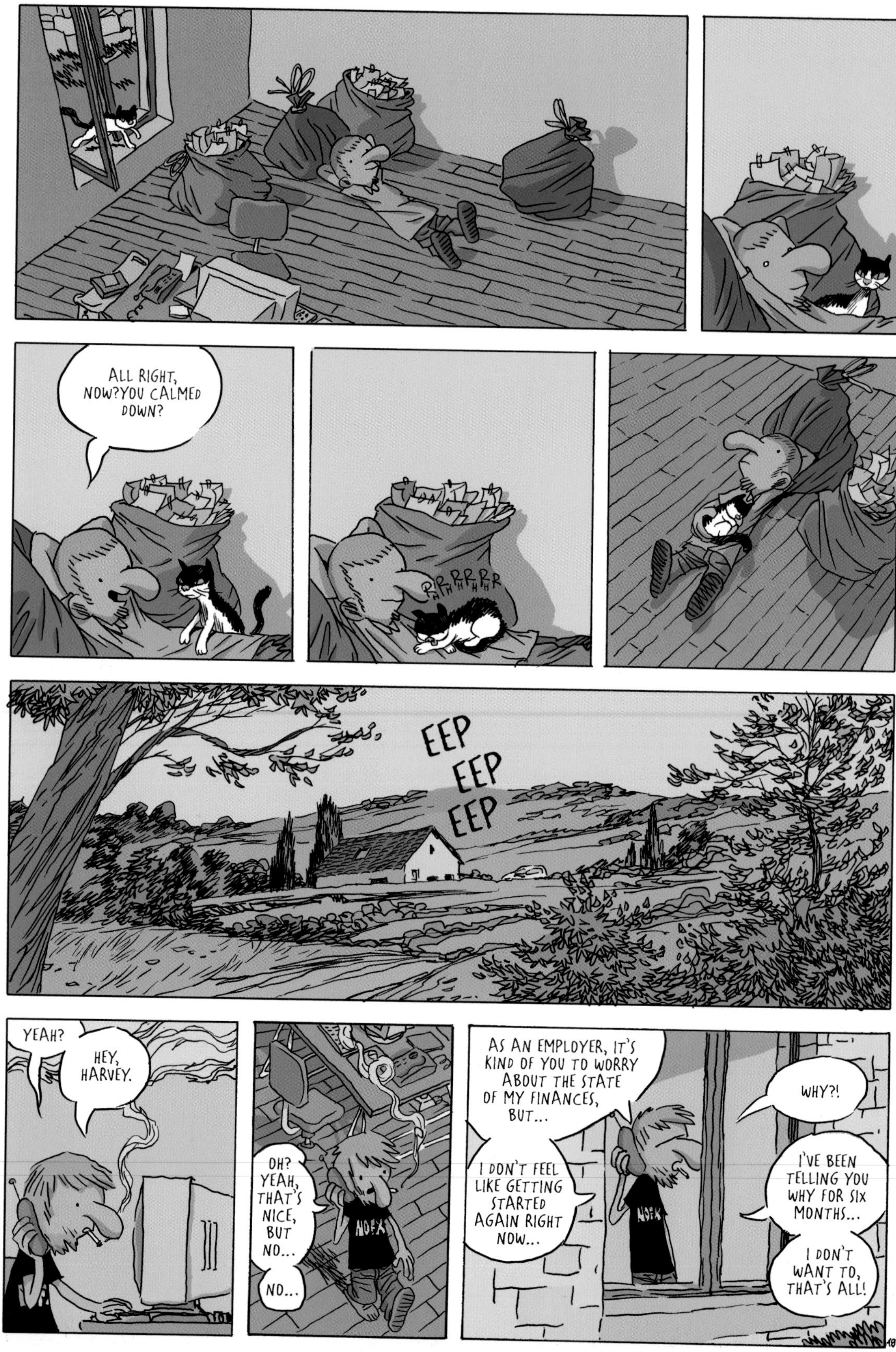

ALL RIGHT, NOW?YOU CALMED DOWN?
RRRRRR HHHHH
EEP
EEP
EEP
YEAH?
HEY, HARVEY.
OH? YEAH, THAT'S NICE, BUT NO...
NO...
AS AN EMPLOYER, IT'S KIND OF YOU TO WORRY ABOUT THE STATE OF MY FINANCES, BUT...
I DON'T FEEL LIKE GETTING STARTED AGAIN RIGHT NOW...
WHY?!
I'VE BEEN TELLING YOU WHY FOR SIX MONTHS...
I DON'T WANT TO, THAT'S ALL!

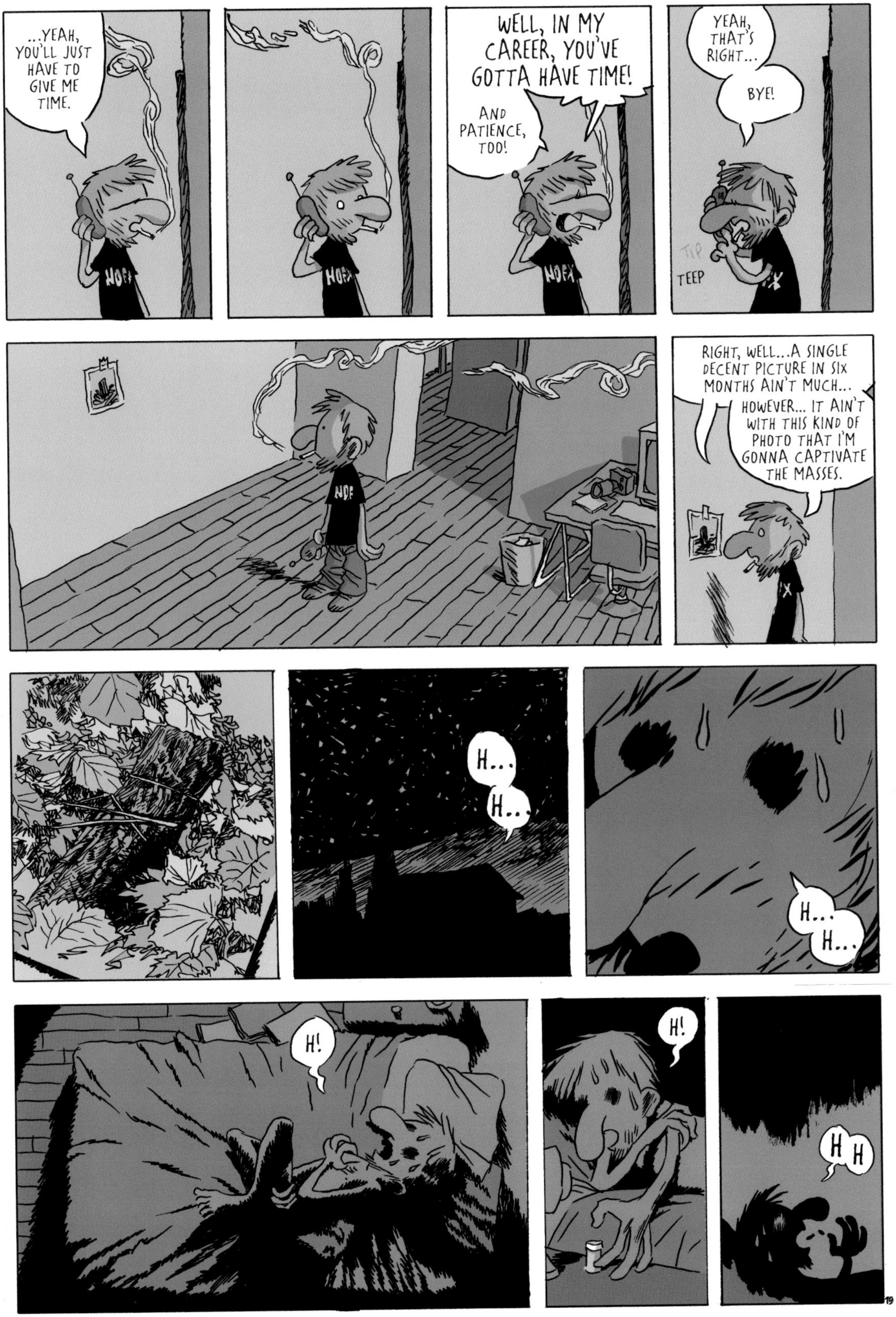
...YEAH, YOU'LL JUST HAVE TO GIVE ME TIME.
WELL, IN MY CAREER, YOU'VE GOTTA HAVE TIME!
AND PATIENCE, TOO!
YEAH, THAT'S RIGHT...
BYE!
TIP
TEEP
RIGHT, WELL...A SINGLE DECENT PICTURE IN SIX MONTHS AIN'T MUCH...
HOWEVER... IT AIN'T WITH THIS KIND OF PHOTO THAT I'M GONNA CAPTIVATE THE MASSES.
H...
H...
H...
H...
H!
H!
H H

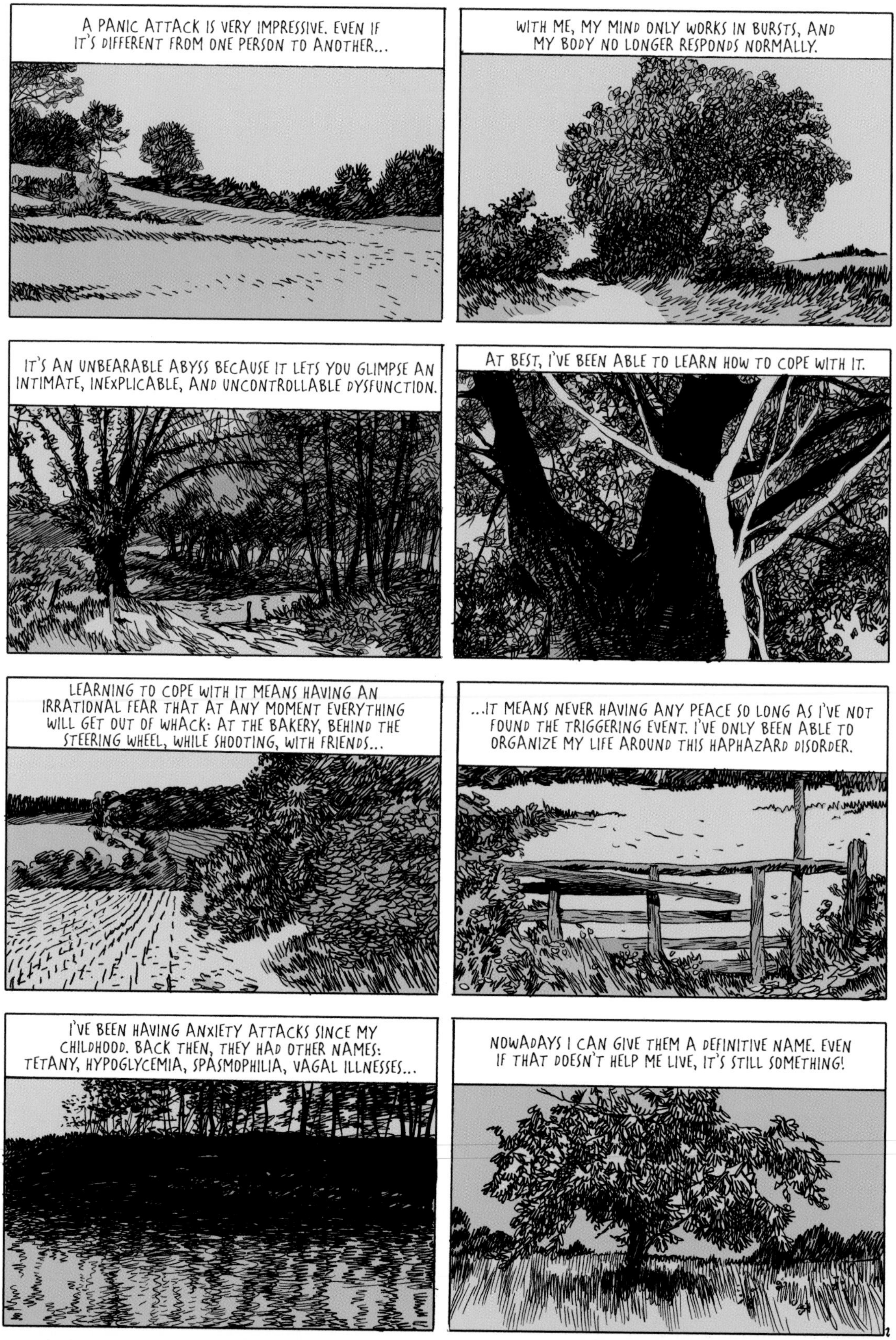
A PANIC ATTACK IS VERY IMPRESSIVE. EVEN IF IT'S DIFFERENT FROM ONE PERSON TO ANOTHER...
WITH ME, MY MIND ONLY WORKS IN BURSTS, AND MY BODY NO LONGER RESPONDS NORMALLY.
IT'S AN UNBEARABLE ABYSS BECAUSE IT LETS YOU GLIMPSE AN INTIMATE, INEXPLICABLE, AND UNCONTROLLABLE DYSFUNCTION.
AT BEST, I'VE BEEN ABLE TO LEARN HOW TO COPE WITH IT.
LEARNING TO COPE WITH IT MEANS HAVING AN IRRATIONAL FEAR THAT AT ANY MOMENT EVERYTHING WILL GET OUT OF WHACK: AT THE BAKERY, BEHIND THE STEERING WHEEL, WHILE SHOOTING, WITH FRIENDS...
...IT MEANS NEVER HAVING ANY PEACE SO LONG AS I'VE NOT FOUND THE TRIGGERING EVENT. I'VE ONLY BEEN ABLE TO ORGANIZE MY LIFE AROUND THIS HAPHAZARD DISORDER.
I'VE BEEN HAVING ANXIETY ATTACKS SINCE MY CHILDHOOD. BACK THEN, THEY HAD OTHER NAMES: TETANY, HYPOGLYCEMIA, SPASMOPHILIA, VAGAL ILLNESSES...
NOWADAYS I CAN GIVE THEM A DEFINITIVE NAME. EVEN IF THAT DOESN'T HELP ME LIVE, IT'S STILL SOMETHING!

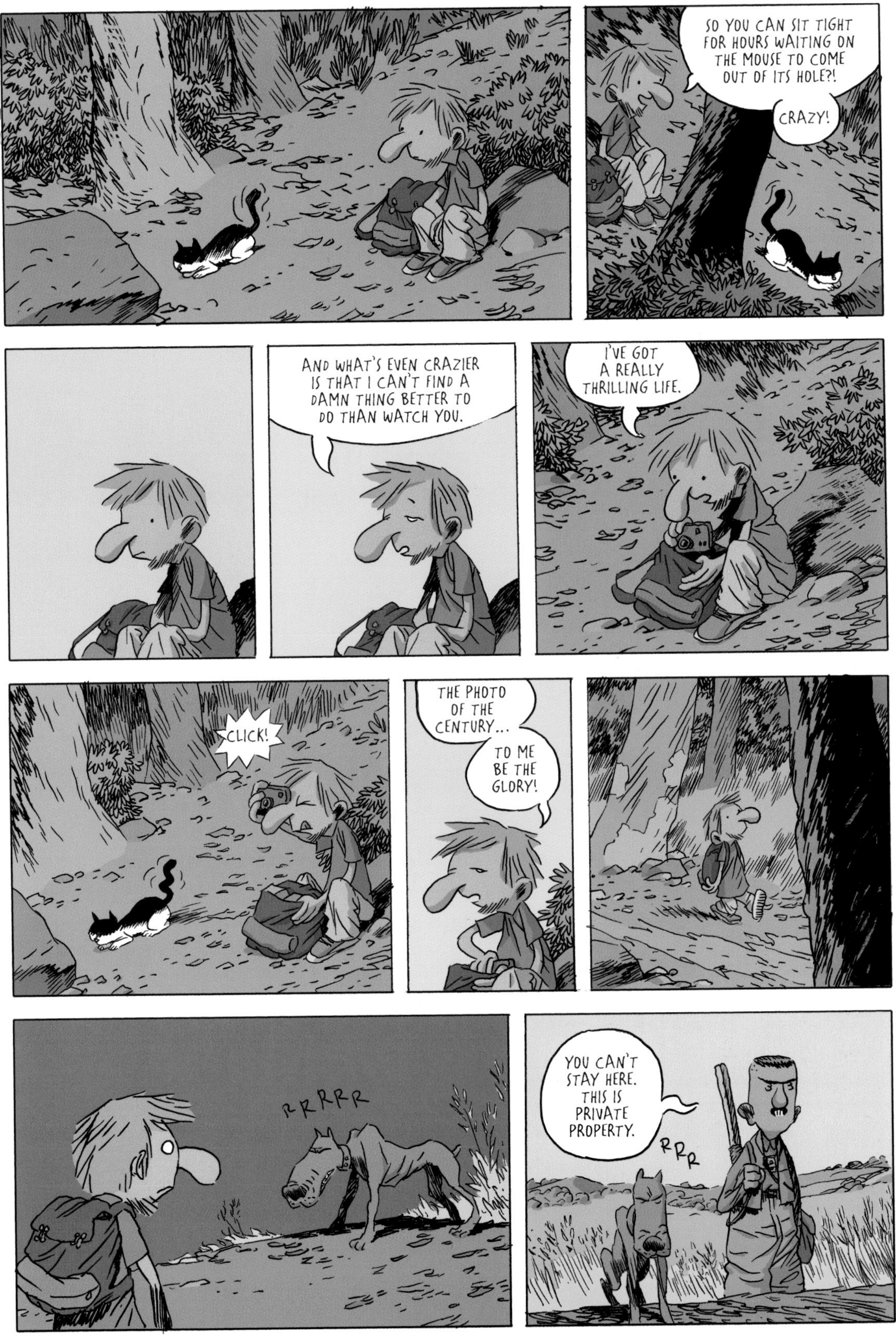

SO YOU CAN SIT TIGHT FOR HOURS WAITING ON THE MOUSE TO COME OUT OF ITS HOLE?!
CRAZY!
AND WHAT'S EVEN CRAZIER IS THAT I CAN'T FIND A DAMN THING BETTER TO DO THAN WATCH YOU.
I'VE GOT A REALLY THRILLING LIFE.
CLICK!
THE PHOTO OF THE CENTURY...
TO ME BE THE GLORY!
RRRRR
YOU CAN'T STAY HERE. THIS IS PRIVATE PROPERTY.
RRR

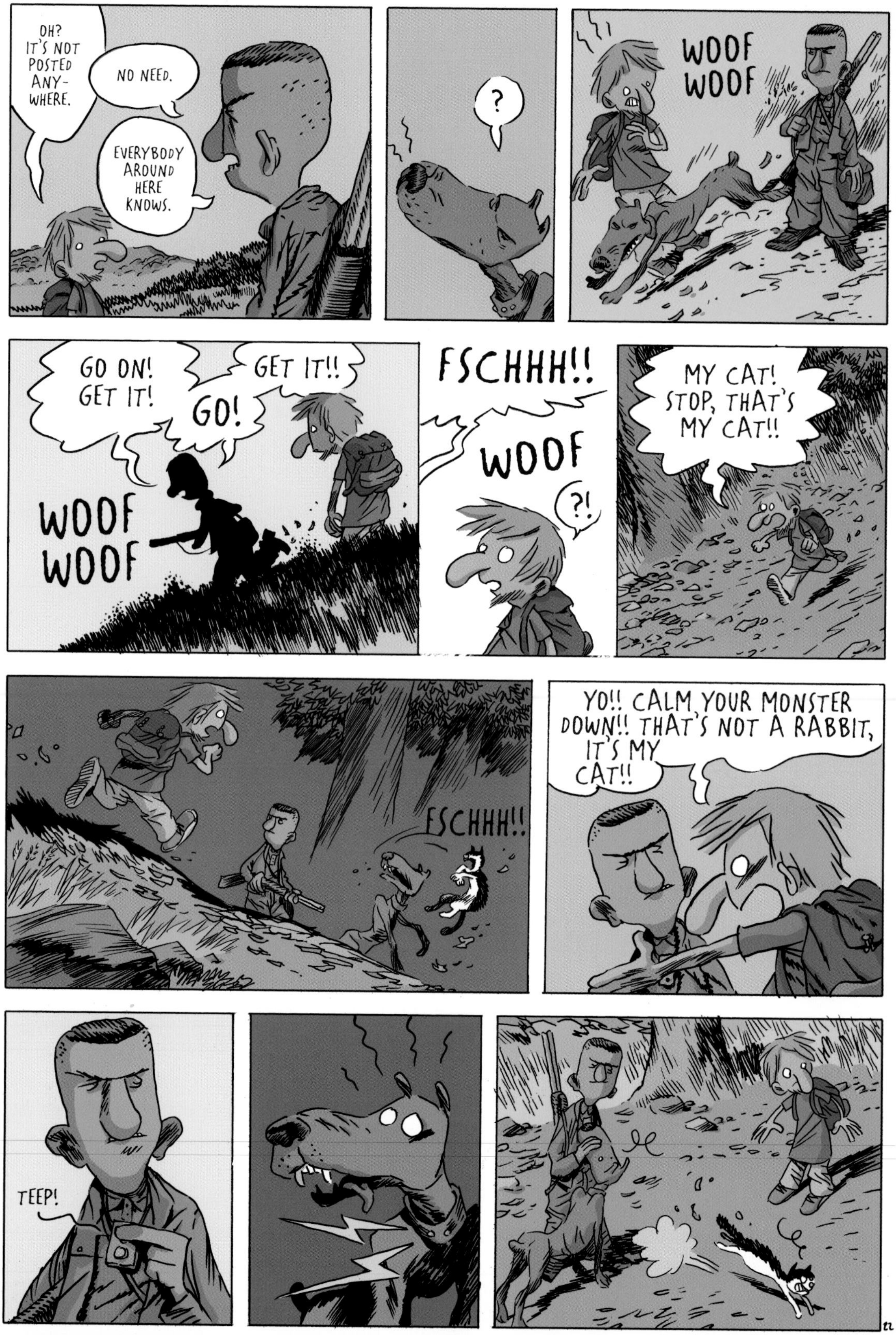
OH? IT'S NOT POSTED ANY- WHERE.
NO NEED.
EVERYBODY AROUND HERE KNOWS.
?
WOOF WOOF
GO ON! GET IT!
GO!
GET IT!!
WOOF WOOF
FSCHHH!!
WOOF
?!
MY CAT! STOP, THAT'S MY CAT!!
FSCHHH!!
YO!! CALM YOUR MONSTER DOWN!! THAT'S NOT A RABBIT, IT'S MY CAT!!
TEEP!

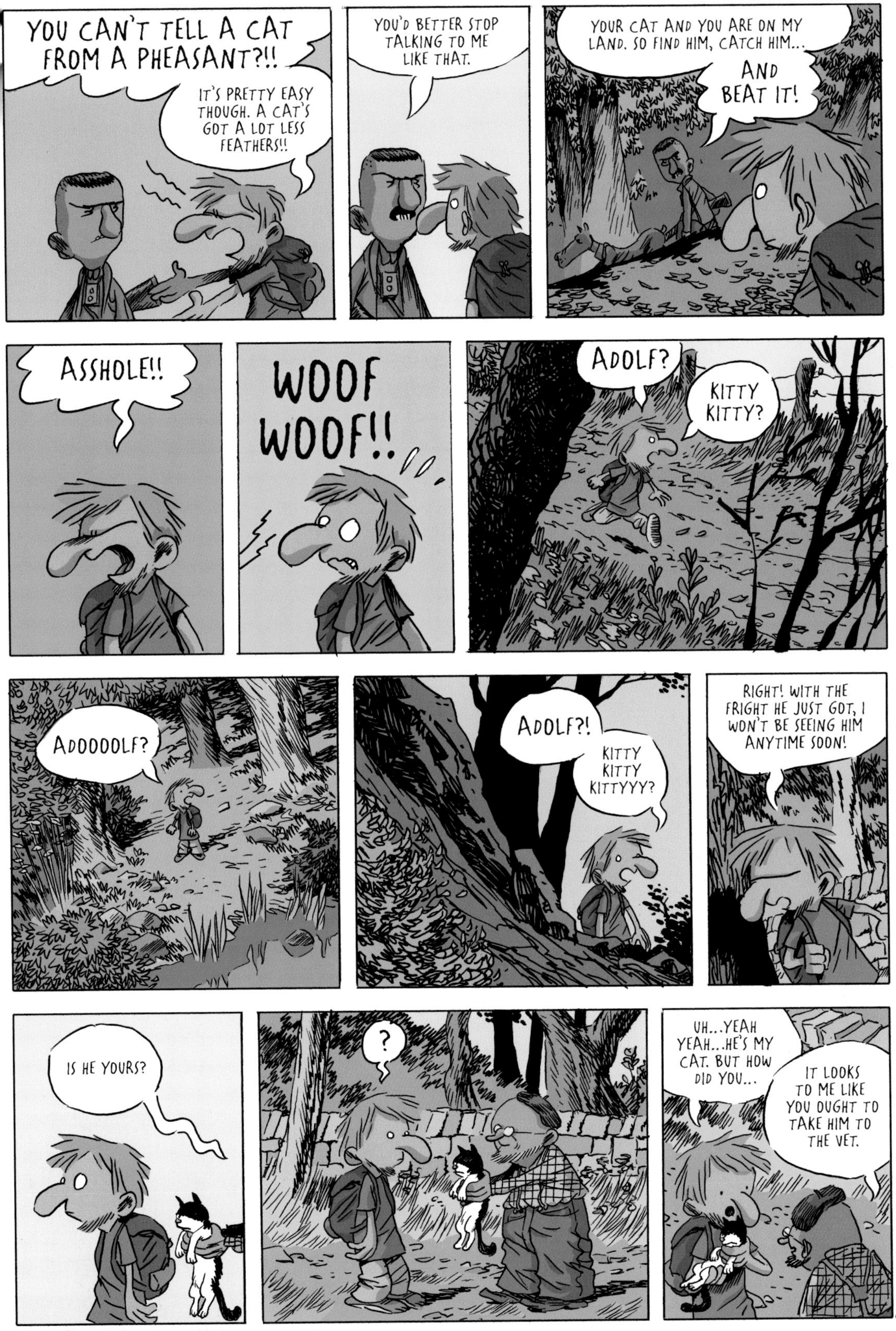
YOU CAN'T TELL A CAT FROM A PHEASANT?!!
IT'S PRETTY EASY THOUGH. A CAT'S GOT A LOT LESS FEATHERS!!
YOU'D BETTER STOP TALKING TO ME LIKE THAT.
YOUR CAT AND YOU ARE ON MY LAND. SO FIND HIM, CATCH HIM...
AND BEAT IT!
ASSHOLE!!
WOOF WOOF!!
ADOLF?
KITTY KITTY?
ADOOOOLF?
ADOLF?!
KITTY KITTY KITTYYY?
RIGHT! WITH THE FRIGHT HE JUST GOT, I WON'T BE SEEING HIM ANYTIME SOON!
IS HE YOURS?
?
UH...YEAH YEAH...HE'S MY CAT. BUT HOW DID YOU...
IT LOOKS TO ME LIKE YOU OUGHT TO TAKE HIM TO THE VET.

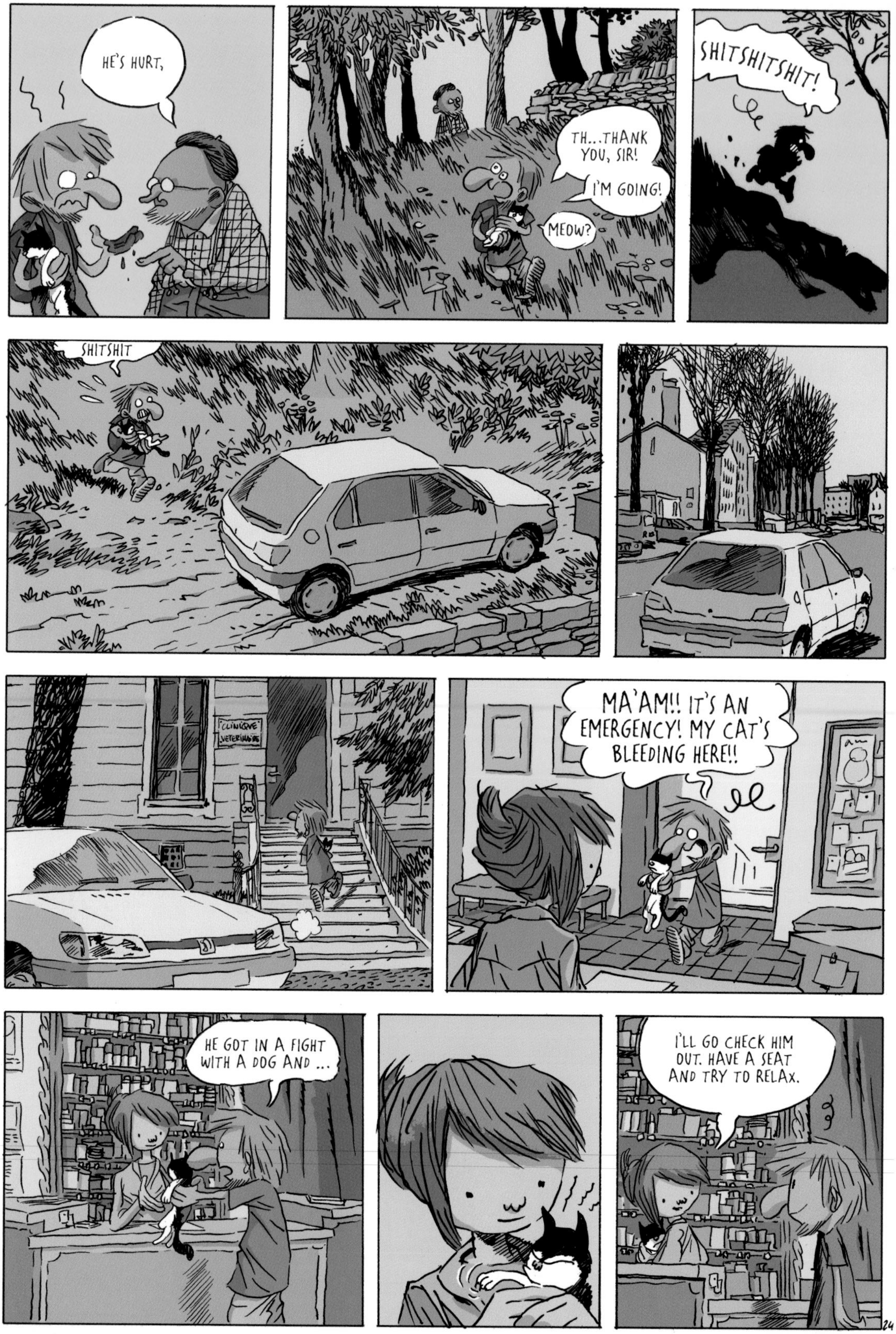
HE'S HURT,
TH...THANK YOU, SIR!
I'M GOING!
MEOW?
SHITSHITSHIT!
SHITSHIT
CLINIQUE VETERINAIRE
MA'AM!! IT'S AN EMERGENCY! MY CAT'S BLEEDING HERE!!
HE GOT IN A FIGHT WITH A DOG AND ...
I'LL GO CHECK HIM OUT. HAVE A SEAT AND TRY TO RELAX.

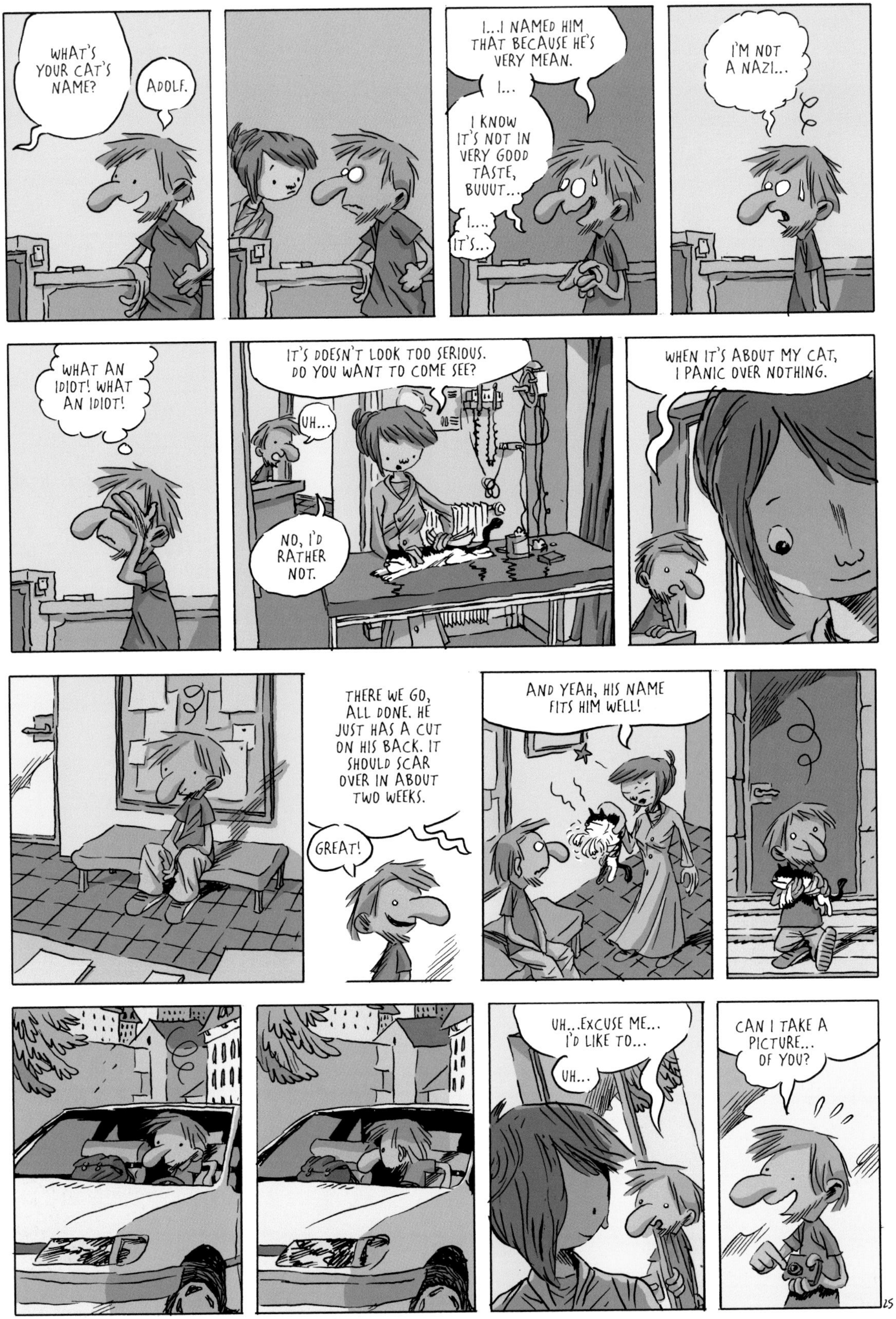

WHAT'S YOUR CAT'S NAME?
ADOLF.
I...I NAMED HIM THAT BECAUSE HE'S VERY MEAN.
I...
I KNOW IT'S NOT IN VERY GOOD TASTE, BUUUT...
I....
IT'S...
I'M NOT A NAZI...
WHAT AN IDIOT! WHAT AN IDIOT!
IT'S DOESN'T LOOK TOO SERIOUS. DO YOU WANT TO COME SEE?
UH...
NO, I'D RATHER NOT.
WHEN IT'S ABOUT MY CAT, I PANIC OVER NOTHING.
THERE WE GO, ALL DONE. HE JUST HAS A CUT ON HIS BACK. IT SHOULD SCAR OVER IN ABOUT TWO WEEKS.
GREAT!
AND YEAH, HIS NAME FITS HIM WELL!
UH...EXCUSE ME... I'D LIKE TO...
UH...
CAN I TAKE A PICTURE... OF YOU?

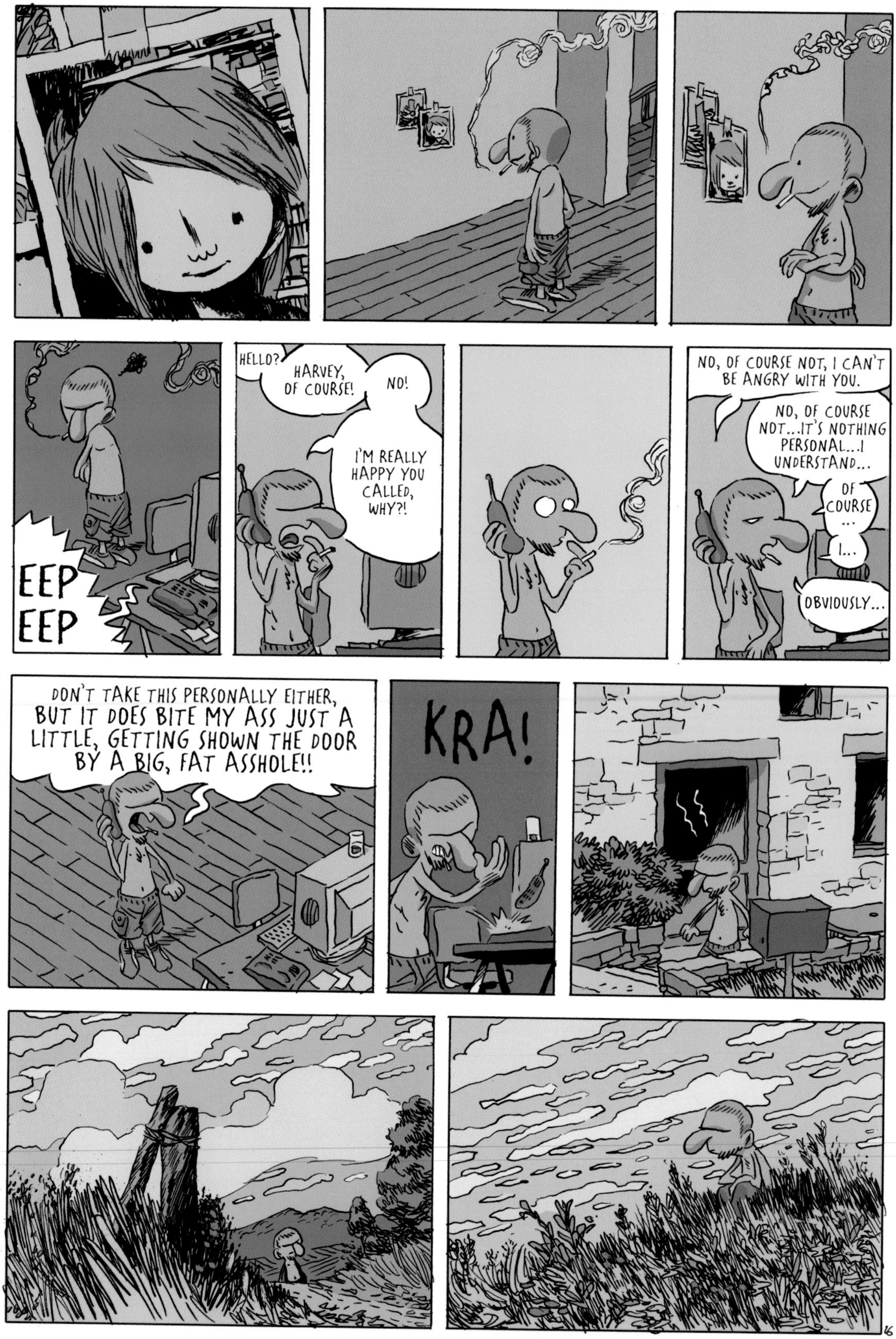
EEP
EEP
HELLO?
HARVEY, OF COURSE!
NO!
I'M REALLY HAPPY YOU CALLED, WHY?!
NO, OF COURSE NOT, I CAN'T BE ANGRY WITH YOU.
NO, OF COURSE NOT...IT'S NOTHING PERSONAL...I UNDERSTAND...
OF COURSE ...
I...
OBVIOUSLY...
DON'T TAKE THIS PERSONALLY EITHER, BUT IT DOES BITE MY ASS JUST A LITTLE, GETTING SHOWN THE DOOR BY A BIG, FAT ASSHOLE!!
KRA!

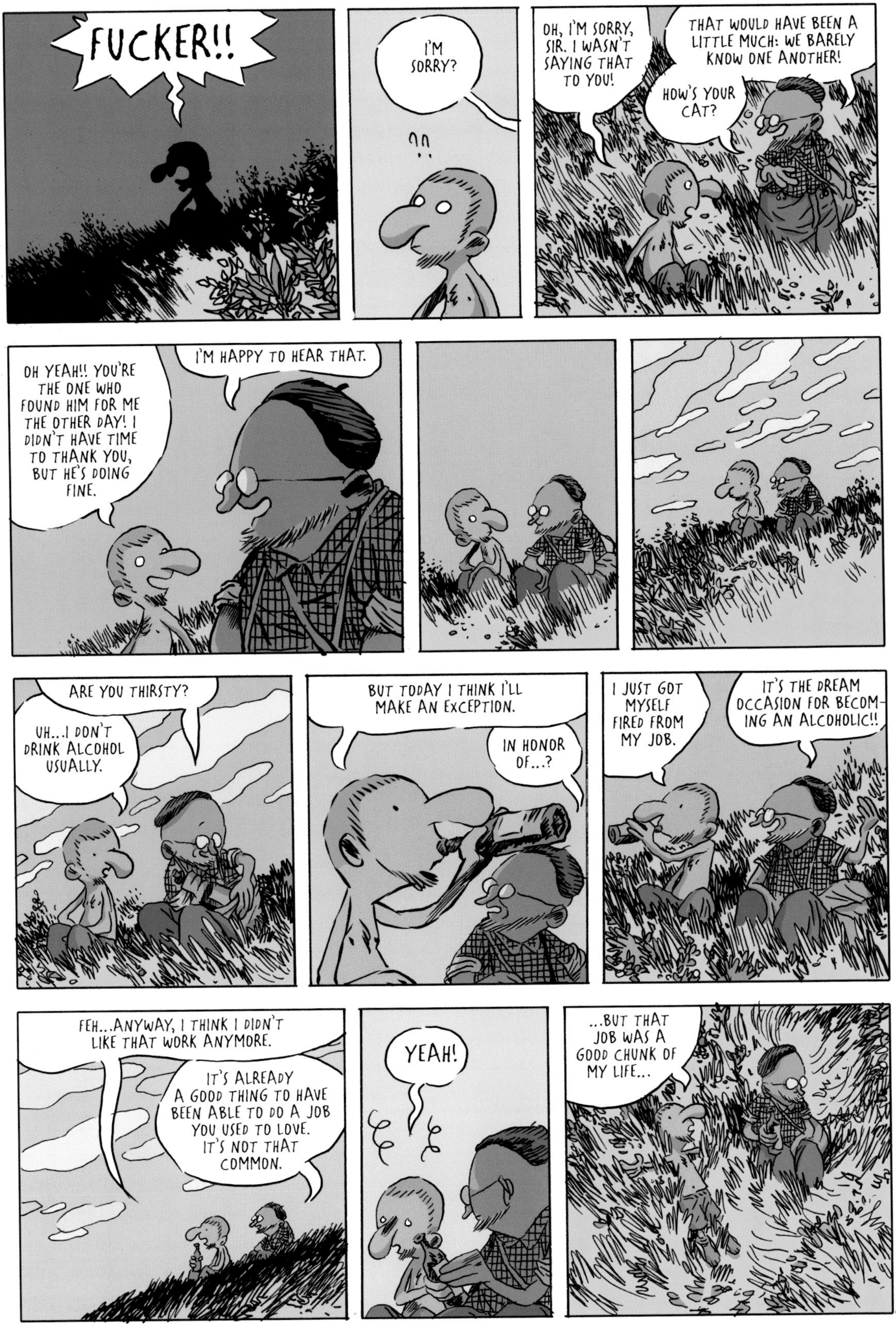
FUCKER!!
I'M SORRY?
OH, I'M SORRY, SIR. I WASN'T SAYING THAT TO YOU!
THAT WOULD HAVE BEEN A LITTLE MUCH: WE BARELY KNOW ONE ANOTHER!
HOW'S YOUR CAT?
OH YEAH!! YOU'RE THE ONE WHO FOUND HIM FOR ME THE OTHER DAY! I DIDN'T HAVE TIME TO THANK YOU, BUT HE'S DOING FINE.
I'M HAPPY TO HEAR THAT.
ARE YOU THIRSTY?
UH...I DON'T DRINK ALCOHOL USUALLY.
BUT TODAY I THINK I'LL MAKE AN EXCEPTION.
IN HONOR OF...?
I JUST GOT MYSELF FIRED FROM MY JOB.
IT'S THE DREAM OCCASION FOR BECOMING AN ALCOHOLIC!!
FEH...ANYWAY, I THINK I DIDN'T LIKE THAT WORK ANYMORE.
IT'S ALREADY A GOOD THING TO HAVE BEEN ABLE TO DO A JOB YOU USED TO LOVE. IT'S NOT THAT COMMON.
YEAH!
...BUT THAT JOB WAS A GOOD CHUNK OF MY LIFE...

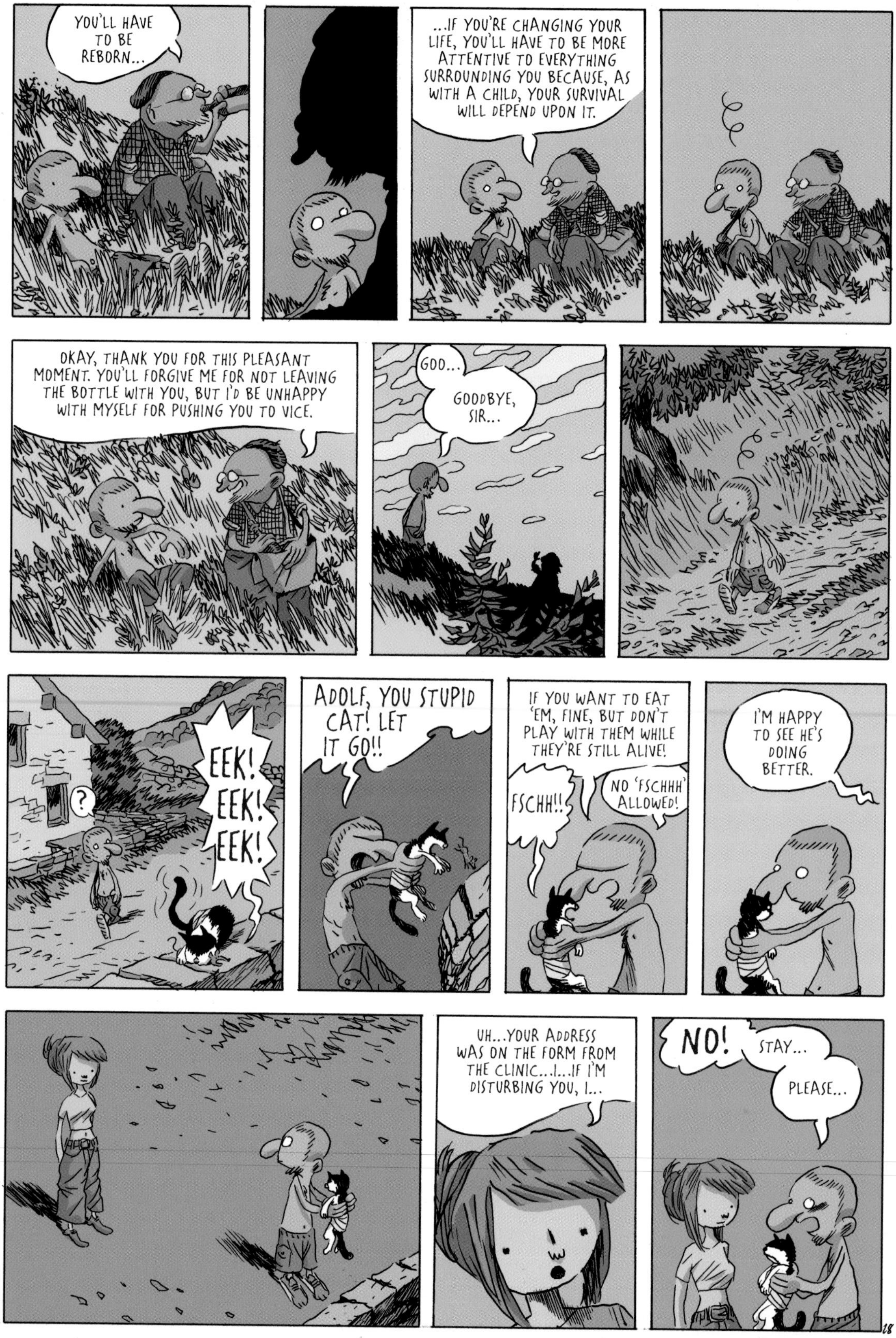

YOU'LL HAVE TO BE REBORN...
...IF YOU'RE CHANGING YOUR LIFE, YOU'LL HAVE TO BE MORE ATTENTIVE TO EVERYTHING SURROUNDING YOU BECAUSE, AS WITH A CHILD, YOUR SURVIVAL WILL DEPEND UPON IT.
OKAY, THANK YOU FOR THIS PLEASANT MOMENT. YOU'LL FORGIVE ME FOR NOT LEAVING THE BOTTLE WITH YOU, BUT I'D BE UNHAPPY WITH MYSELF FOR PUSHING YOU TO VICE.
GOO...
GOODBYE, SIR...
?
EEK! EEK! EEK!
ADOLF, YOU STUPID CAT! LET IT GO!!
IF YOU WANT TO EAT 'EM, FINE, BUT DON'T PLAY WITH THEM WHILE THEY'RE STILL ALIVE!
FSCHH!!
NO 'FSCHHH' ALLOWED!
I'M HAPPY TO SEE HE'S DOING BETTER.
UH...YOUR ADDRESS WAS ON THE FORM FROM THE CLINIC...I...IF I'M DISTURBING YOU, I...
NO!
STAY...
PLEASE...

I'VE HAD EIGHT YEARS OF ANALYSIS WITHOUT EVER TALKING ABOUT WOMEN. WHAT A FEAT...

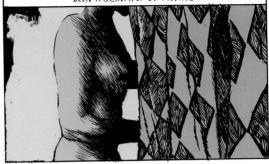

MY LOVE LIFE HAS SHOWN ME THAT I LOVE SOLITUDE. SINCE PRESENCE ANNOYS ME SO MUCH, I'VE ALWAYS BEEN FASCINATED BY ABSENCE.

IT'S HARD TALKING TO A WOMAN I LOVE ABOUT THE INCREDIBLE COMPLEXITY INTO WHICH THAT RELATIONSHIP THRUSTS ME.

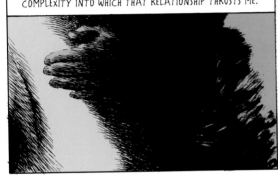

THEY'VE NEVER BEEN ABLE TO LONG TOLERATE MY COMPLETE INABILITY FOR A MINIMUM OF SERENITY...

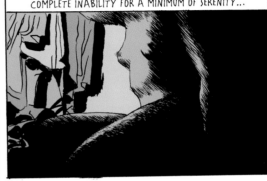

I CAN'T SAY I BLAME THEM. I CAN'T STAND MYSELF ALL THAT MUCH EITHER.

WITHOUT EVEN MENTIONING SEXUALITY, WHICH FOR ME REMAINS SOMETHING MYSTERIOUS, ATTRACTIVE, YET VERY INTIMATELY VIOLENT.

IT'S PAINFUL ENOUGH FOR ME TO ADOPT EVEN BLAND BEHAVIOR WITH THE SUPERMARKET CASHIER ABOUT WHOM I KNOW NOTHING. SO HOW CAN I RESOLVE TO DO SO WITH SOMEONE WHOM I KNOW GENITALLY?

I STILL HAVE LOTS OF THINGS TO SHED LIGHT ON, IF I DON'T WANT TO BE REINCARNATED AS SEWER SCUM...

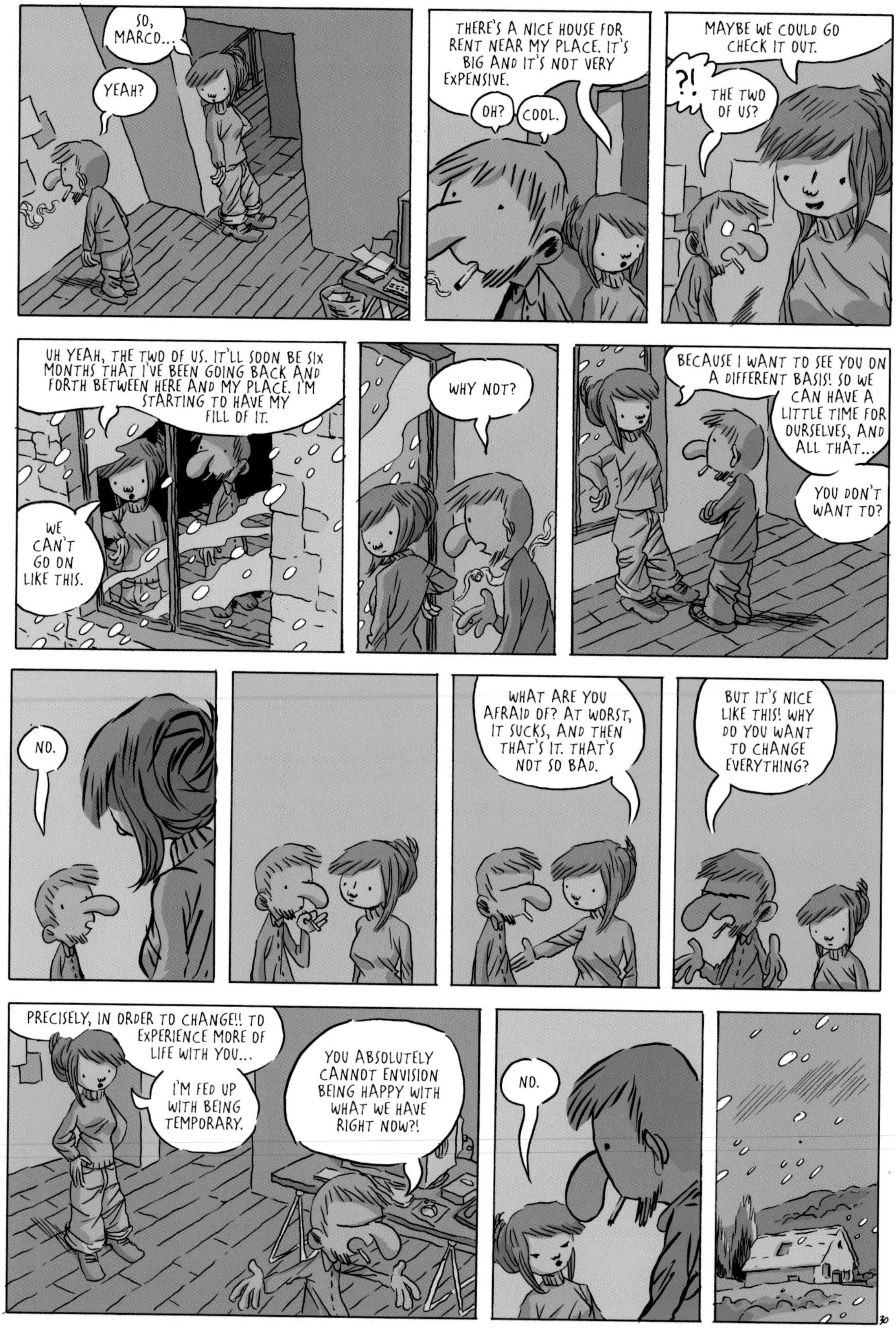

SO, MARCO...
YEAH?
THERE'S A NICE HOUSE FOR RENT NEAR MY PLACE. IT'S BIG AND IT'S NOT VERY EXPENSIVE.
OH?
COOL.
MAYBE WE COULD GO CHECK IT OUT.
?!
THE TWO OF US?
UH YEAH, THE TWO OF US. IT'LL SOON BE SIX MONTHS THAT I'VE BEEN GOING BACK AND FORTH BETWEEN HERE AND MY PLACE. I'M STARTING TO HAVE MY FILL OF IT.
WE CAN'T GO ON LIKE THIS.
WHY NOT?
BECAUSE I WANT TO SEE YOU ON A DIFFERENT BASIS! SO WE CAN HAVE A LITTLE TIME FOR OURSELVES, AND ALL THAT...
YOU DON'T WANT TO?
NO.
WHAT ARE YOU AFRAID OF? AT WORST, IT SUCKS, AND THEN THAT'S IT. THAT'S NOT SO BAD.
BUT IT'S NICE LIKE THIS! WHY DO YOU WANT TO CHANGE EVERYTHING?
PRECISELY, IN ORDER TO CHANGE!! TO EXPERIENCE MORE OF LIFE WITH YOU...
I'M FED UP WITH BEING TEMPORARY.
YOU ABSOLUTELY CANNOT ENVISION BEING HAPPY WITH WHAT WE HAVE RIGHT NOW?!
NO.

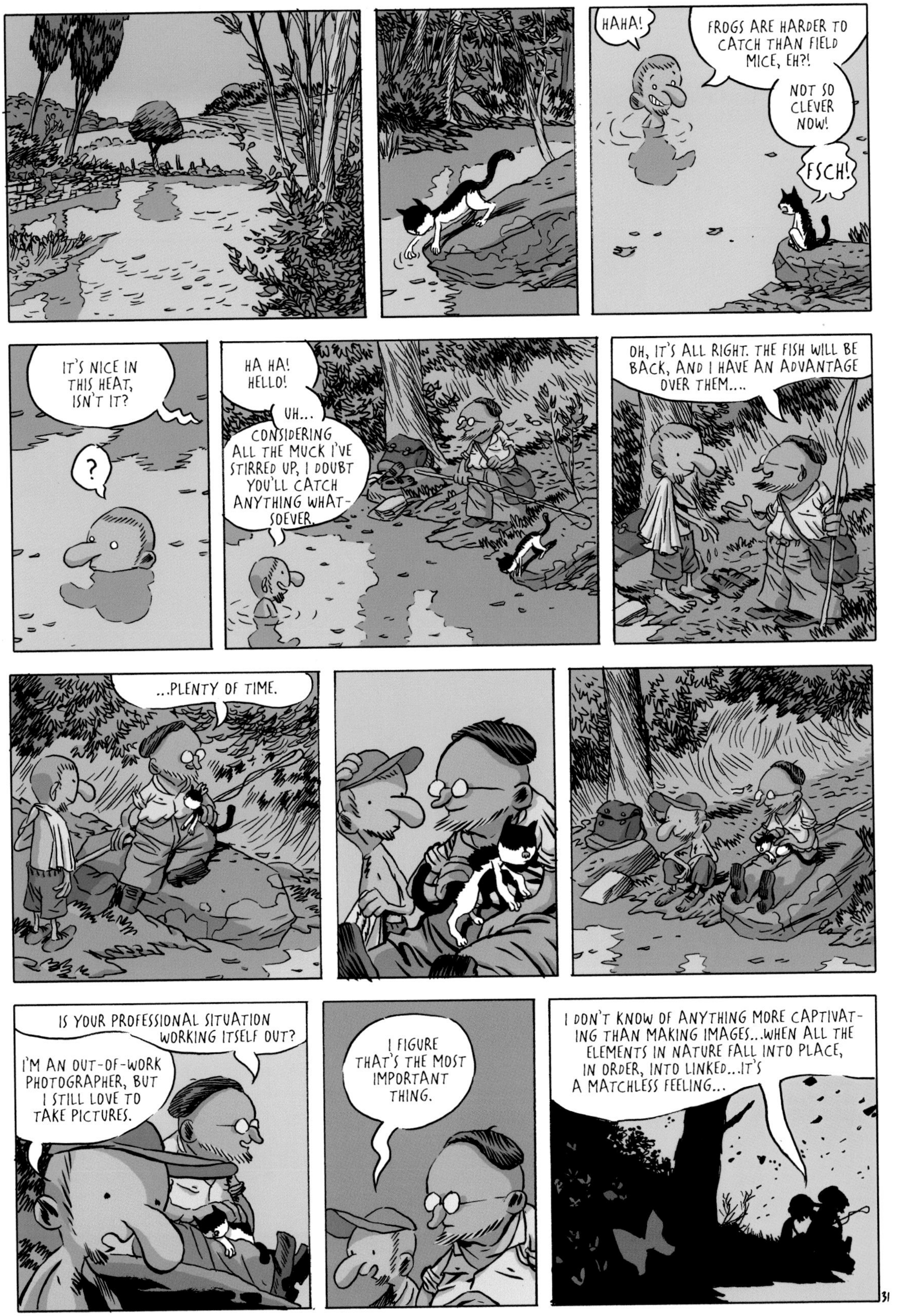
HAHA!
FROGS ARE HARDER TO CATCH THAN FIELD MICE, EH?!
NOT SO CLEVER NOW!
FSCH!
IT'S NICE IN THIS HEAT, ISN'T IT?
?
HA HA! HELLO!
UH...
CONSIDERING ALL THE MUCK I'VE STIRRED UP, I DOUBT YOU'LL CATCH ANYTHING WHATSOEVER.
OH, IT'S ALL RIGHT. THE FISH WILL BE BACK, AND I HAVE AN ADVANTAGE OVER THEM....
...PLENTY OF TIME.
IS YOUR PROFESSIONAL SITUATION WORKING ITSELF OUT?
I'M AN OUT-OF-WORK PHOTOGRAPHER, BUT I STILL LOVE TO TAKE PICTURES.
I FIGURE THAT'S THE MOST IMPORTANT THING.
I DON'T KNOW OF ANYTHING MORE CAPTIVATING THAN MAKING IMAGES...WHEN ALL THE ELEMENTS IN NATURE FALL INTO PLACE, IN ORDER, INTO LINKED...IT'S A MATCHLESS FEELING...

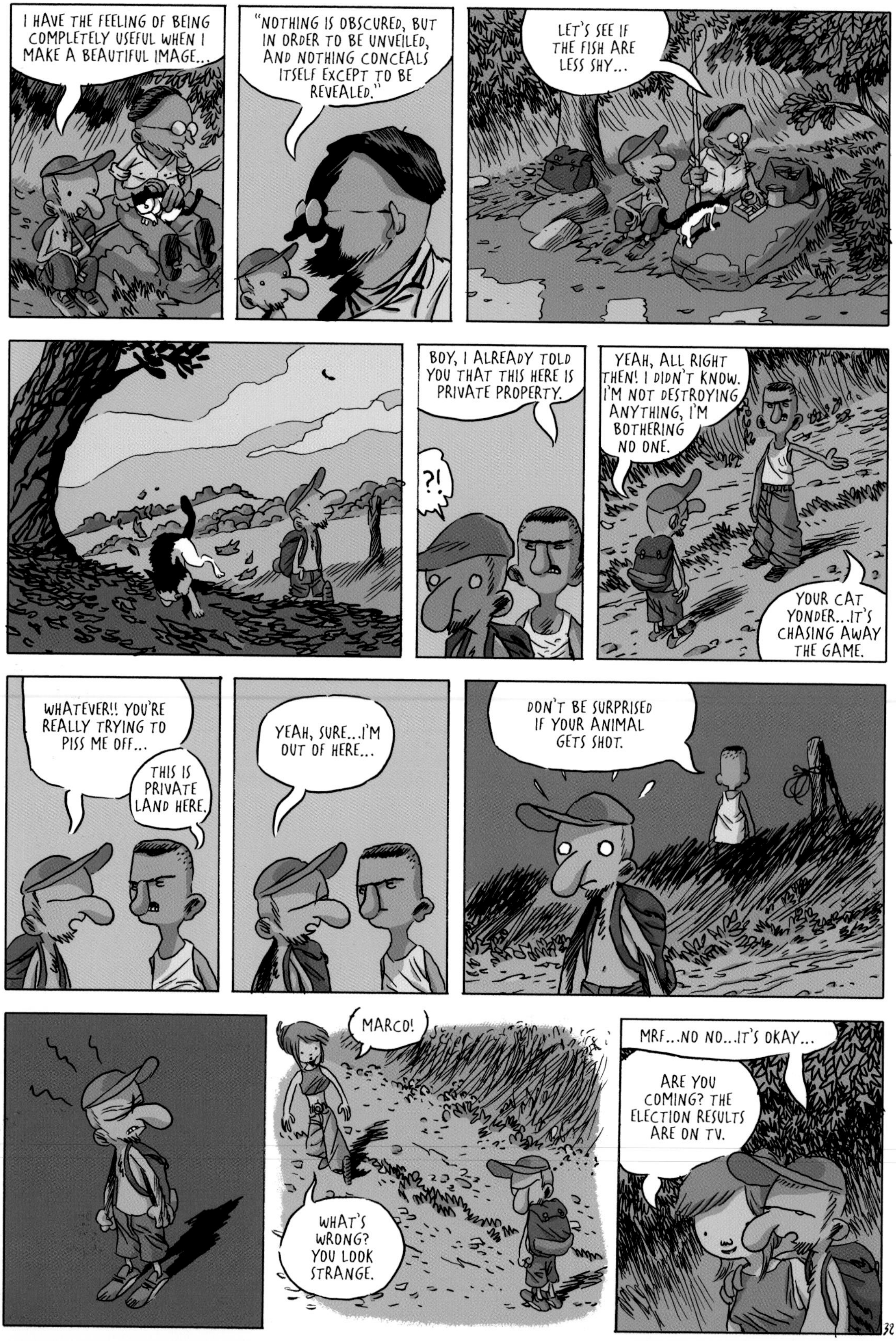

I HAVE THE FEELING OF BEING COMPLETELY USEFUL WHEN I MAKE A BEAUTIFUL IMAGE...
"NOTHING IS OBSCURED, BUT IN ORDER TO BE UNVEILED, AND NOTHING CONCEALS ITSELF EXCEPT TO BE REVEALED."
LET'S SEE IF THE FISH ARE LESS SHY...
BOY, I ALREADY TOLD YOU THAT THIS HERE IS PRIVATE PROPERTY.
?!
YEAH, ALL RIGHT THEN! I DIDN'T KNOW. I'M NOT DESTROYING ANYTHING, I'M BOTHERING NO ONE.
YOUR CAT YONDER...IT'S CHASING AWAY THE GAME.
WHATEVER!! YOU'RE REALLY TRYING TO PISS ME OFF...
THIS IS PRIVATE LAND HERE.
YEAH, SURE...I'M OUT OF HERE...
DON'T BE SURPRISED IF YOUR ANIMAL GETS SHOT.
MARCO!
WHAT'S WRONG? YOU LOOK STRANGE.
MRF...NO NO...IT'S OKAY...
ARE YOU COMING? THE ELECTION RESULTS ARE ON TV.

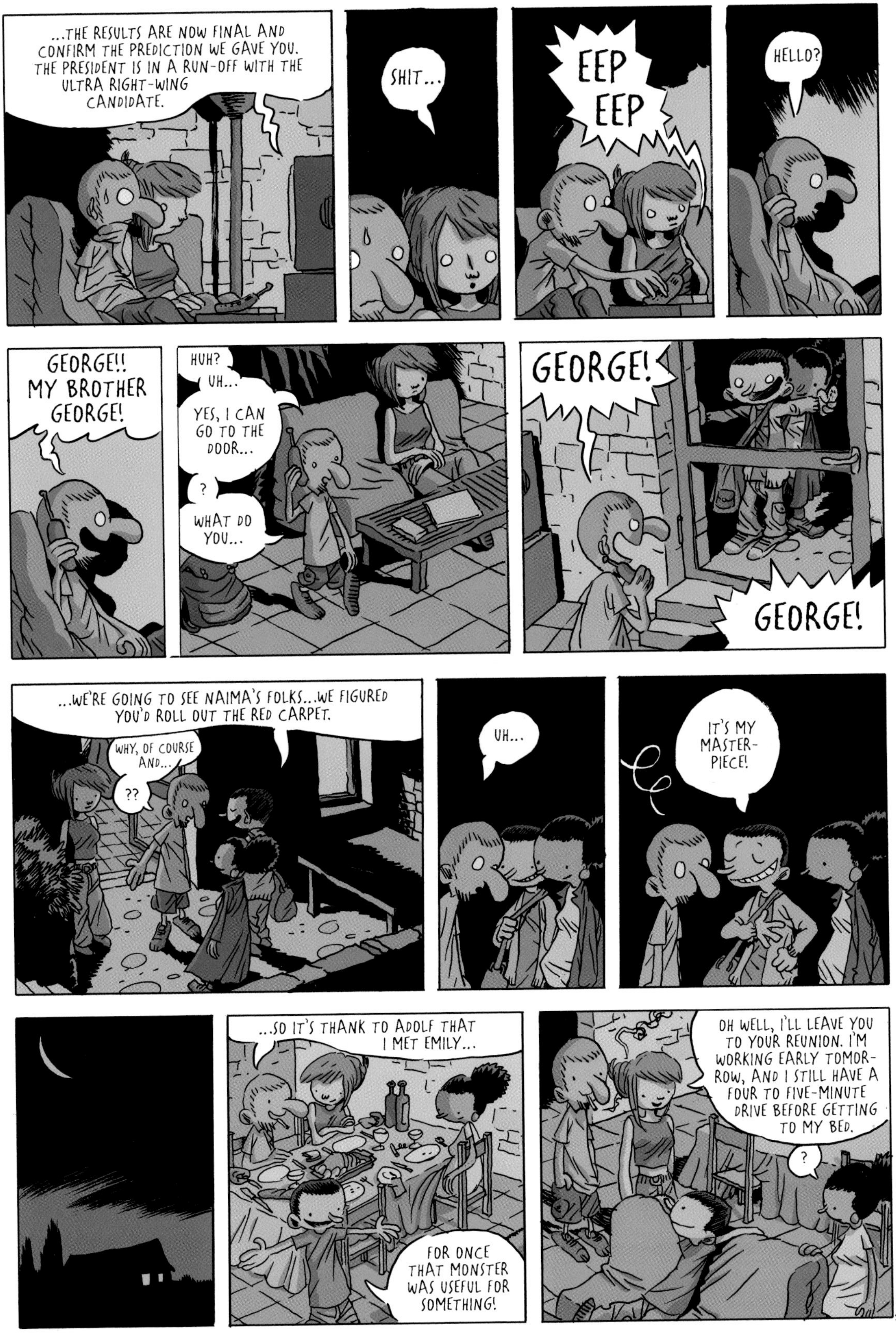
...THE RESULTS ARE NOW FINAL AND CONFIRM THE PREDICTION WE GAVE YOU. THE PRESIDENT IS IN A RUN-OFF WITH THE ULTRA RIGHT-WING CANDIDATE.
SHIT...
EEP EEP
HELLO?
GEORGE!! MY BROTHER GEORGE!
HUH?
UH...
YES, I CAN GO TO THE DOOR...
?
WHAT DO YOU...
GEORGE!
GEORGE!
...WE'RE GOING TO SEE NAIMA'S FOLKS...WE FIGURED YOU'D ROLL OUT THE RED CARPET.
WHY, OF COURSE AND...
??
UH...
IT'S MY MASTER-PIECE!
...SO IT'S THANK TO ADOLF THAT I MET EMILY...
FOR ONCE THAT MONSTER WAS USEFUL FOR SOMETHING!
OH WELL, I'LL LEAVE YOU TO YOUR REUNION. I'M WORKING EARLY TOMOR-ROW, AND I STILL HAVE A FOUR TO FIVE-MINUTE DRIVE BEFORE GETTING TO MY BED.
?

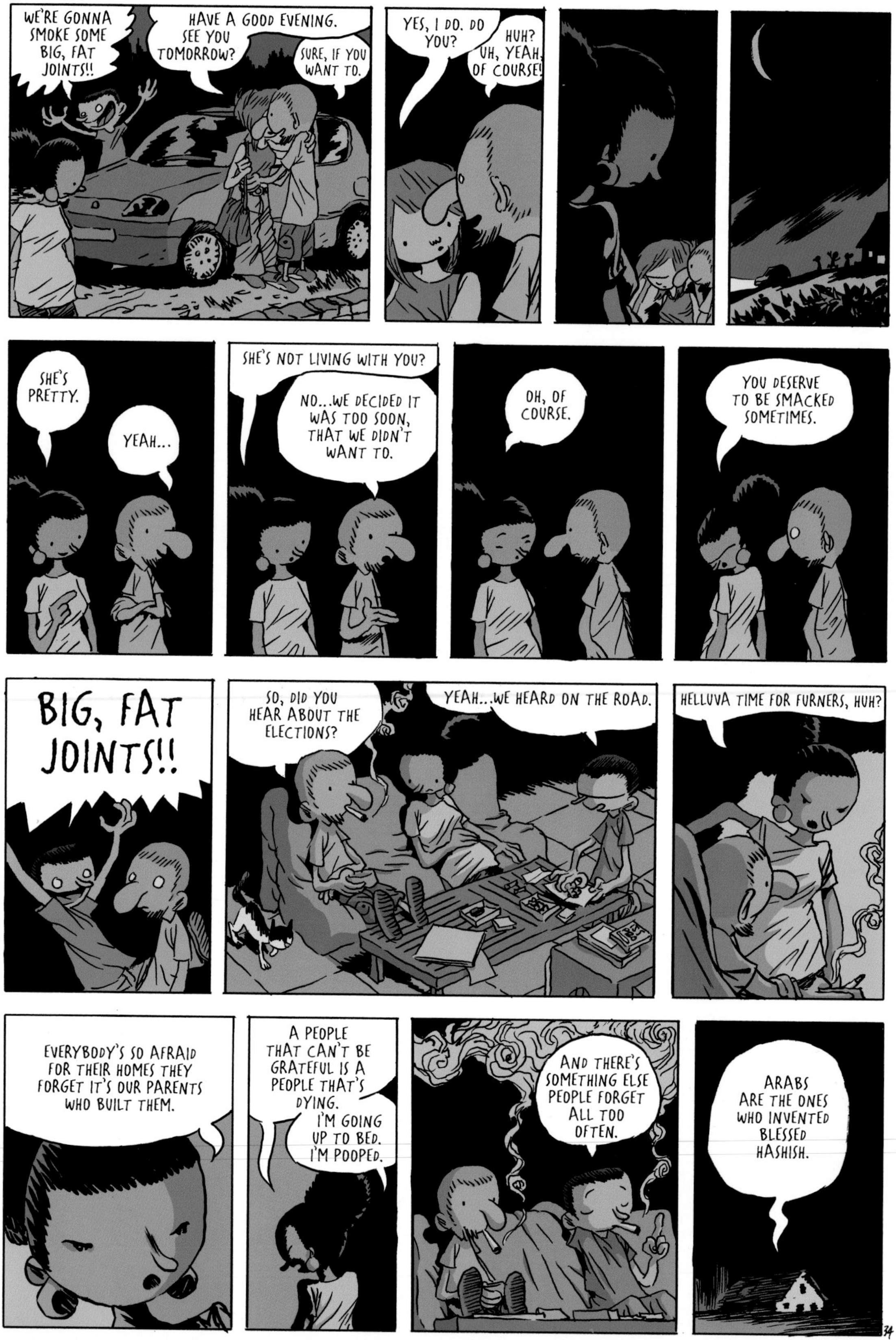
WE'RE GONNA SMOKE SOME BIG, FAT JOINTS!!
HAVE A GOOD EVENING. SEE YOU TOMORROW?
SURE, IF YOU WANT TO.
YES, I DO. DO YOU?
HUH? UH, YEAH. OF COURSE!
SHE'S PRETTY.
YEAH...
SHE'S NOT LIVING WITH YOU?
NO...WE DECIDED IT WAS TOO SOON, THAT WE DIDN'T WANT TO.
OH, OF COURSE.
YOU DESERVE TO BE SMACKED SOMETIMES.
BIG, FAT JOINTS!!
SO, DID YOU HEAR ABOUT THE ELECTIONS?
YEAH...WE HEARD ON THE ROAD.
HELLUVA TIME FOR FURNERS, HUH?
EVERYBODY'S SO AFRAID FOR THEIR HOMES THEY FORGET IT'S OUR PARENTS WHO BUILT THEM.
A PEOPLE THAT CAN'T BE GRATEFUL IS A PEOPLE THAT'S DYING.
I'M GOING UP TO BED. I'M POOPED.
AND THERE'S SOMETHING ELSE PEOPLE FORGET ALL TOO OFTEN.
ARABS ARE THE ONES WHO INVENTED BLESSED HASHISH.

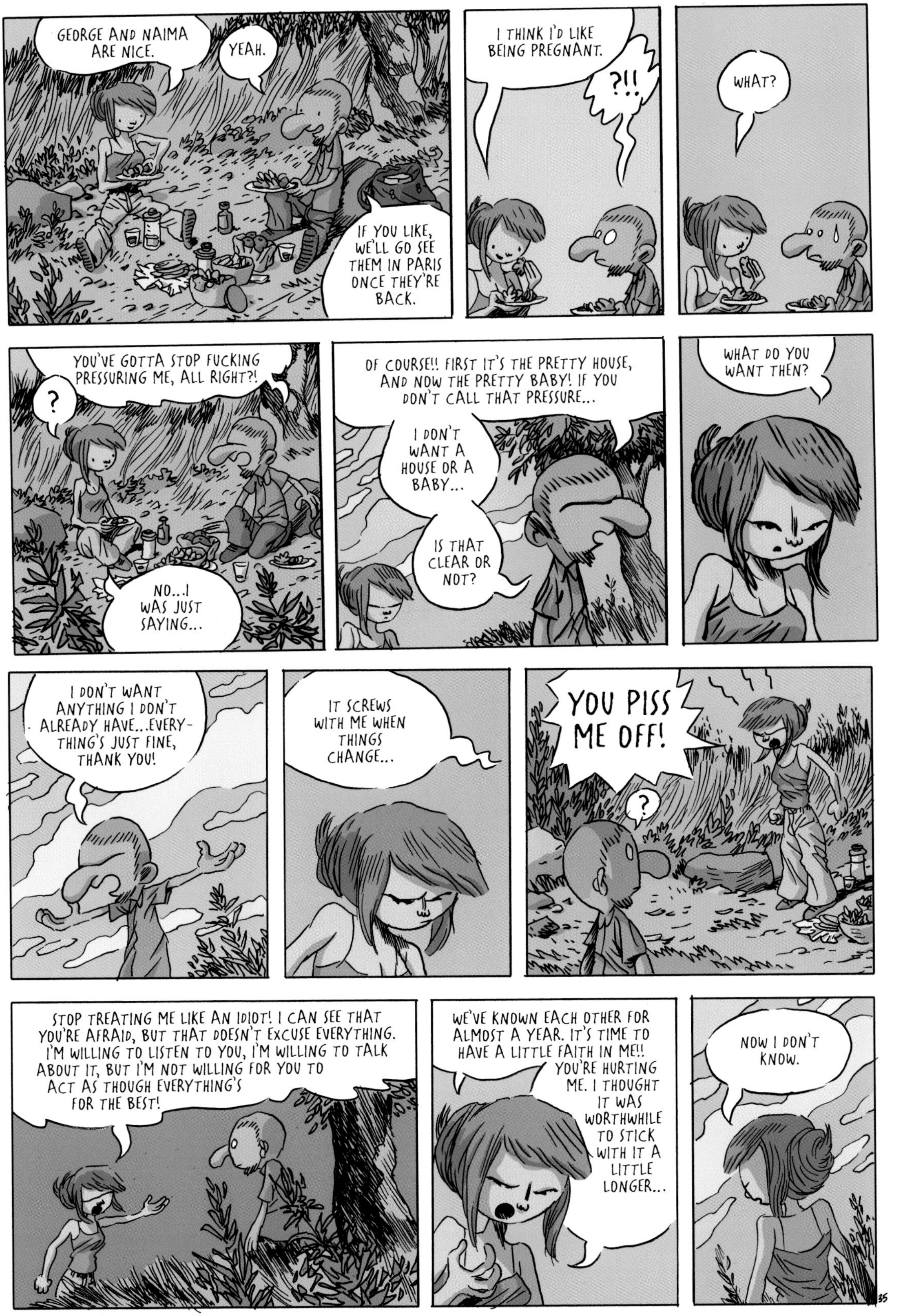
GEORGE AND NAIMA ARE NICE.
YEAH.
IF YOU LIKE, WE'LL GO SEE THEM IN PARIS ONCE THEY'RE BACK.
I THINK I'D LIKE BEING PREGNANT.
?!!
WHAT?
YOU'VE GOTTA STOP FUCKING PRESSURING ME, ALL RIGHT?!
?
NO...I WAS JUST SAYING...
OF COURSE!! FIRST IT'S THE PRETTY HOUSE, AND NOW THE PRETTY BABY! IF YOU DON'T CALL THAT PRESSURE...
I DON'T WANT A HOUSE OR A BABY...
IS THAT CLEAR OR NOT?
WHAT DO YOU WANT THEN?
I DON'T WANT ANYTHING I DON'T ALREADY HAVE...EVERYTHING'S JUST FINE, THANK YOU!
IT SCREWS WITH ME WHEN THINGS CHANGE...
YOU PISS ME OFF!
?
STOP TREATING ME LIKE AN IDIOT! I CAN SEE THAT YOU'RE AFRAID, BUT THAT DOESN'T EXCUSE EVERYTHING. I'M WILLING TO LISTEN TO YOU, I'M WILLING TO TALK ABOUT IT, BUT I'M NOT WILLING FOR YOU TO ACT AS THOUGH EVERYTHING'S FOR THE BEST!
WE'VE KNOWN EACH OTHER FOR ALMOST A YEAR. IT'S TIME TO HAVE A LITTLE FAITH IN ME!! YOU'RE HURTING ME. I THOUGHT IT WAS WORTHWHILE TO STICK WITH IT A LITTLE LONGER...
NOW I DON'T KNOW.

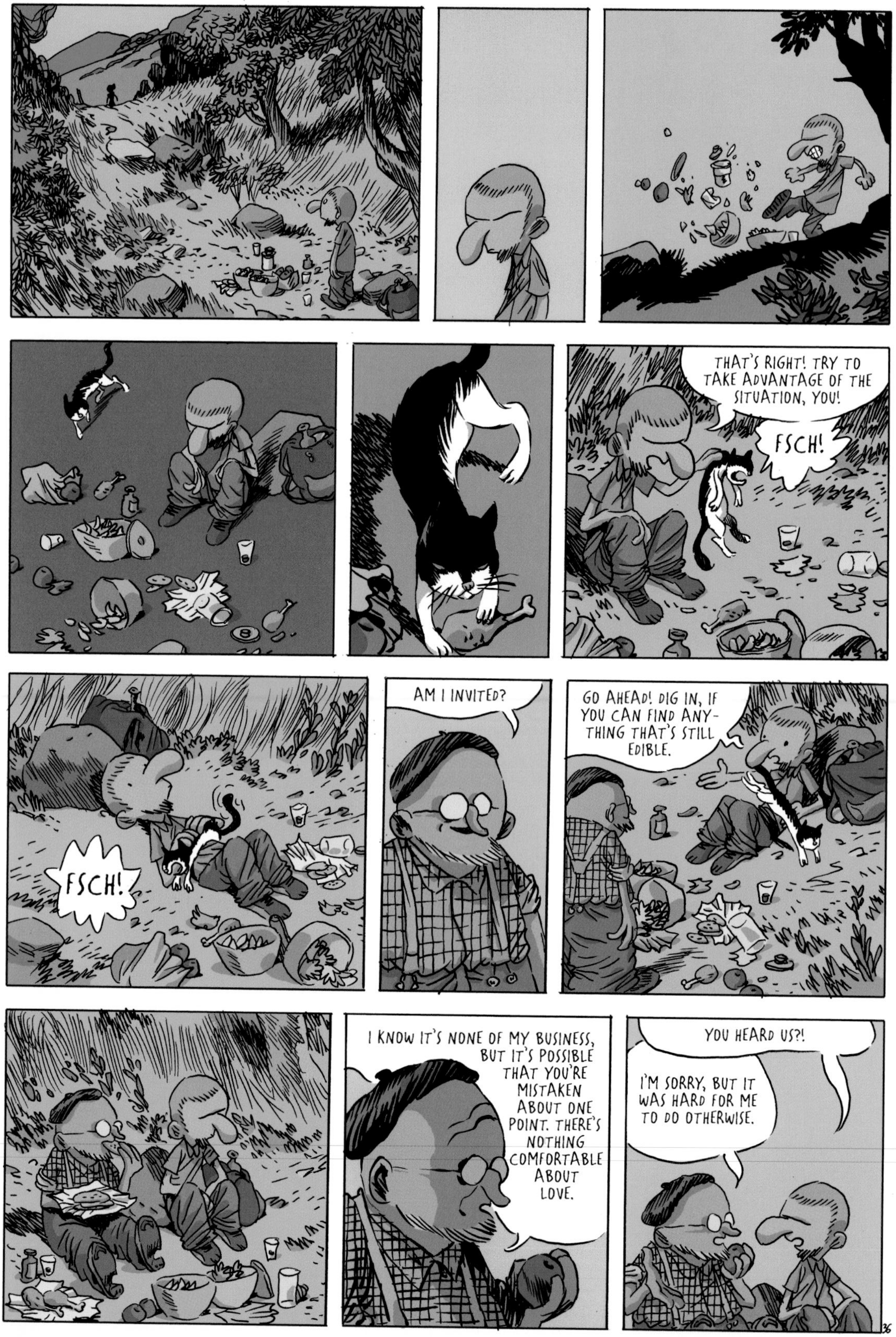
THAT'S RIGHT! TRY TO TAKE ADVANTAGE OF THE SITUATION, YOU!
FSCH!
FSCH!
AM I INVITED?
GO AHEAD! DIG IN, IF YOU CAN FIND ANYTHING THAT'S STILL EDIBLE.
I KNOW IT'S NONE OF MY BUSINESS, BUT IT'S POSSIBLE THAT YOU'RE MISTAKEN ABOUT ONE POINT. THERE'S NOTHING COMFORTABLE ABOUT LOVE.
YOU HEARD US?!
I'M SORRY, BUT IT WAS HARD FOR ME TO DO OTHERWISE.

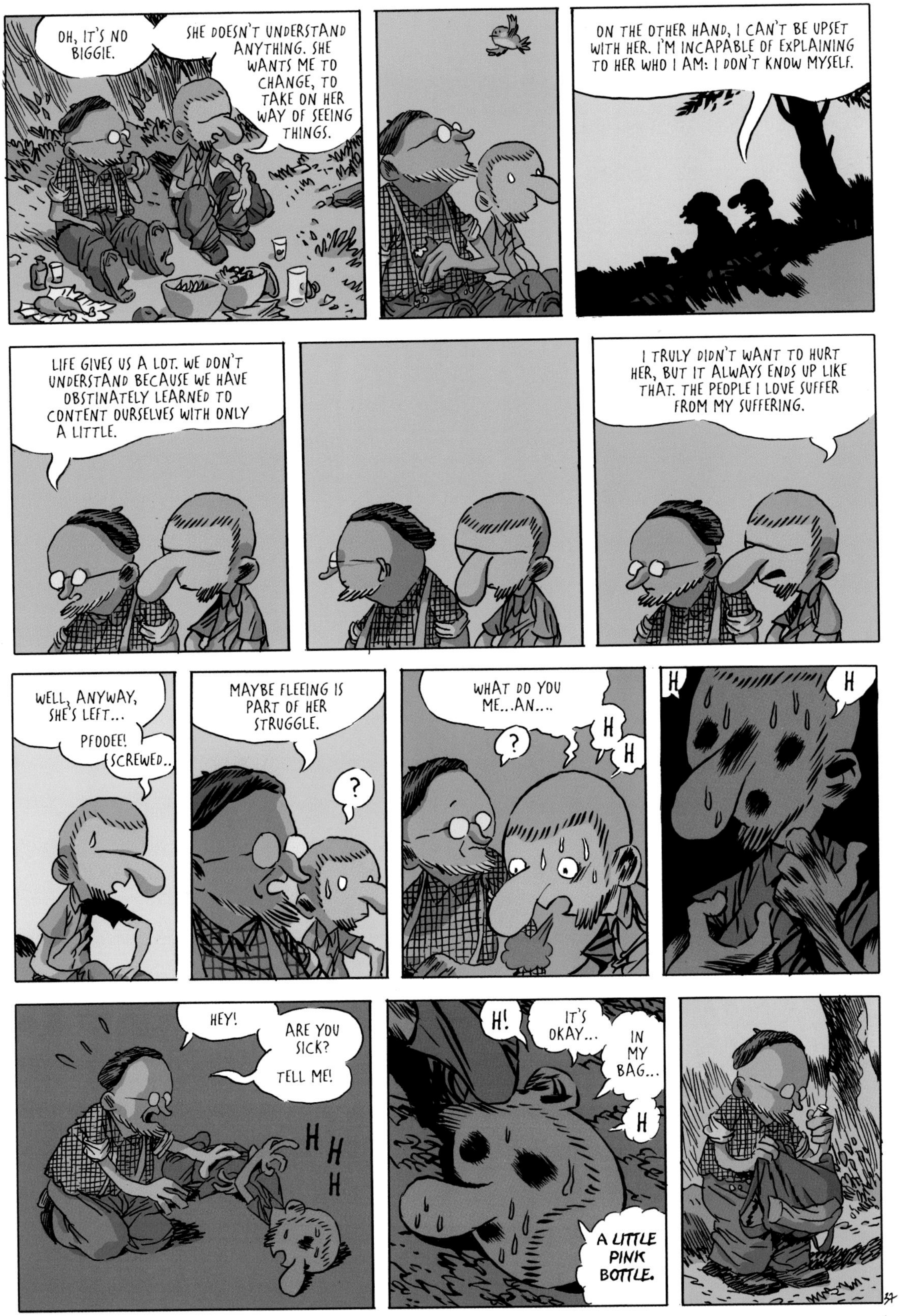
OH, IT'S NO BIGGIE.
SHE DOESN'T UNDERSTAND ANYTHING. SHE WANTS ME TO CHANGE, TO TAKE ON HER WAY OF SEEING THINGS.
ON THE OTHER HAND, I CAN'T BE UPSET WITH HER. I'M INCAPABLE OF EXPLAINING TO HER WHO I AM: I DON'T KNOW MYSELF.
LIFE GIVES US A LOT. WE DON'T UNDERSTAND BECAUSE WE HAVE OBSTINATELY LEARNED TO CONTENT OURSELVES WITH ONLY A LITTLE.
I TRULY DIDN'T WANT TO HURT HER, BUT IT ALWAYS ENDS UP LIKE THAT. THE PEOPLE I LOVE SUFFER FROM MY SUFFERING.
WELL, ANYWAY, SHE'S LEFT...
PFOOEE!
SCREWED...
MAYBE FLEEING IS PART OF HER STRUGGLE.
?
WHAT DO YOU ME...AN....
?
H
H
H
H
HEY!
ARE YOU SICK?
TELL ME!
H
H
H
H!
IT'S OKAY...
IN MY BAG...
H
A LITTLE PINK BOTTLE.

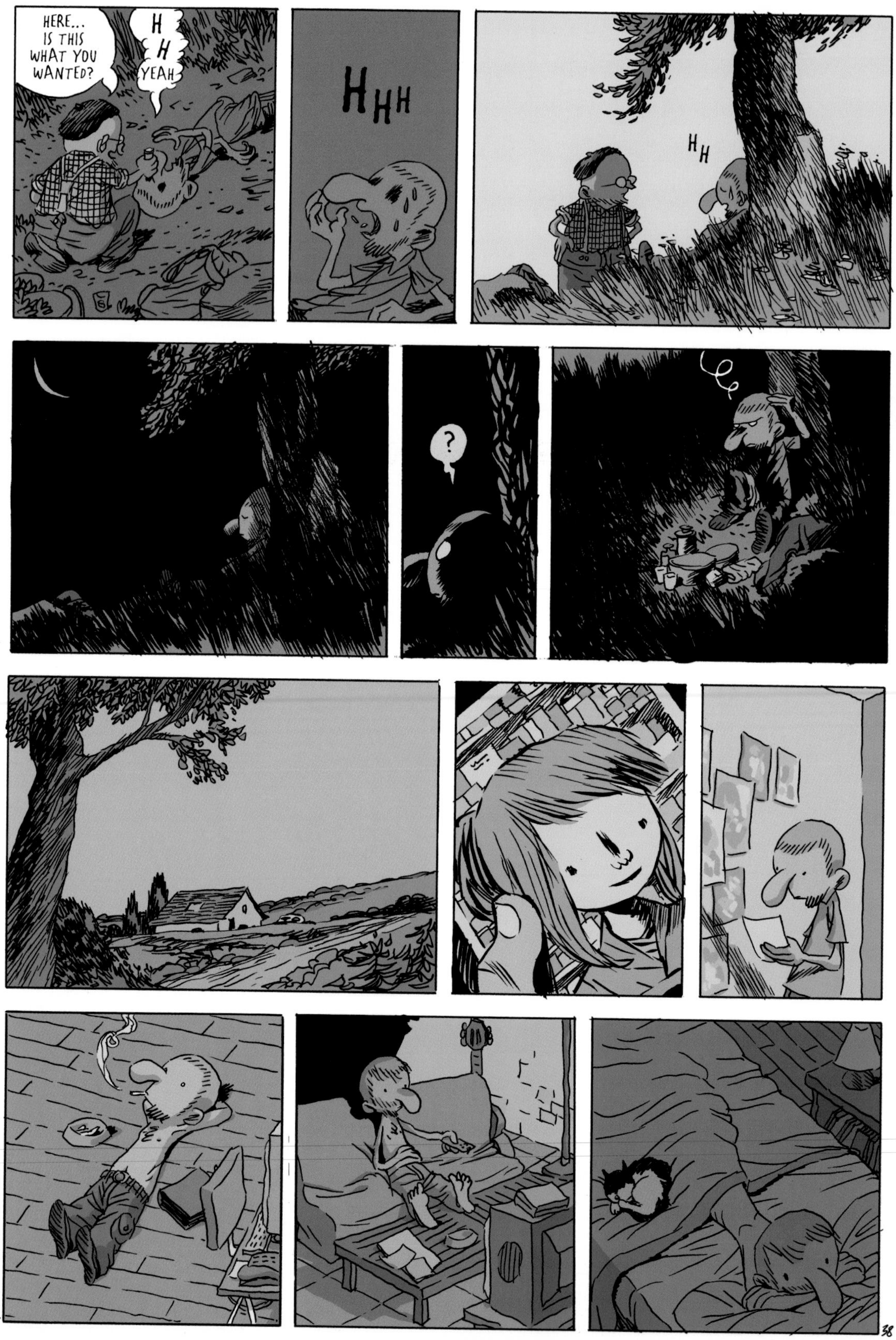
HERE... IS THIS WHAT YOU WANTED?
H H YEAH
HHH
HH
?

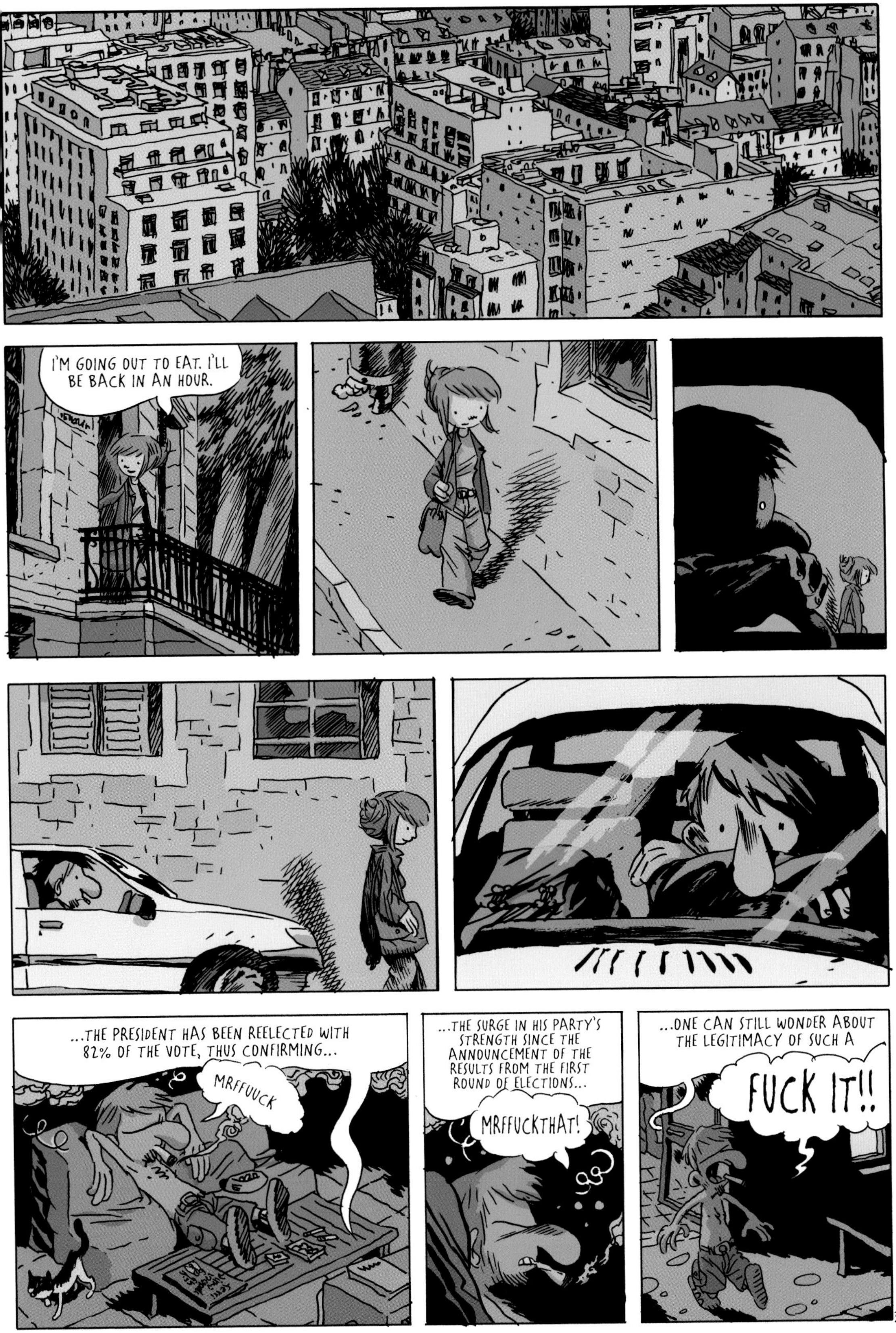
I'M GOING OUT TO EAT. I'LL BE BACK IN AN HOUR.
...THE PRESIDENT HAS BEEN REELECTED WITH 82% OF THE VOTE, THUS CONFIRMING...
MRFFUUCK
...THE SURGE IN HIS PARTY'S STRENGTH SINCE THE ANNOUNCEMENT OF THE RESULTS FROM THE FIRST ROUND OF ELECTIONS...
MRFFUCKTHAT!
...ONE CAN STILL WONDER ABOUT THE LEGITIMACY OF SUCH A
FUCK IT!!

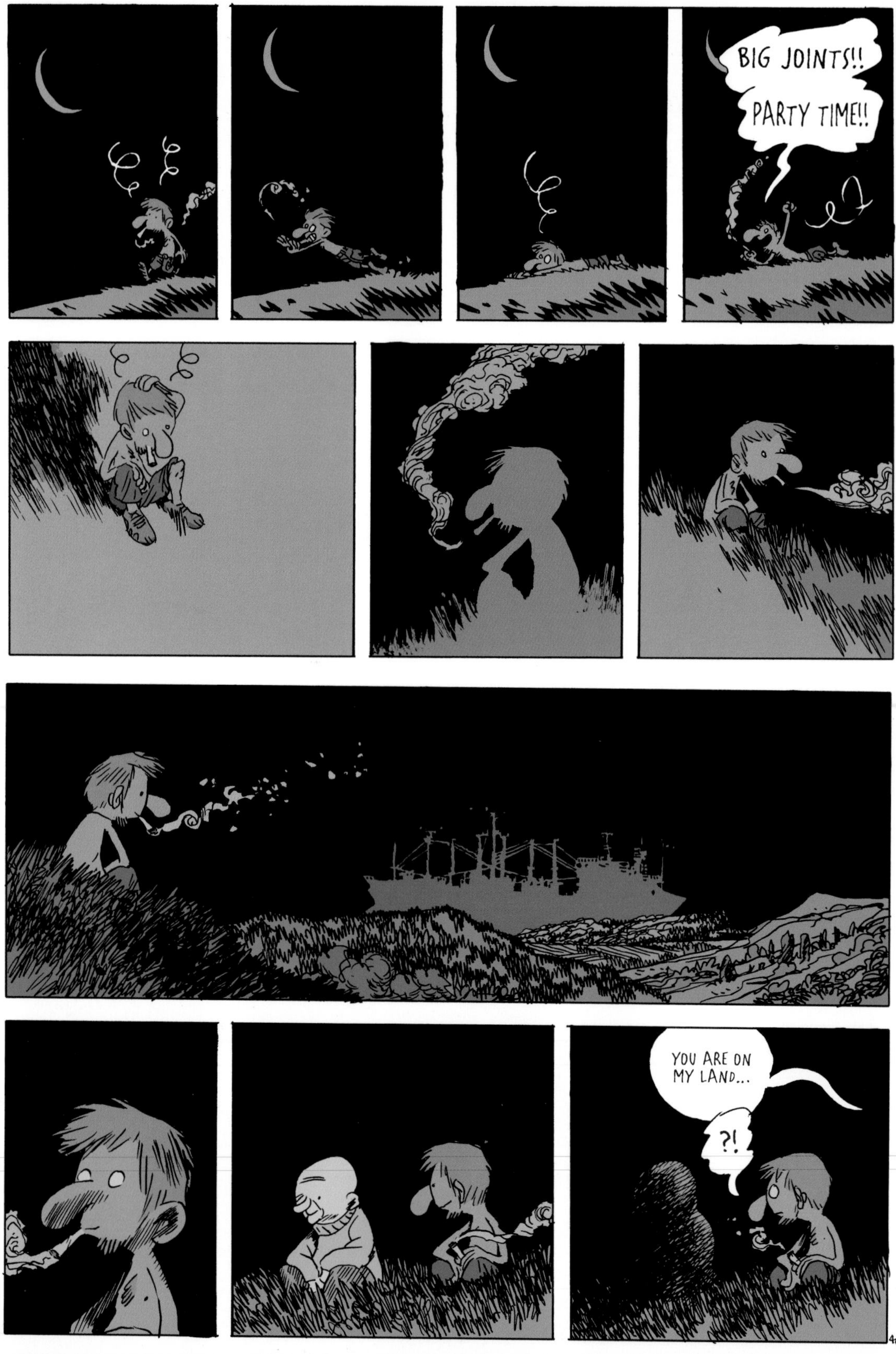
BIG JOINTS!!
PARTY TIME!!
YOU ARE ON MY LAND...
?!

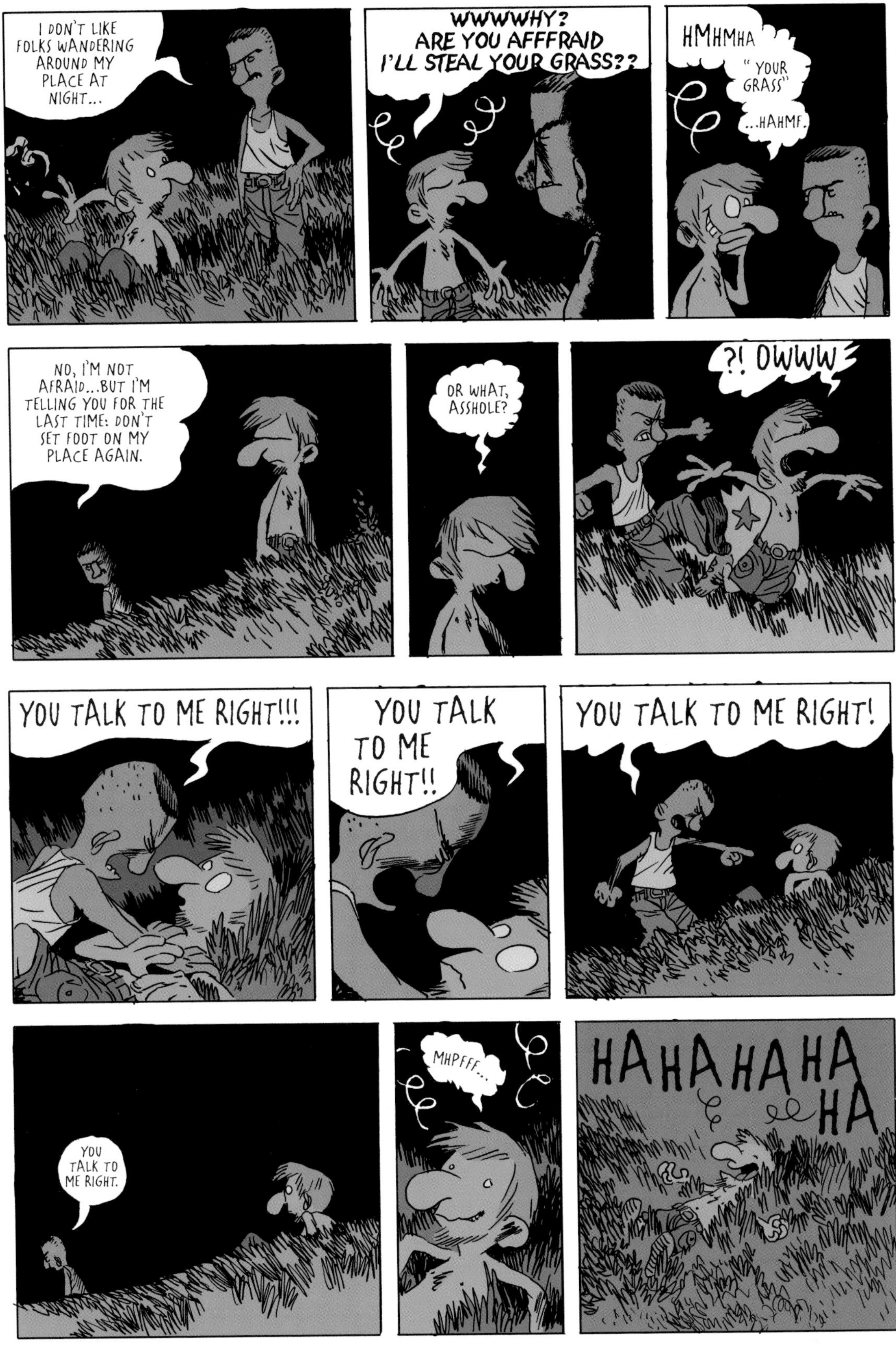
I DON'T LIKE FOLKS WANDERING AROUND MY PLACE AT NIGHT...
WWWWHY? ARE YOU AFFFRAID I'LL STEAL YOUR GRASS??
HMHMHA
"YOUR GRASS"
...HAHMF.
NO, I'M NOT AFRAID...BUT I'M TELLING YOU FOR THE LAST TIME: DON'T SET FOOT ON MY PLACE AGAIN.
OR WHAT, ASSHOLE?
?! OWWW
YOU TALK TO ME RIGHT!!!
YOU TALK TO ME RIGHT!!
YOU TALK TO ME RIGHT!
YOU TALK TO ME RIGHT.
MHPFFF...
HAHAHAHAHA HA

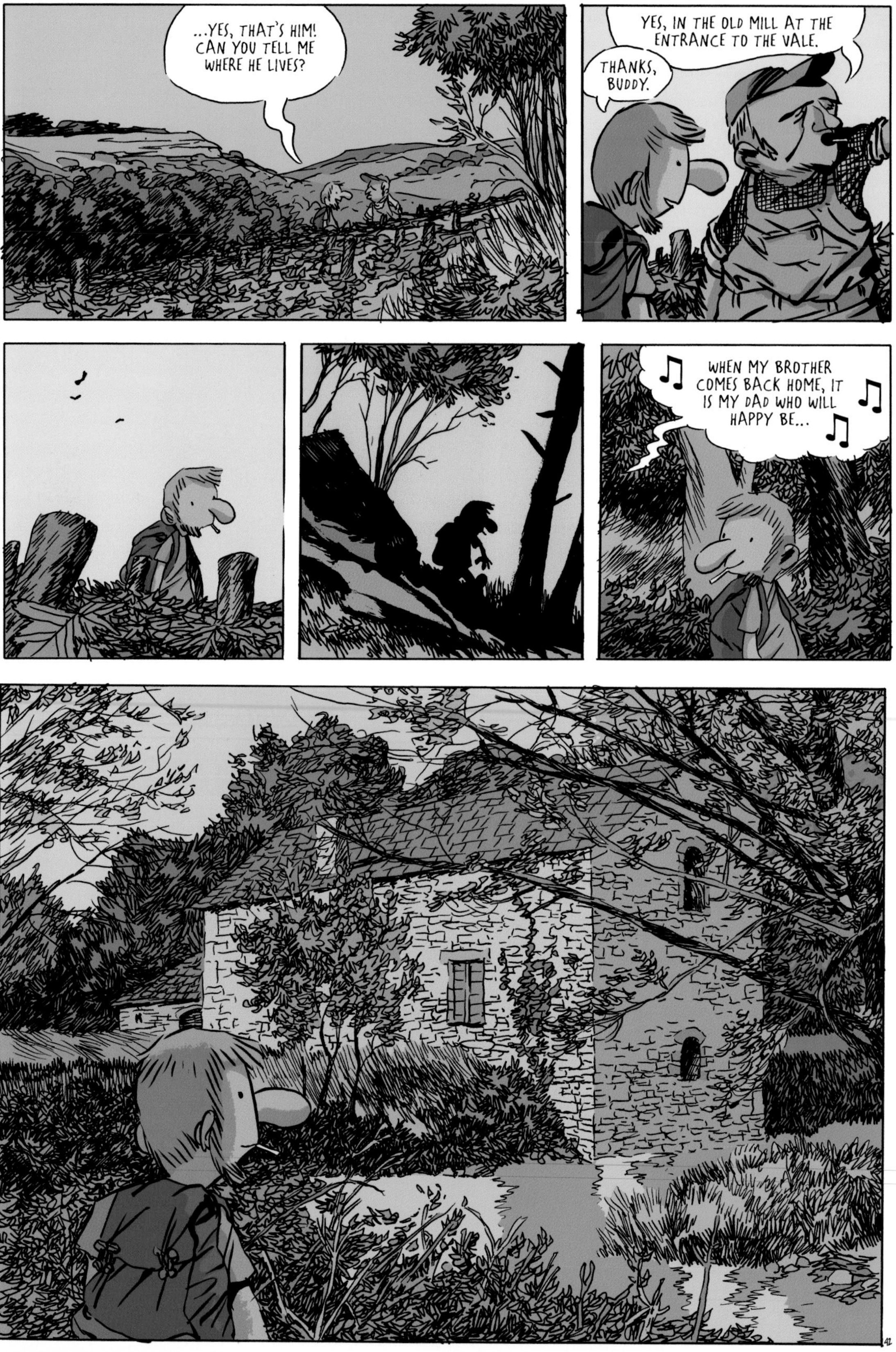
...YES, THAT'S HIM! CAN YOU TELL ME WHERE HE LIVES?
YES, IN THE OLD MILL AT THE ENTRANCE TO THE VALE.
THANKS, BUDDY.
WHEN MY BROTHER COMES BACK HOME, IT IS MY DAD WHO WILL HAPPY BE...

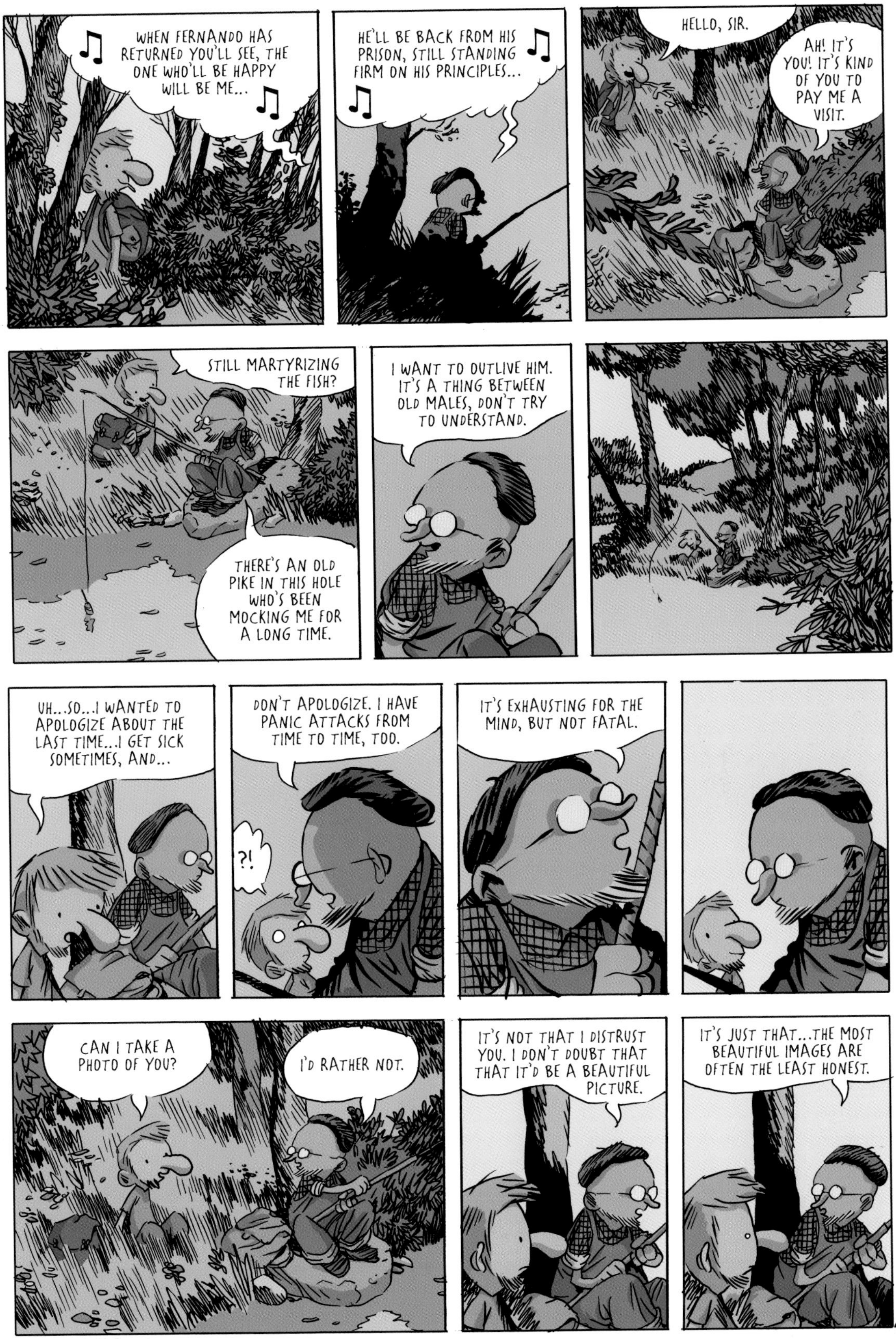
WHEN FERNANDO HAS RETURNED YOU'LL SEE, THE ONE WHO'LL BE HAPPY WILL BE ME...
HE'LL BE BACK FROM HIS PRISON, STILL STANDING FIRM ON HIS PRINCIPLES...
HELLO, SIR.
AH! IT'S YOU! IT'S KIND OF YOU TO PAY ME A VISIT.
STILL MARTYRIZING THE FISH?
THERE'S AN OLD PIKE IN THIS HOLE WHO'S BEEN MOCKING ME FOR A LONG TIME.
I WANT TO OUTLIVE HIM. IT'S A THING BETWEEN OLD MALES, DON'T TRY TO UNDERSTAND.
UH...SO...I WANTED TO APOLOGIZE ABOUT THE LAST TIME...I GET SICK SOMETIMES, AND...
DON'T APOLOGIZE. I HAVE PANIC ATTACKS FROM TIME TO TIME, TOO.
?!
IT'S EXHAUSTING FOR THE MIND, BUT NOT FATAL.
CAN I TAKE A PHOTO OF YOU?
I'D RATHER NOT.
IT'S NOT THAT I DISTRUST YOU. I DON'T DOUBT THAT THAT IT'D BE A BEAUTIFUL PICTURE.
IT'S JUST THAT...THE MOST BEAUTIFUL IMAGES ARE OFTEN THE LEAST HONEST.

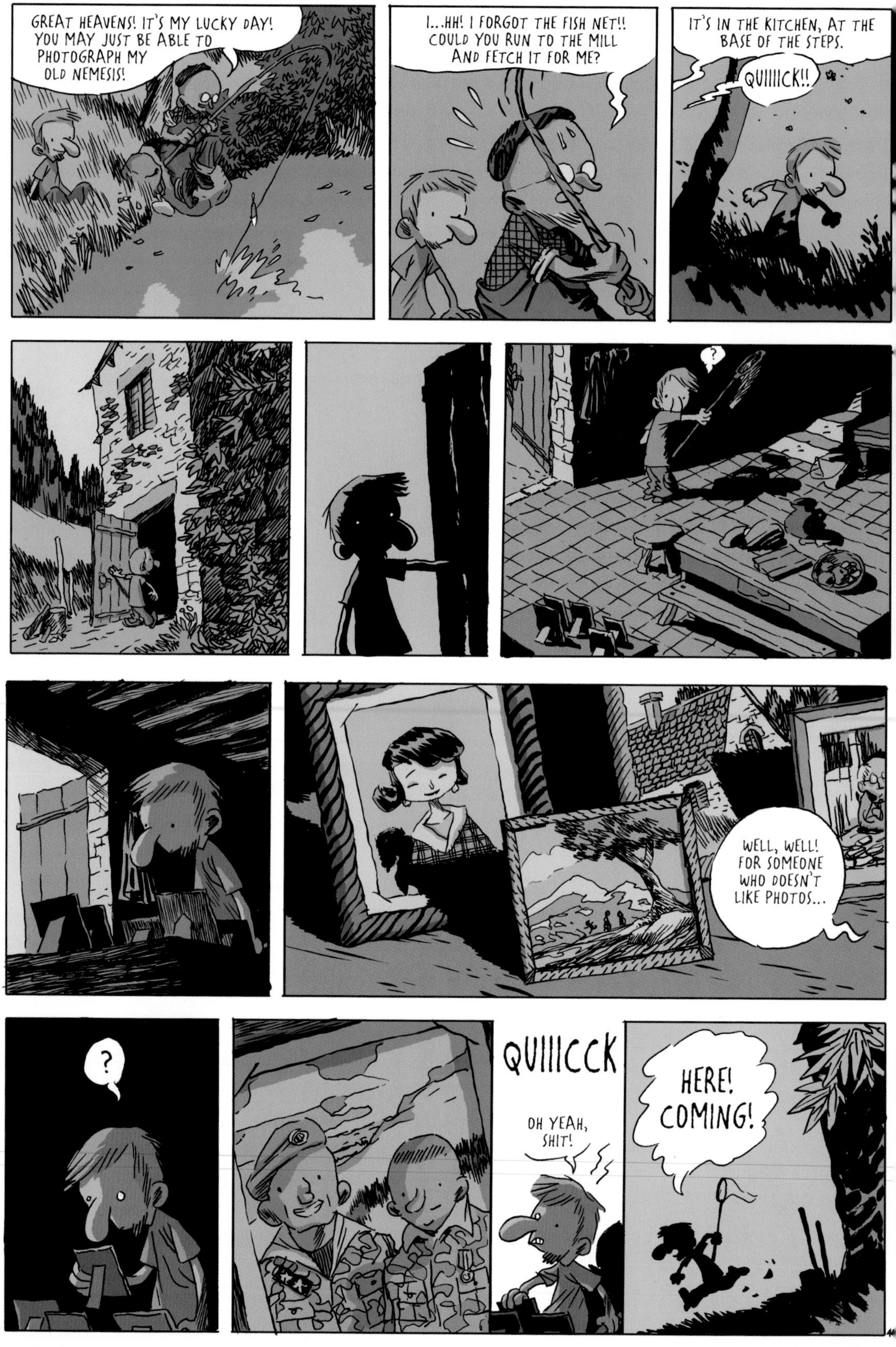
GREAT HEAVENS! IT'S MY LUCKY DAY! YOU MAY JUST BE ABLE TO PHOTOGRAPH MY OLD NEMESIS!
I...HH! I FORGOT THE FISH NET!! COULD YOU RUN TO THE MILL AND FETCH IT FOR ME?
IT'S IN THE KITCHEN, AT THE BASE OF THE STEPS.
QUIIIICK!!
?
WELL, WELL! FOR SOMEONE WHO DOESN'T LIKE PHOTOS...
?
QUIIICCK
OH YEAH, SHIT!
HERE! COMING!

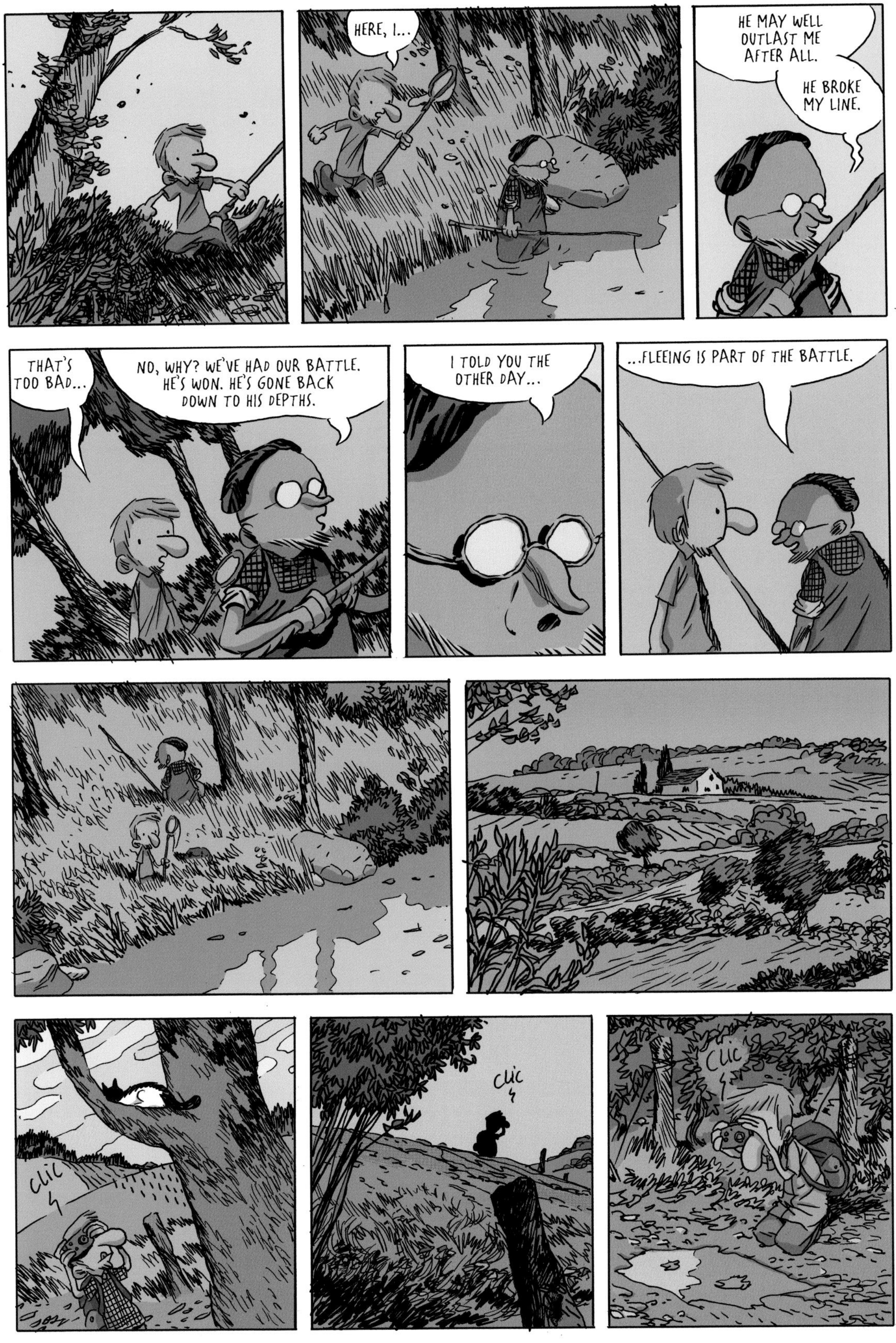
HERE, I...
HE MAY WELL OUTLAST ME AFTER ALL.
HE BROKE MY LINE.
THAT'S TOO BAD...
NO, WHY? WE'VE HAD OUR BATTLE. HE'S WON. HE'S GONE BACK DOWN TO HIS DEPTHS.
I TOLD YOU THE OTHER DAY...
...FLEEING IS PART OF THE BATTLE.
CLIC
CLIC
CLIC

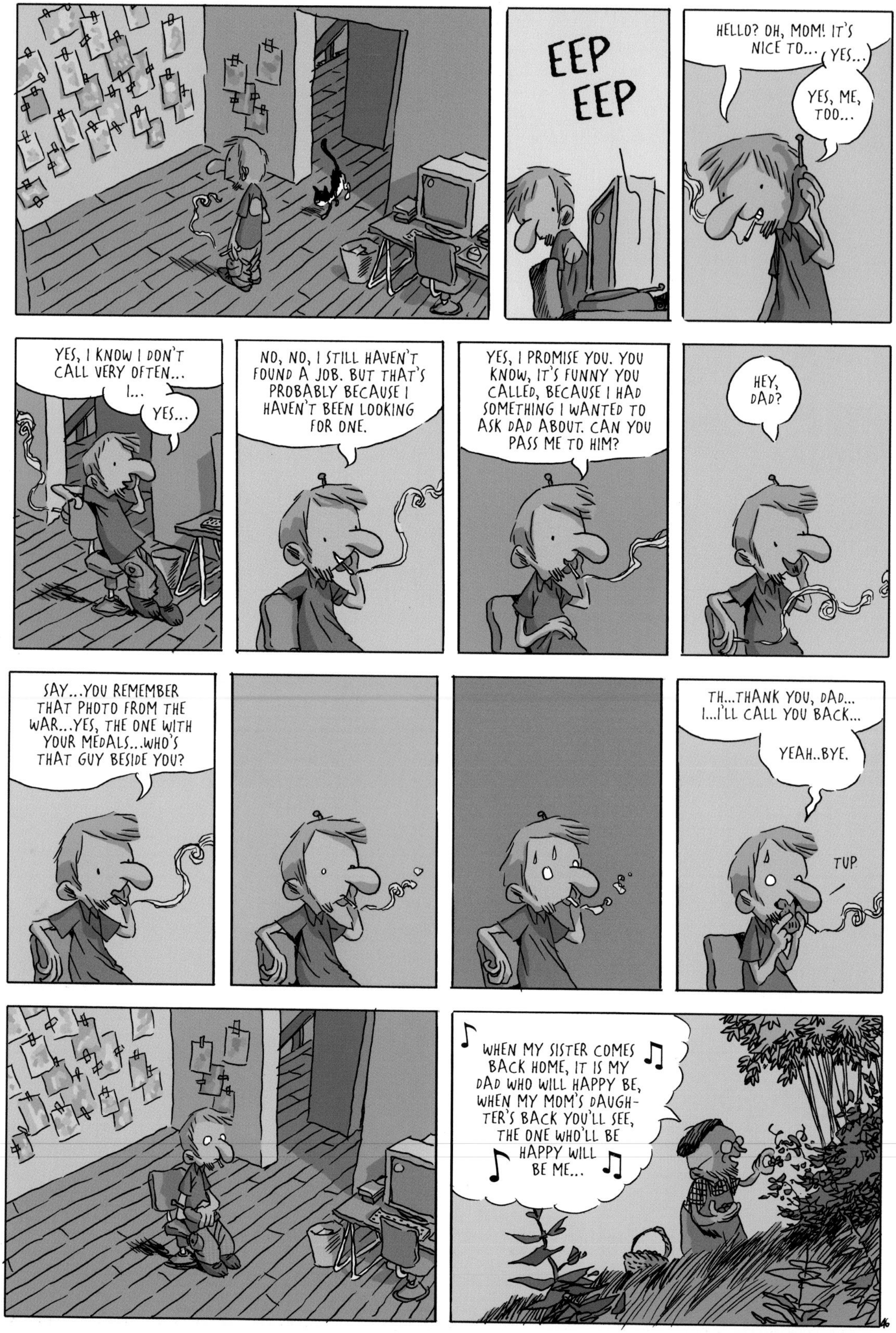
EEP
EEP
HELLO? OH, MOM! IT'S NICE TO...
YES...
YES, ME, TOO...
YES, I KNOW I DON'T CALL VERY OFTEN...
I...
YES...
NO, NO, I STILL HAVEN'T FOUND A JOB. BUT THAT'S PROBABLY BECAUSE I HAVEN'T BEEN LOOKING FOR ONE.
YES, I PROMISE YOU. YOU KNOW, IT'S FUNNY YOU CALLED, BECAUSE I HAD SOMETHING I WANTED TO ASK DAD ABOUT. CAN YOU PASS ME TO HIM?
HEY, DAD?
SAY...YOU REMEMBER THAT PHOTO FROM THE WAR...YES, THE ONE WITH YOUR MEDALS...WHO'S THAT GUY BESIDE YOU?
TH...THANK YOU, DAD... I...I'LL CALL YOU BACK...
YEAH..BYE.
TUP
WHEN MY SISTER COMES BACK HOME, IT IS MY DAD WHO WILL HAPPY BE, WHEN MY MOM'S DAUGHTER'S BACK YOU'LL SEE, THE ONE WHO'LL BE HAPPY WILL BE ME...

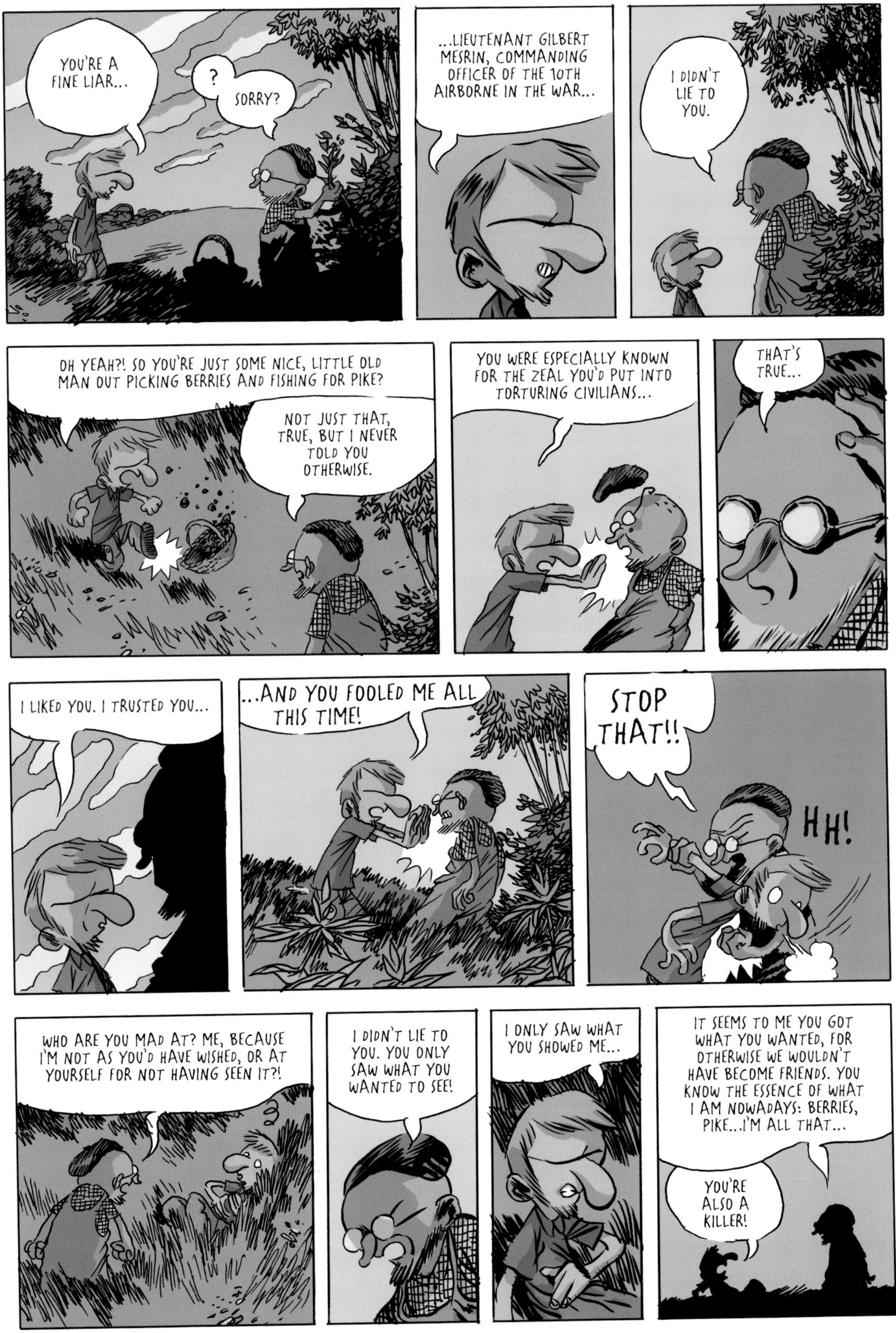

YOU'RE A FINE LIAR...
?
SORRY?
...LIEUTENANT GILBERT MESRIN, COMMANDING OFFICER OF THE 10TH AIRBORNE IN THE WAR...
I DIDN'T LIE TO YOU.
OH YEAH?! SO YOU'RE JUST SOME NICE, LITTLE OLD MAN OUT PICKING BERRIES AND FISHING FOR PIKE?
NOT JUST THAT, TRUE, BUT I NEVER TOLD YOU OTHERWISE.
YOU WERE ESPECIALLY KNOWN FOR THE ZEAL YOU'D PUT INTO TORTURING CIVILIANS...
THAT'S TRUE...
I LIKED YOU. I TRUSTED YOU...
...AND YOU FOOLED ME ALL THIS TIME!
STOP THAT!!
HH!
WHO ARE YOU MAD AT? ME, BECAUSE I'M NOT AS YOU'D HAVE WISHED, OR AT YOURSELF FOR NOT HAVING SEEN IT?!
I DIDN'T LIE TO YOU. YOU ONLY SAW WHAT YOU WANTED TO SEE!
I ONLY SAW WHAT YOU SHOWED ME...
IT SEEMS TO ME YOU GOT WHAT YOU WANTED, FOR OTHERWISE WE WOULDN'T HAVE BECOME FRIENDS. YOU KNOW THE ESSENCE OF WHAT I AM NOWADAYS: BERRIES, PIKE...I'M ALL THAT...
YOU'RE ALSO A KILLER!

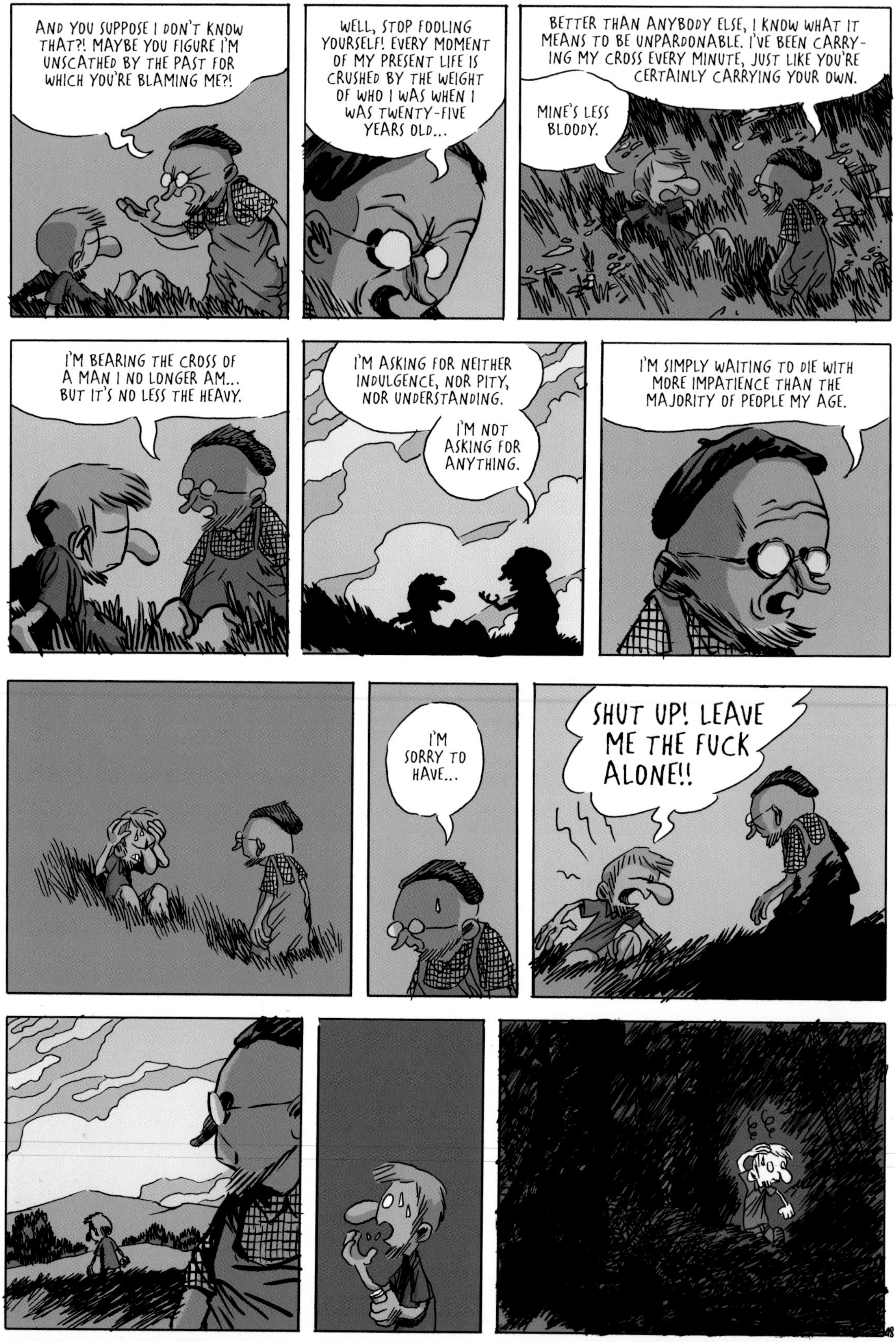
AND YOU SUPPOSE I DON'T KNOW THAT?! MAYBE YOU FIGURE I'M UNSCATHED BY THE PAST FOR WHICH YOU'RE BLAMING ME?!
WELL, STOP FOOLING YOURSELF! EVERY MOMENT OF MY PRESENT LIFE IS CRUSHED BY THE WEIGHT OF WHO I WAS WHEN I WAS TWENTY-FIVE YEARS OLD...
BETTER THAN ANYBODY ELSE, I KNOW WHAT IT MEANS TO BE UNPARDONABLE. I'VE BEEN CARRYING MY CROSS EVERY MINUTE, JUST LIKE YOU'RE CERTAINLY CARRYING YOUR OWN.
MINE'S LESS BLOODY.
I'M BEARING THE CROSS OF A MAN I NO LONGER AM... BUT IT'S NO LESS THE HEAVY.
I'M ASKING FOR NEITHER INDULGENCE, NOR PITY, NOR UNDERSTANDING.
I'M NOT ASKING FOR ANYTHING.
I'M SIMPLY WAITING TO DIE WITH MORE IMPATIENCE THAN THE MAJORITY OF PEOPLE MY AGE.
I'M SORRY TO HAVE...
SHUT UP! LEAVE ME THE FUCK ALONE!!

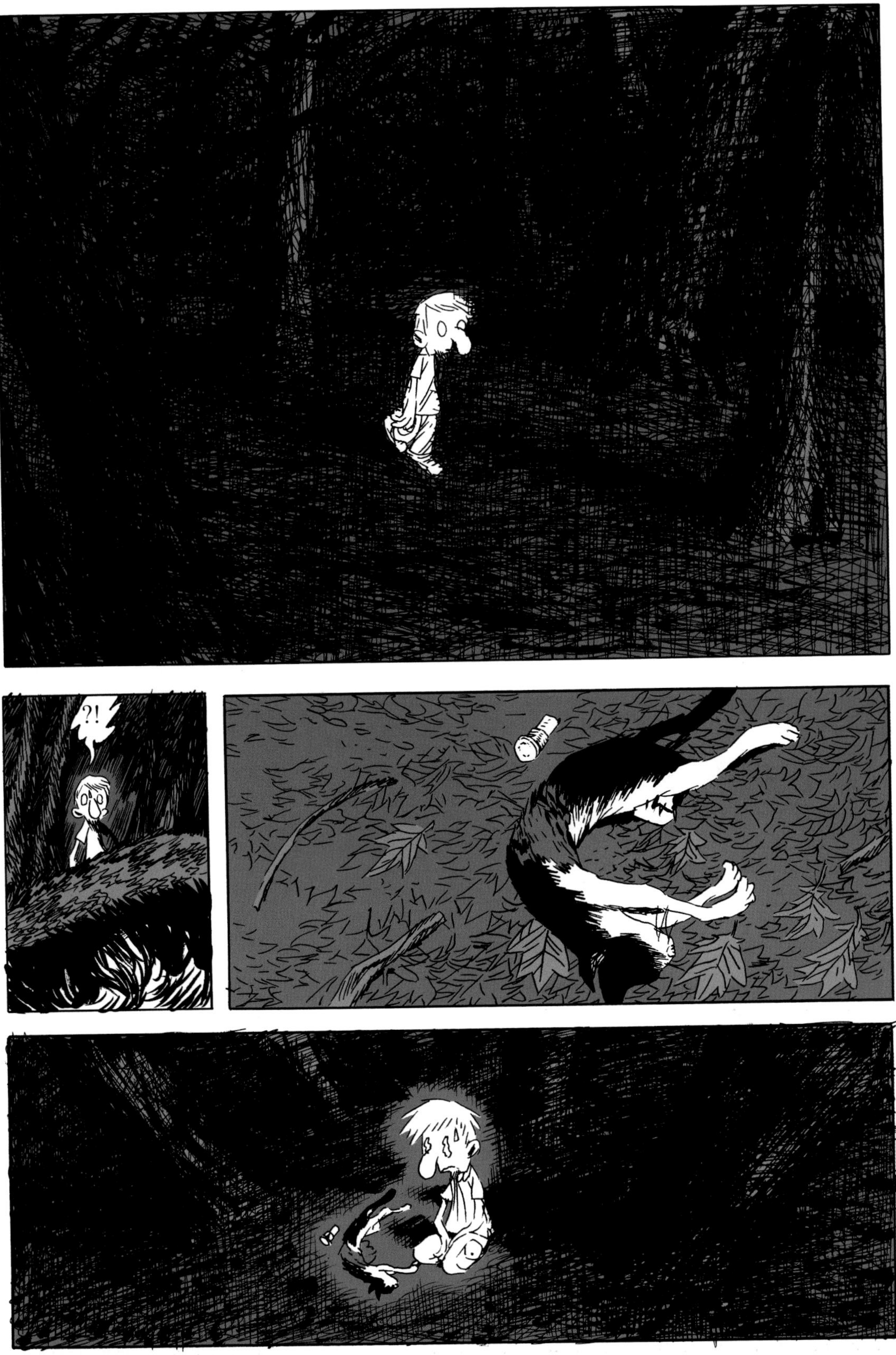
?!

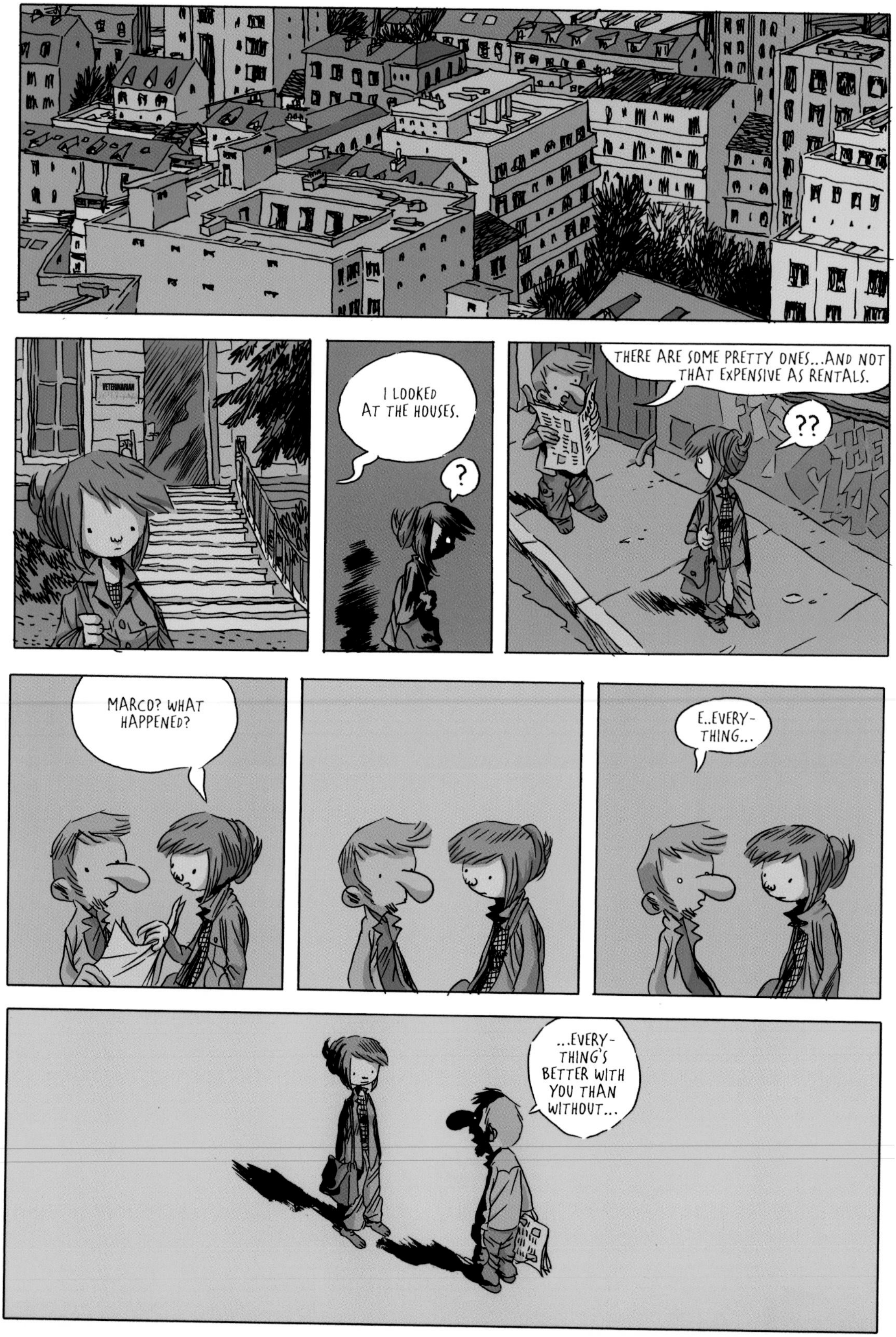
VETERINARIAN
I LOOKED AT THE HOUSES.
?
THERE ARE SOME PRETTY ONES...AND NOT THAT EXPENSIVE AS RENTALS.
??
MARCO? WHAT HAPPENED?
E..EVERY-THING...
...EVERY-THING'S BETTER WITH YOU THAN WITHOUT...

Ordinary Victories

2. Negligible amounts

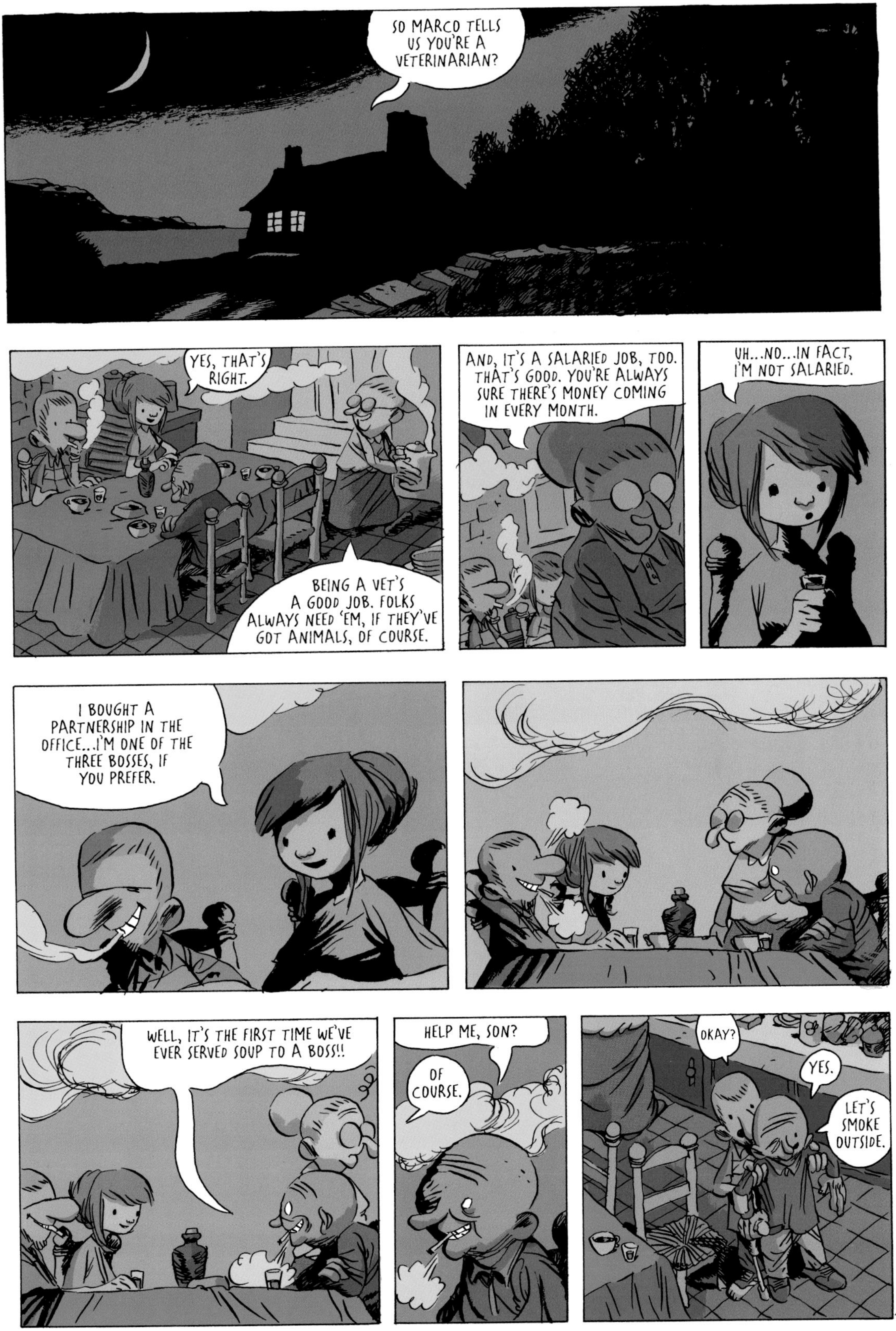

SO MARCO TELLS US YOU'RE A VETERINARIAN?
YES, THAT'S RIGHT.
BEING A VET'S A GOOD JOB. FOLKS ALWAYS NEED 'EM, IF THEY'VE GOT ANIMALS, OF COURSE.
AND, IT'S A SALARIED JOB, TOO. THAT'S GOOD. YOU'RE ALWAYS SURE THERE'S MONEY COMING IN EVERY MONTH.
UH...NO...IN FACT, I'M NOT SALARIED.
I BOUGHT A PARTNERSHIP IN THE OFFICE...I'M ONE OF THE THREE BOSSES, IF YOU PREFER.
WELL, IT'S THE FIRST TIME WE'VE EVER SERVED SOUP TO A BOSS!!
HELP ME, SON?
OF COURSE.
OKAY?
YES.
LET'S SMOKE OUTSIDE.

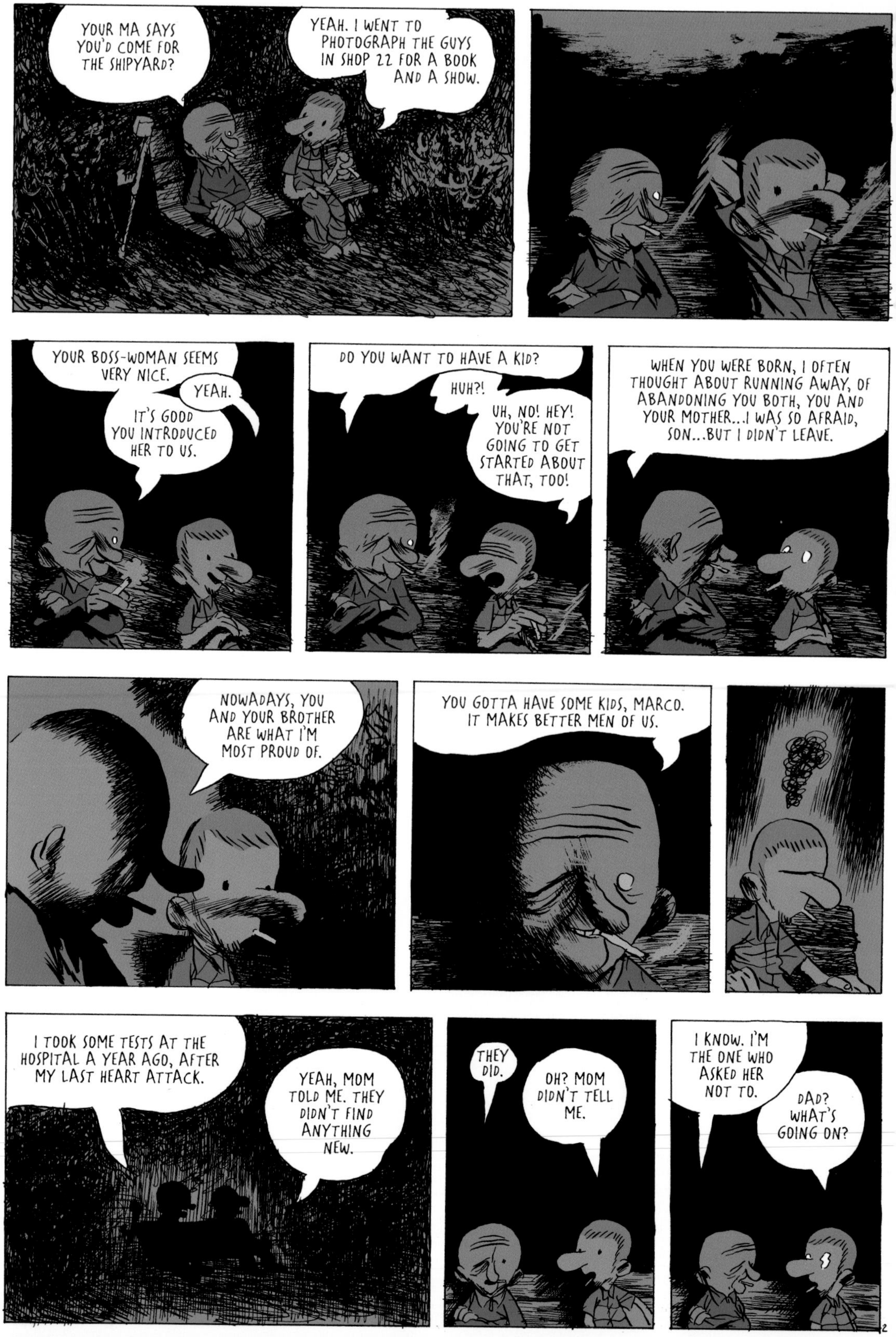

YOUR MA SAYS YOU'D COME FOR THE SHIPYARD?
YEAH. I WENT TO PHOTOGRAPH THE GUYS IN SHOP 22 FOR A BOOK AND A SHOW.
YOUR BOSS-WOMAN SEEMS VERY NICE.
YEAH.
IT'S GOOD YOU INTRODUCED HER TO US.
DO YOU WANT TO HAVE A KID?
HUH?!
UH, NO! HEY! YOU'RE NOT GOING TO GET STARTED ABOUT THAT, TOO!
WHEN YOU WERE BORN, I OFTEN THOUGHT ABOUT RUNNING AWAY, OF ABANDONING YOU BOTH, YOU AND YOUR MOTHER...I WAS SO AFRAID, SON...BUT I DIDN'T LEAVE.
NOWADAYS, YOU AND YOUR BROTHER ARE WHAT I'M MOST PROUD OF.
YOU GOTTA HAVE SOME KIDS, MARCO. IT MAKES BETTER MEN OF US.
I TOOK SOME TESTS AT THE HOSPITAL A YEAR AGO, AFTER MY LAST HEART ATTACK.
YEAH, MOM TOLD ME. THEY DIDN'T FIND ANYTHING NEW.
THEY DID.
OH? MOM DIDN'T TELL ME.
I KNOW. I'M THE ONE WHO ASKED HER NOT TO.
DAD? WHAT'S GOING ON?

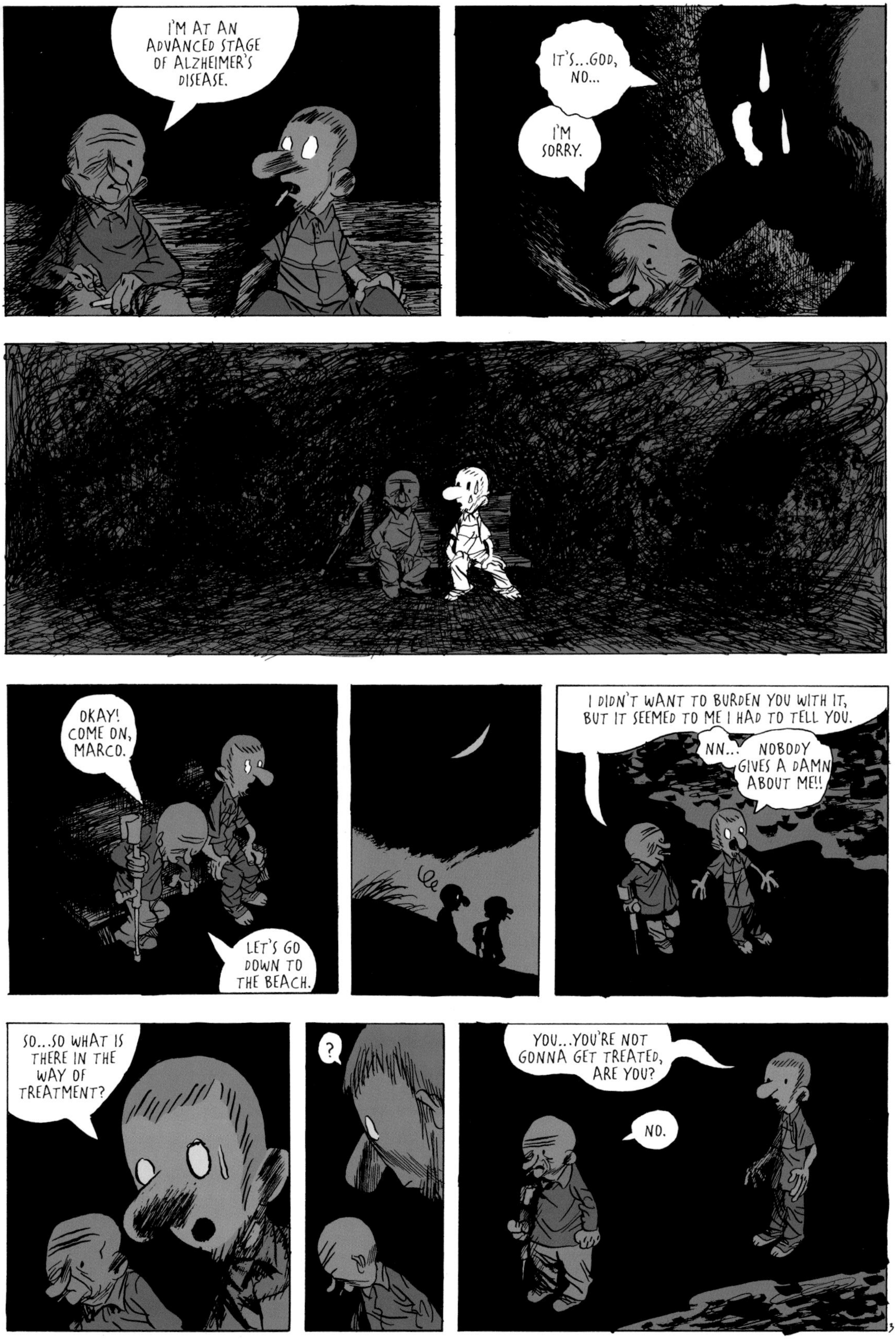
I'M AT AN ADVANCED STAGE OF ALZHEIMER'S DISEASE.
IT'S...GOD, NO...
I'M SORRY.
OKAY! COME ON, MARCO.
LET'S GO DOWN TO THE BEACH.
I DIDN'T WANT TO BURDEN YOU WITH IT, BUT IT SEEMED TO ME I HAD TO TELL YOU.
NN...
NOBODY GIVES A DAMN ABOUT ME!!
SO...SO WHAT IS THERE IN THE WAY OF TREATMENT?
?
YOU...YOU'RE NOT GONNA GET TREATED, ARE YOU?
NO.

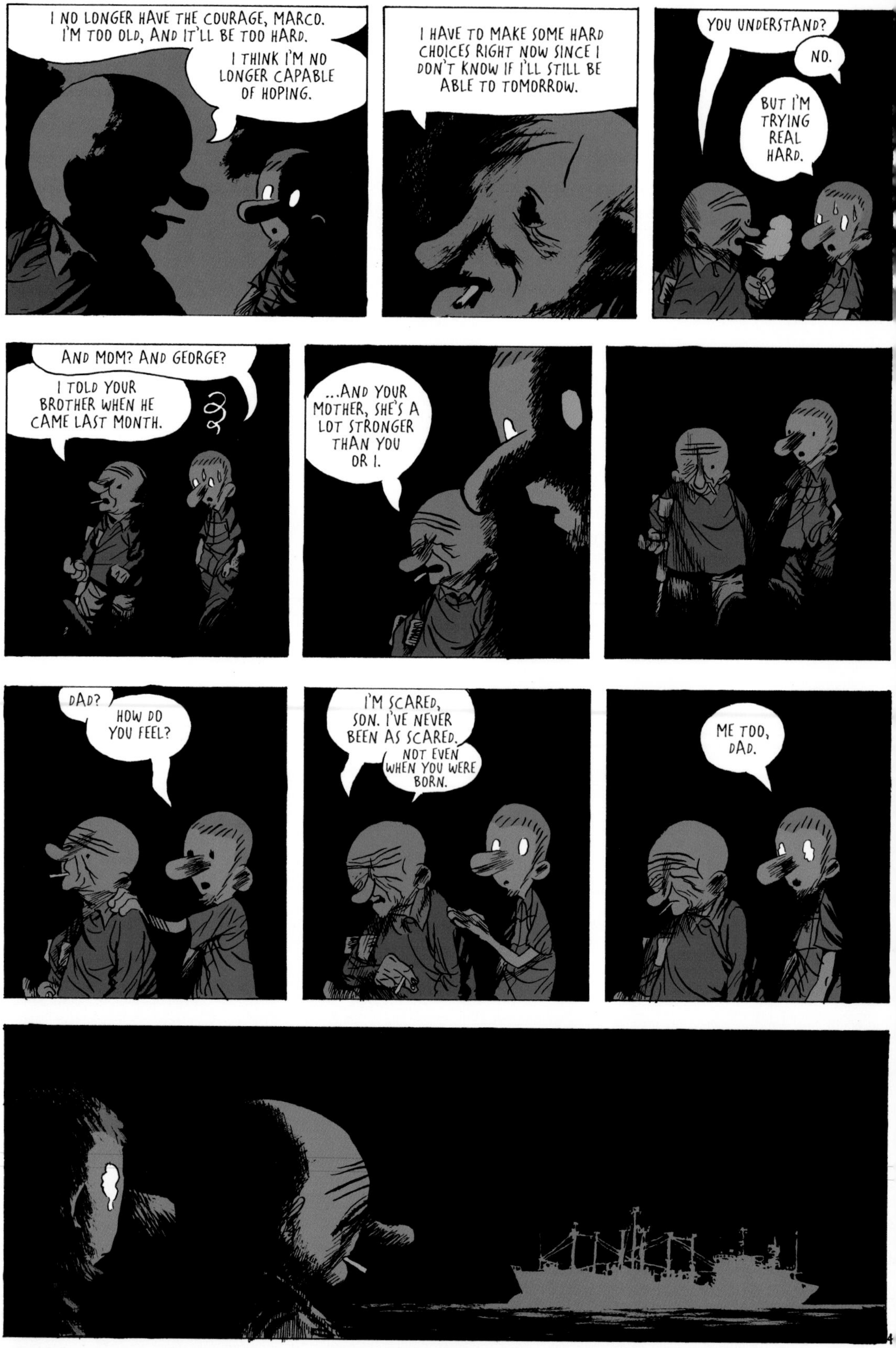

I NO LONGER HAVE THE COURAGE, MARCO. I'M TOO OLD, AND IT'LL BE TOO HARD.
I THINK I'M NO LONGER CAPABLE OF HOPING.
I HAVE TO MAKE SOME HARD CHOICES RIGHT NOW SINCE I DON'T KNOW IF I'LL STILL BE ABLE TO TOMORROW.
YOU UNDERSTAND?
NO.
BUT I'M TRYING REAL HARD.
AND MOM? AND GEORGE?
I TOLD YOUR BROTHER WHEN HE CAME LAST MONTH.
...AND YOUR MOTHER, SHE'S A LOT STRONGER THAN YOU OR I.
DAD?
HOW DO YOU FEEL?
I'M SCARED, SON. I'VE NEVER BEEN AS SCARED.
NOT EVEN WHEN YOU WERE BORN.
ME TOO, DAD.

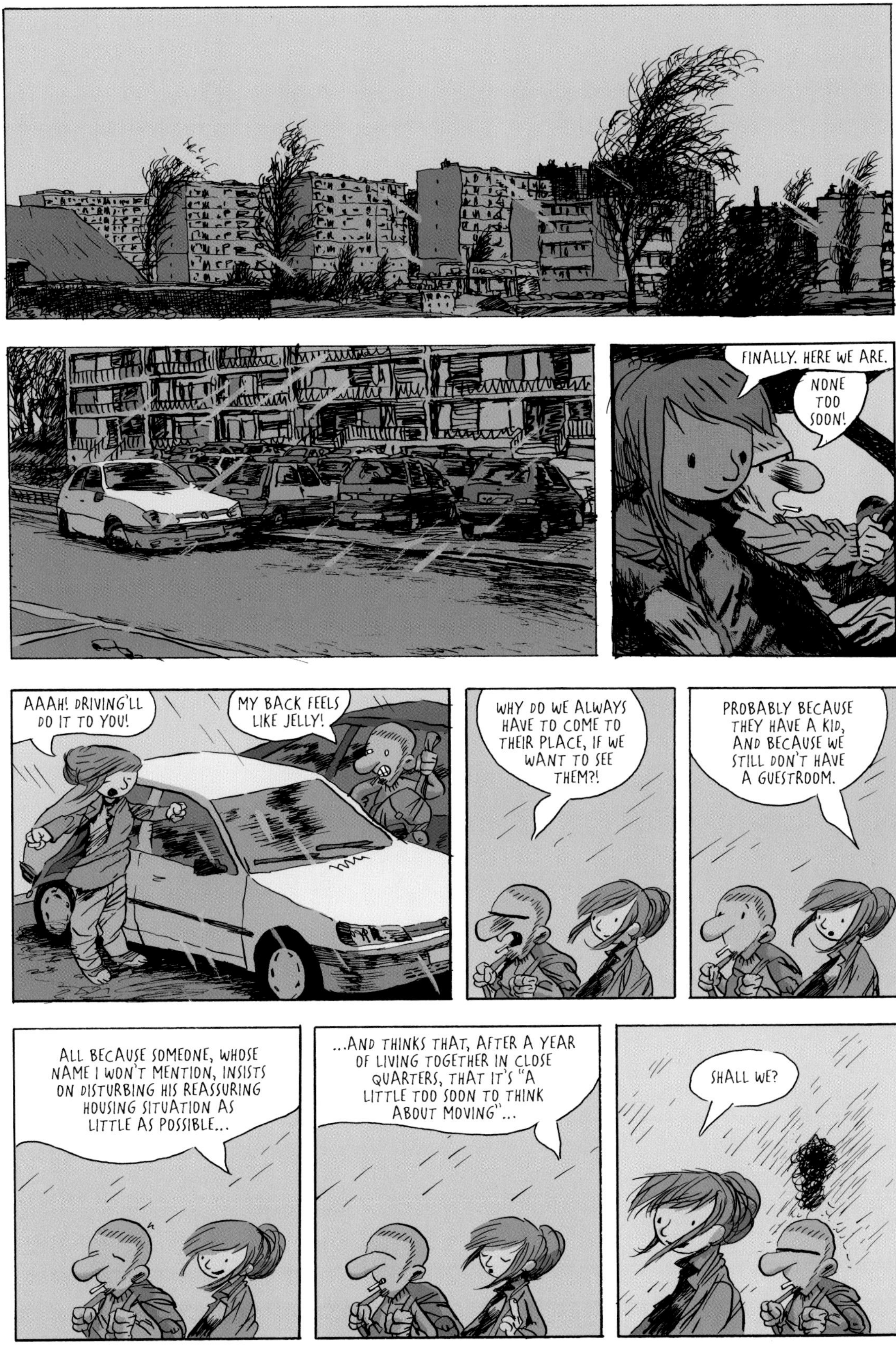

FINALLY. HERE WE ARE.
NONE TOO SOON!
AAAH! DRIVING'LL DO IT TO YOU!
MY BACK FEELS LIKE JELLY!
WHY DO WE ALWAYS HAVE TO COME TO THEIR PLACE, IF WE WANT TO SEE THEM?!
PROBABLY BECAUSE THEY HAVE A KID, AND BECAUSE WE STILL DON'T HAVE A GUESTROOM.
ALL BECAUSE SOMEONE, WHOSE NAME I WON'T MENTION, INSISTS ON DISTURBING HIS REASSURING HOUSING SITUATION AS LITTLE AS POSSIBLE...
...AND THINKS THAT, AFTER A YEAR OF LIVING TOGETHER IN CLOSE QUARTERS, THAT IT'S "A LITTLE TOO SOON TO THINK ABOUT MOVING"...
SHALL WE?

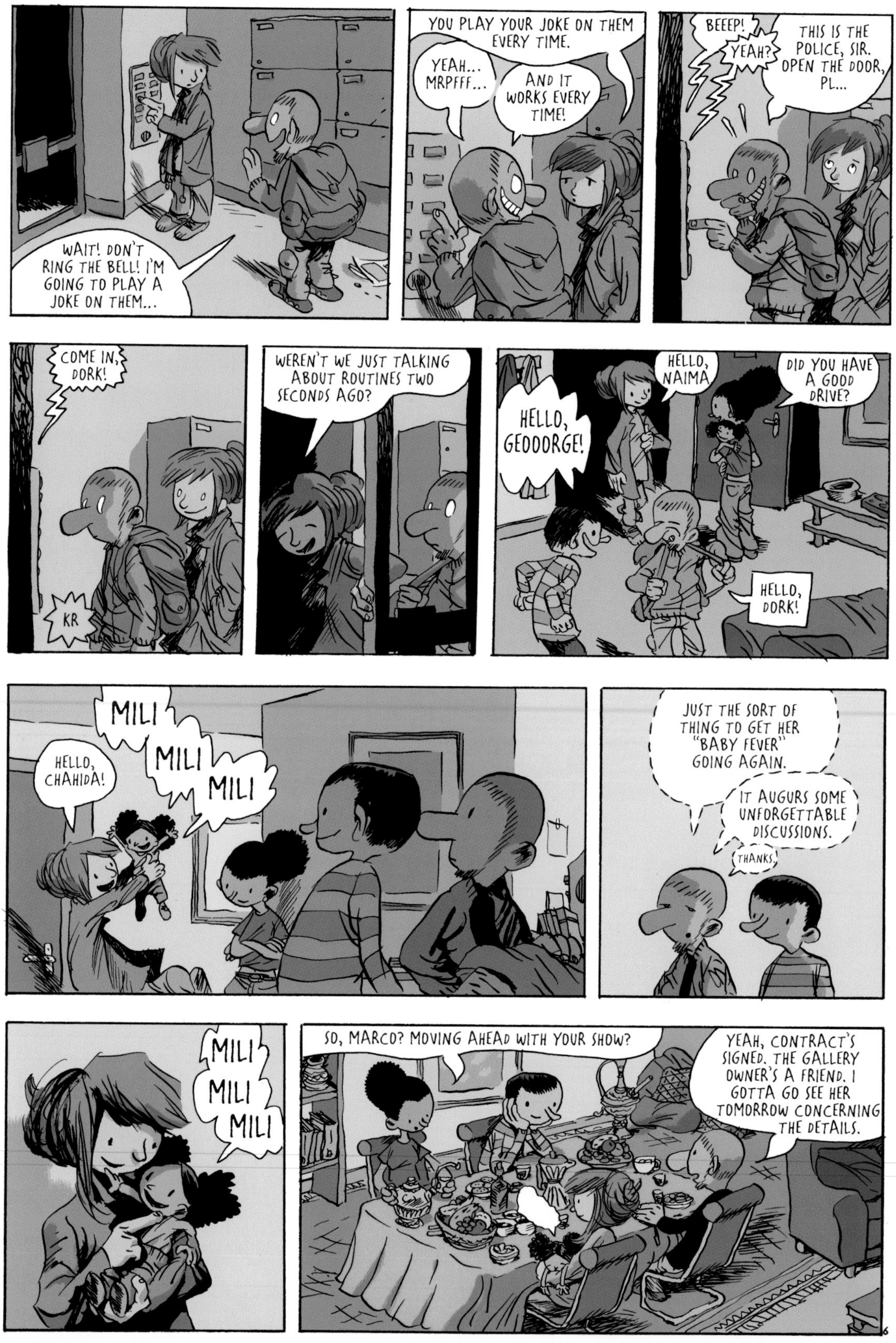
WAIT! DON'T RING THE BELL! I'M GOING TO PLAY A JOKE ON THEM...
YOU PLAY YOUR JOKE ON THEM EVERY TIME.
YEAH... MRPFFF...
AND IT WORKS EVERY TIME!
BEEEP!
YEAH?
THIS IS THE POLICE, SIR. OPEN THE DOOR, PL...
COME IN, DORK!
KR
WEREN'T WE JUST TALKING ABOUT ROUTINES TWO SECONDS AGO?
HELLO, NAIMA
HELLO, GEOOORGE!
DID YOU HAVE A GOOD DRIVE?
HELLO, DORK!
HELLO, CHAHIDA!
MILI
MILI
MILI
JUST THE SORT OF THING TO GET HER "BABY FEVER" GOING AGAIN.
IT AUGURS SOME UNFORGETTABLE DISCUSSIONS.
THANKS.
MILI
MILI
MILI
SO, MARCO? MOVING AHEAD WITH YOUR SHOW?
YEAH, CONTRACT'S SIGNED. THE GALLERY OWNER'S A FRIEND. I GOTTA GO SEE HER TOMORROW CONCERNING THE DETAILS.

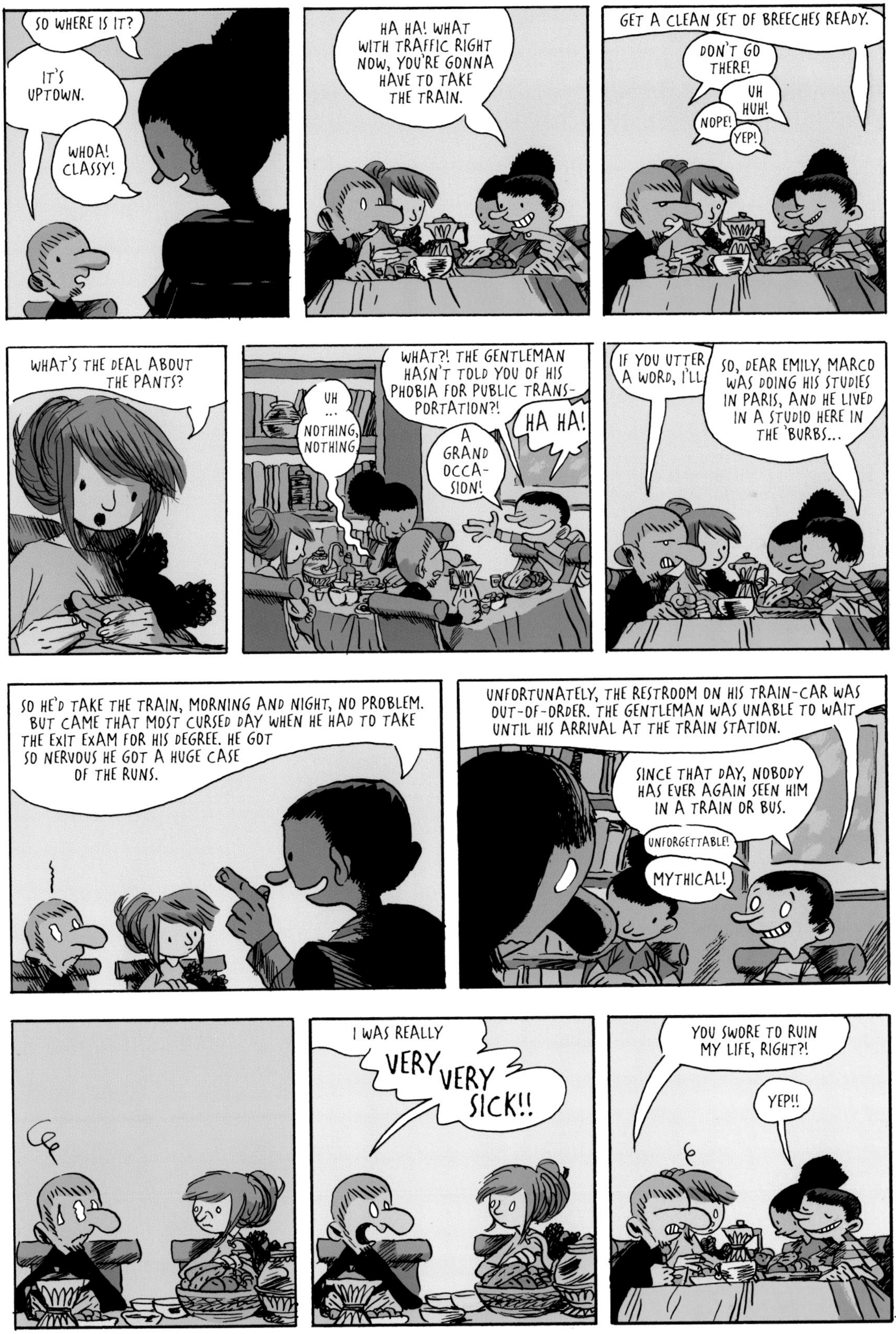

SO WHERE IS IT?
IT'S UPTOWN.
WHOA! CLASSY!
HA HA! WHAT WITH TRAFFIC RIGHT NOW, YOU'RE GONNA HAVE TO TAKE THE TRAIN.
GET A CLEAN SET OF BREECHES READY.
DON'T GO THERE!
UH HUH!
NOPE!
YEP!
WHAT'S THE DEAL ABOUT THE PANTS?
UH ... NOTHING, NOTHING.
WHAT?! THE GENTLEMAN HASN'T TOLD YOU OF HIS PHOBIA FOR PUBLIC TRANS-PORTATION?!
A GRAND OCCA-SION!
HA HA!
IF YOU UTTER A WORD, I'LL
SO, DEAR EMILY, MARCO WAS DOING HIS STUDIES IN PARIS, AND HE LIVED IN A STUDIO HERE IN THE 'BURBS...
SO HE'D TAKE THE TRAIN, MORNING AND NIGHT, NO PROBLEM. BUT CAME THAT MOST CURSED DAY WHEN HE HAD TO TAKE THE EXIT EXAM FOR HIS DEGREE. HE GOT SO NERVOUS HE GOT A HUGE CASE OF THE RUNS.
UNFORTUNATELY, THE RESTROOM ON HIS TRAIN-CAR WAS OUT-OF-ORDER. THE GENTLEMAN WAS UNABLE TO WAIT UNTIL HIS ARRIVAL AT THE TRAIN STATION.
SINCE THAT DAY, NOBODY HAS EVER AGAIN SEEN HIM IN A TRAIN OR BUS.
UNFORGETTABLE!
MYTHICAL!
I WAS REALLY VERY VERY SICK!!
YOU SWORE TO RUIN MY LIFE, RIGHT?!
YEP!!

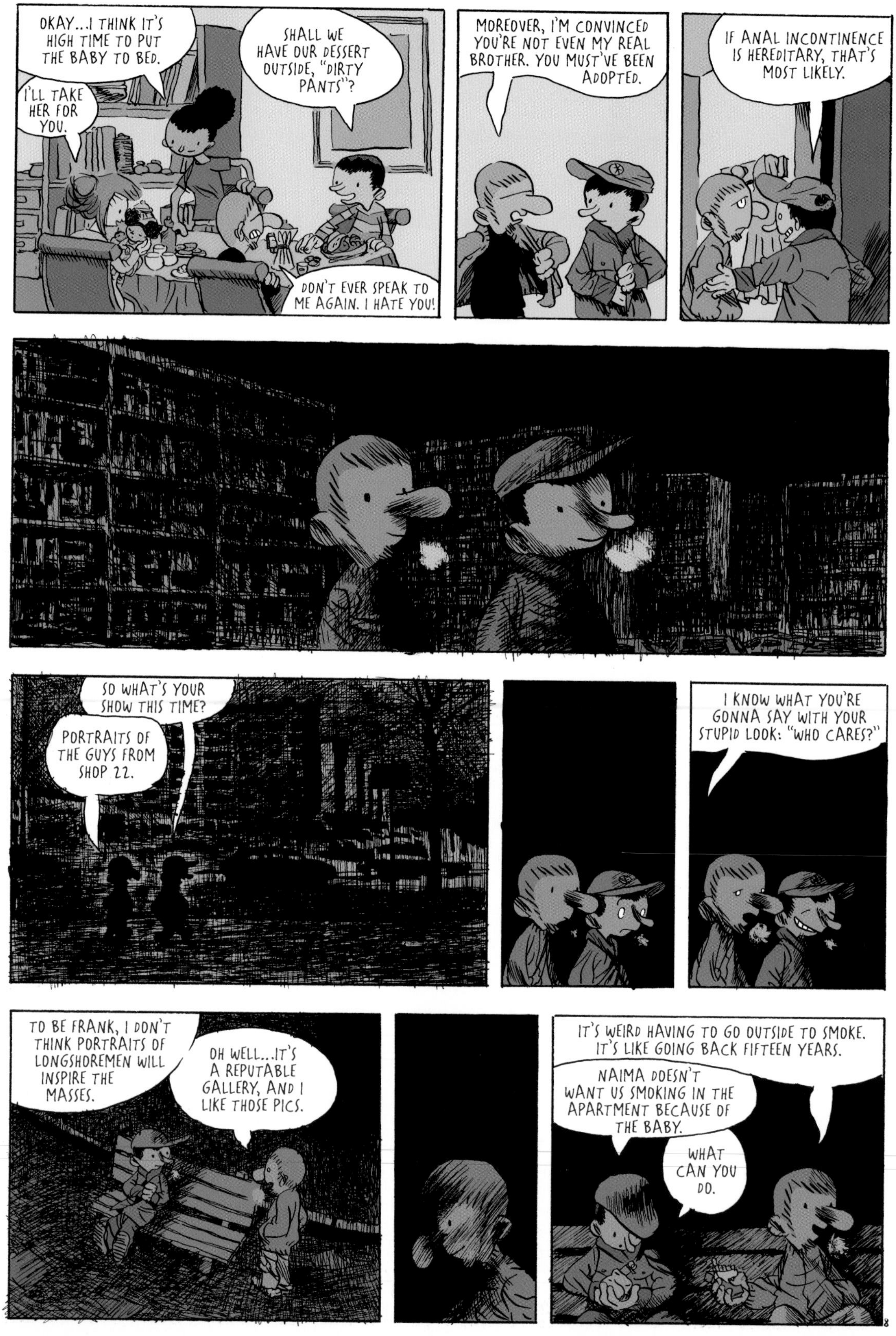

OKAY...I THINK IT'S HIGH TIME TO PUT THE BABY TO BED.
I'LL TAKE HER FOR YOU.
SHALL WE HAVE OUR DESSERT OUTSIDE, "DIRTY PANTS"?
DON'T EVER SPEAK TO ME AGAIN. I HATE YOU!
MOREOVER, I'M CONVINCED YOU'RE NOT EVEN MY REAL BROTHER. YOU MUST'VE BEEN ADOPTED.
IF ANAL INCONTINENCE IS HEREDITARY, THAT'S MOST LIKELY.
SO WHAT'S YOUR SHOW THIS TIME?
PORTRAITS OF THE GUYS FROM SHOP 22.
I KNOW WHAT YOU'RE GONNA SAY WITH YOUR STUPID LOOK: "WHO CARES?"
TO BE FRANK, I DON'T THINK PORTRAITS OF LONGSHOREMEN WILL INSPIRE THE MASSES.
OH WELL...IT'S A REPUTABLE GALLERY, AND I LIKE THOSE PICS.
IT'S WEIRD HAVING TO GO OUTSIDE TO SMOKE. IT'S LIKE GOING BACK FIFTEEN YEARS.
NAIMA DOESN'T WANT US SMOKING IN THE APARTMENT BECAUSE OF THE BABY.
WHAT CAN YOU DO.

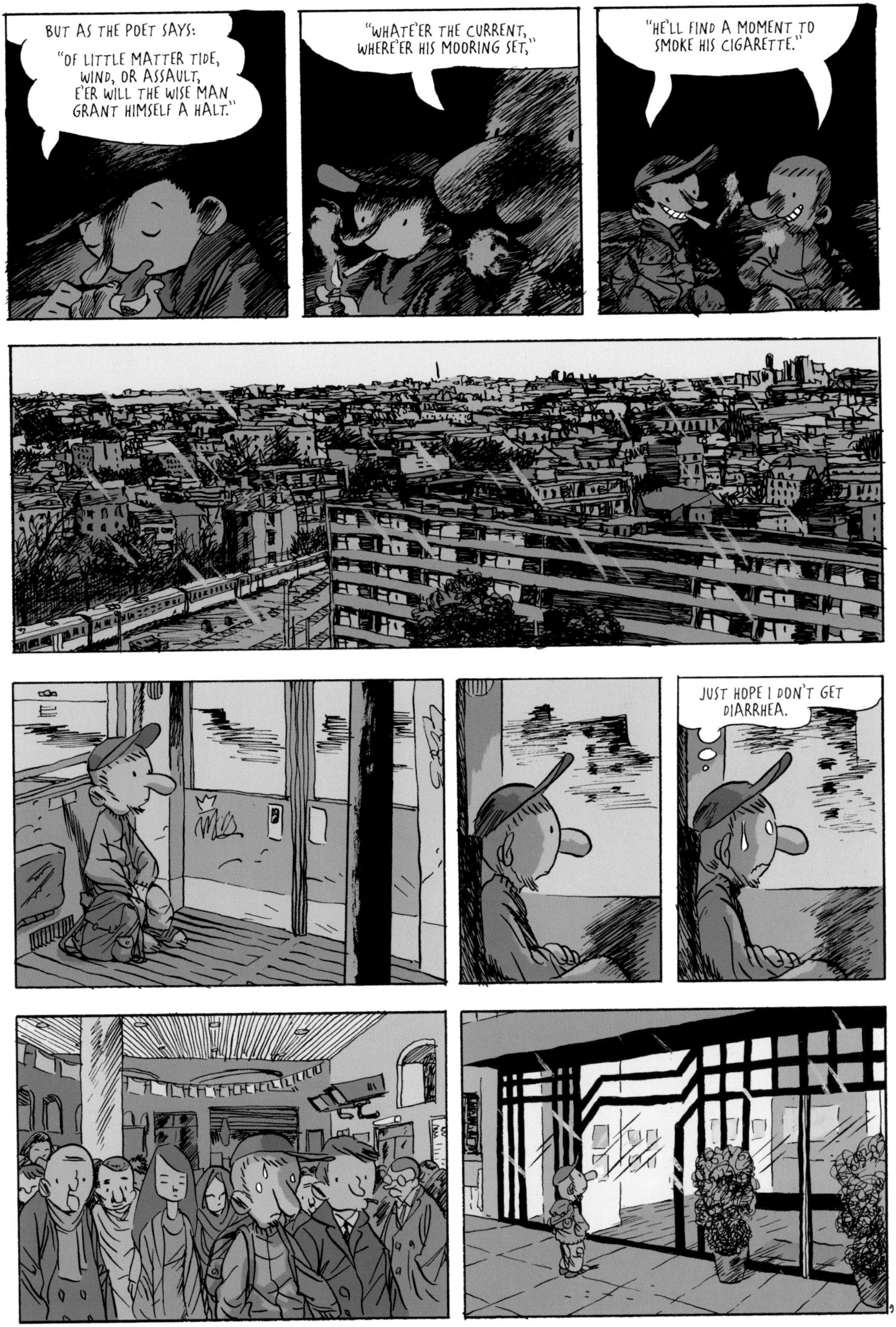
BUT AS THE POET SAYS:
"OF LITTLE MATTER TIDE, WIND, OR ASSAULT, E'ER WILL THE WISE MAN GRANT HIMSELF A HALT."
"WHATE'ER THE CURRENT, WHERE'ER HIS MOORING SET,"
"HE'LL FIND A MOMENT TO SMOKE HIS CIGARETTE."
JUST HOPE I DON'T GET DIARRHEA.

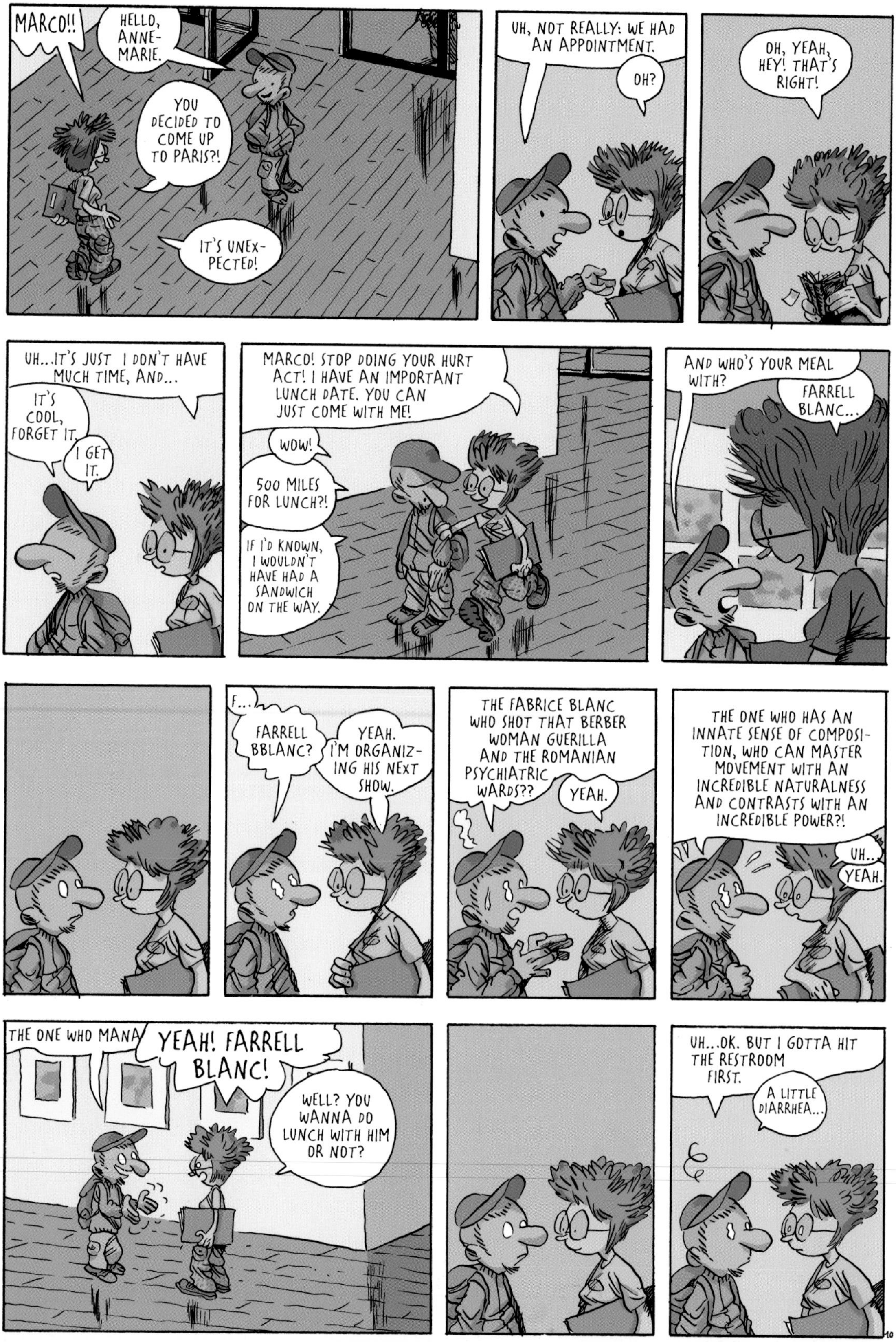
MARCO!!
HELLO, ANNE-MARIE.
YOU DECIDED TO COME UP TO PARIS?!
IT'S UNEXPECTED!
UH, NOT REALLY: WE HAD AN APPOINTMENT.
OH?
OH, YEAH, HEY! THAT'S RIGHT!
UH...IT'S JUST I DON'T HAVE MUCH TIME, AND...
IT'S COOL, FORGET IT.
I GET IT.
MARCO! STOP DOING YOUR HURT ACT! I HAVE AN IMPORTANT LUNCH DATE. YOU CAN JUST COME WITH ME!
WOW!
500 MILES FOR LUNCH?!
IF I'D KNOWN, I WOULDN'T HAVE HAD A SANDWICH ON THE WAY.
AND WHO'S YOUR MEAL WITH?
FARRELL BLANC...
F...
FARRELL BBLANC?
YEAH. I'M ORGANIZING HIS NEXT SHOW.
THE FABRICE BLANC WHO SHOT THAT BERBER WOMAN GUERILLA AND THE ROMANIAN PSYCHIATRIC WARDS??
YEAH.
THE ONE WHO HAS AN INNATE SENSE OF COMPOSITION, WHO CAN MASTER MOVEMENT WITH AN INCREDIBLE NATURALNESS AND CONTRASTS WITH AN INCREDIBLE POWER?!
UH...
YEAH.
THE ONE WHO MANA
YEAH! FARRELL BLANC!
WELL? YOU WANNA DO LUNCH WITH HIM OR NOT?
UH...OK. BUT I GOTTA HIT THE RESTROOM FIRST.
A LITTLE DIARRHEA...

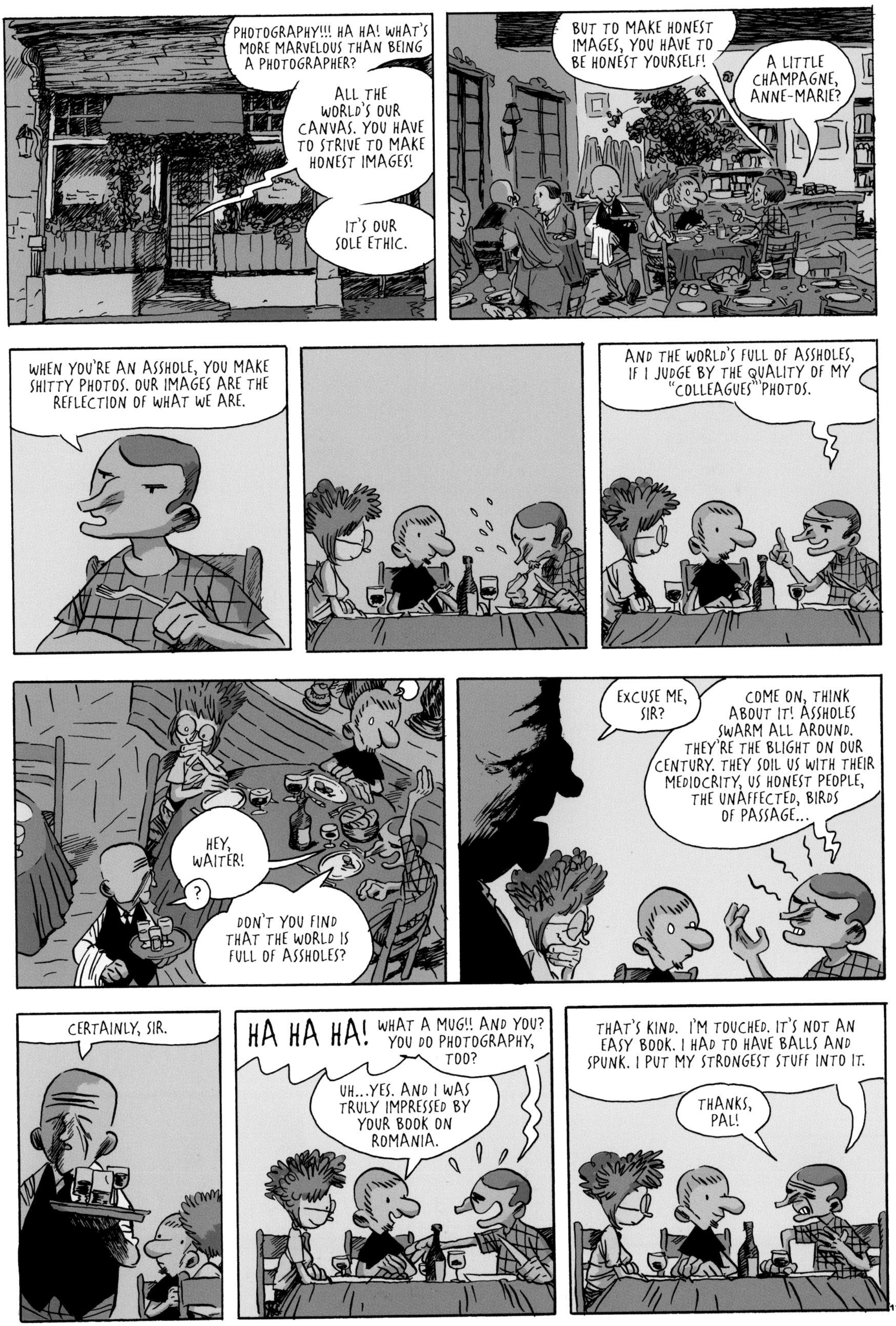
PHOTOGRAPHY!!! HA HA! WHAT'S MORE MARVELOUS THAN BEING A PHOTOGRAPHER?
ALL THE WORLD'S OUR CANVAS. YOU HAVE TO STRIVE TO MAKE HONEST IMAGES!
IT'S OUR SOLE ETHIC.
BUT TO MAKE HONEST IMAGES, YOU HAVE TO BE HONEST YOURSELF!
A LITTLE CHAMPAGNE, ANNE-MARIE?
WHEN YOU'RE AN ASSHOLE, YOU MAKE SHITTY PHOTOS. OUR IMAGES ARE THE REFLECTION OF WHAT WE ARE.
AND THE WORLD'S FULL OF ASSHOLES, IF I JUDGE BY THE QUALITY OF MY "COLLEAGUES'" PHOTOS.
HEY, WAITER!
?
DON'T YOU FIND THAT THE WORLD IS FULL OF ASSHOLES?
EXCUSE ME, SIR?
COME ON, THINK ABOUT IT! ASSHOLES SWARM ALL AROUND. THEY'RE THE BLIGHT ON OUR CENTURY. THEY SOIL US WITH THEIR MEDIOCRITY, US HONEST PEOPLE, THE UNAFFECTED, BIRDS OF PASSAGE...
CERTAINLY, SIR.
HA HA HA!
WHAT A MUG!! AND YOU? YOU DO PHOTOGRAPHY, TOO?
UH...YES. AND I WAS TRULY IMPRESSED BY YOUR BOOK ON ROMANIA.
THAT'S KIND. I'M TOUCHED. IT'S NOT AN EASY BOOK. I HAD TO HAVE BALLS AND SPUNK. I PUT MY STRONGEST STUFF INTO IT.
THANKS, PAL!

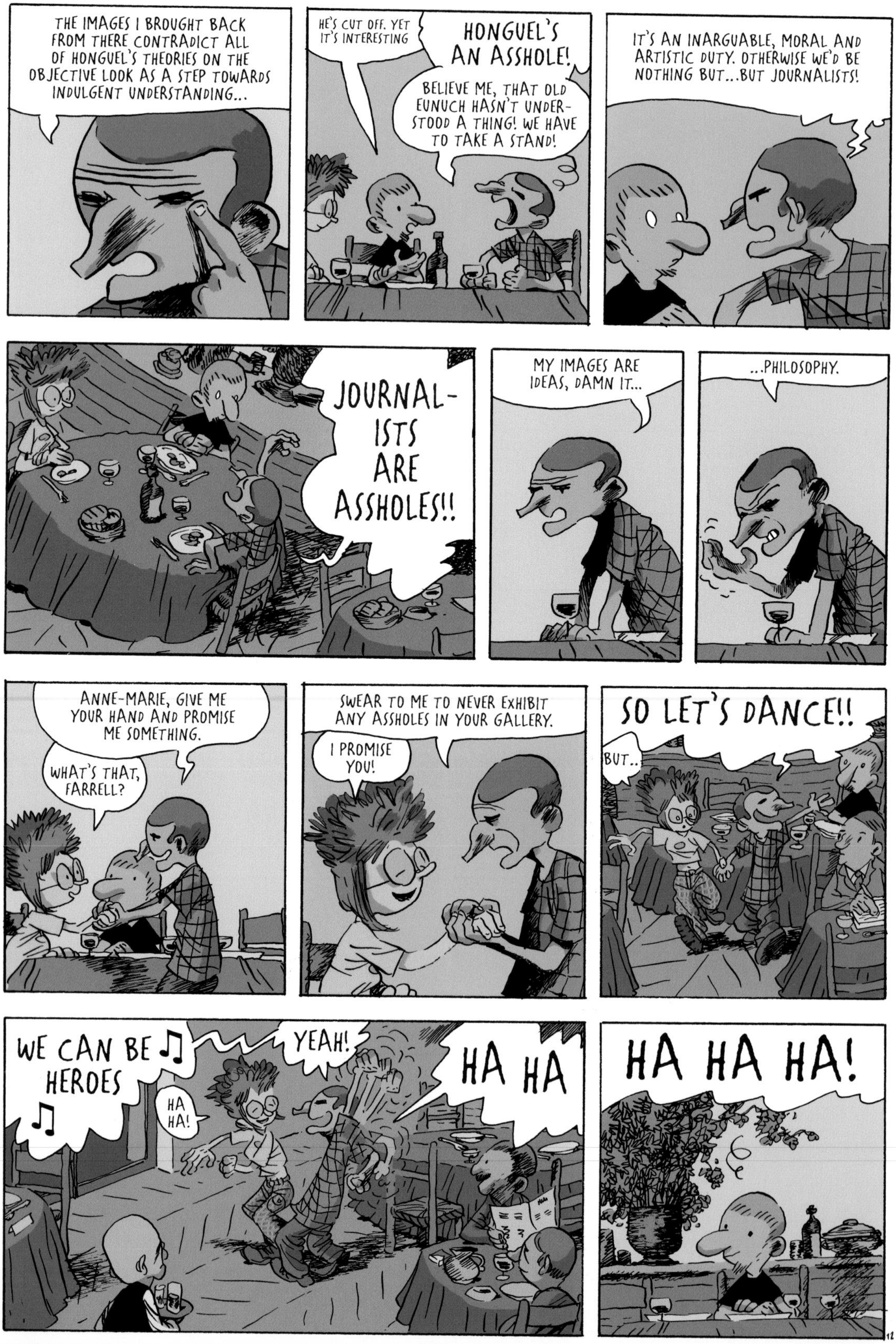
THE IMAGES I BROUGHT BACK FROM THERE CONTRADICT ALL OF HONGUEL'S THEORIES ON THE OBJECTIVE LOOK AS A STEP TOWARDS INDULGENT UNDERSTANDING...
HE'S CUT OFF. YET IT'S INTERESTING
HONGUEL'S AN ASSHOLE!
BELIEVE ME, THAT OLD EUNUCH HASN'T UNDER-STOOD A THING! WE HAVE TO TAKE A STAND!
IT'S AN INARGUABLE, MORAL AND ARTISTIC DUTY. OTHERWISE WE'D BE NOTHING BUT...BUT JOURNALISTS!
JOURNAL-ISTS ARE ASSHOLES!!
MY IMAGES ARE IDEAS, DAMN IT...
...PHILOSOPHY.
ANNE-MARIE, GIVE ME YOUR HAND AND PROMISE ME SOMETHING.
WHAT'S THAT, FARRELL?
SWEAR TO ME TO NEVER EXHIBIT ANY ASSHOLES IN YOUR GALLERY.
I PROMISE YOU!
SO LET'S DANCE!!
BUT...
WE CAN BE ♫ HEROES ♫
YEAH!
HA HA!
HA HA
HA HA HA!

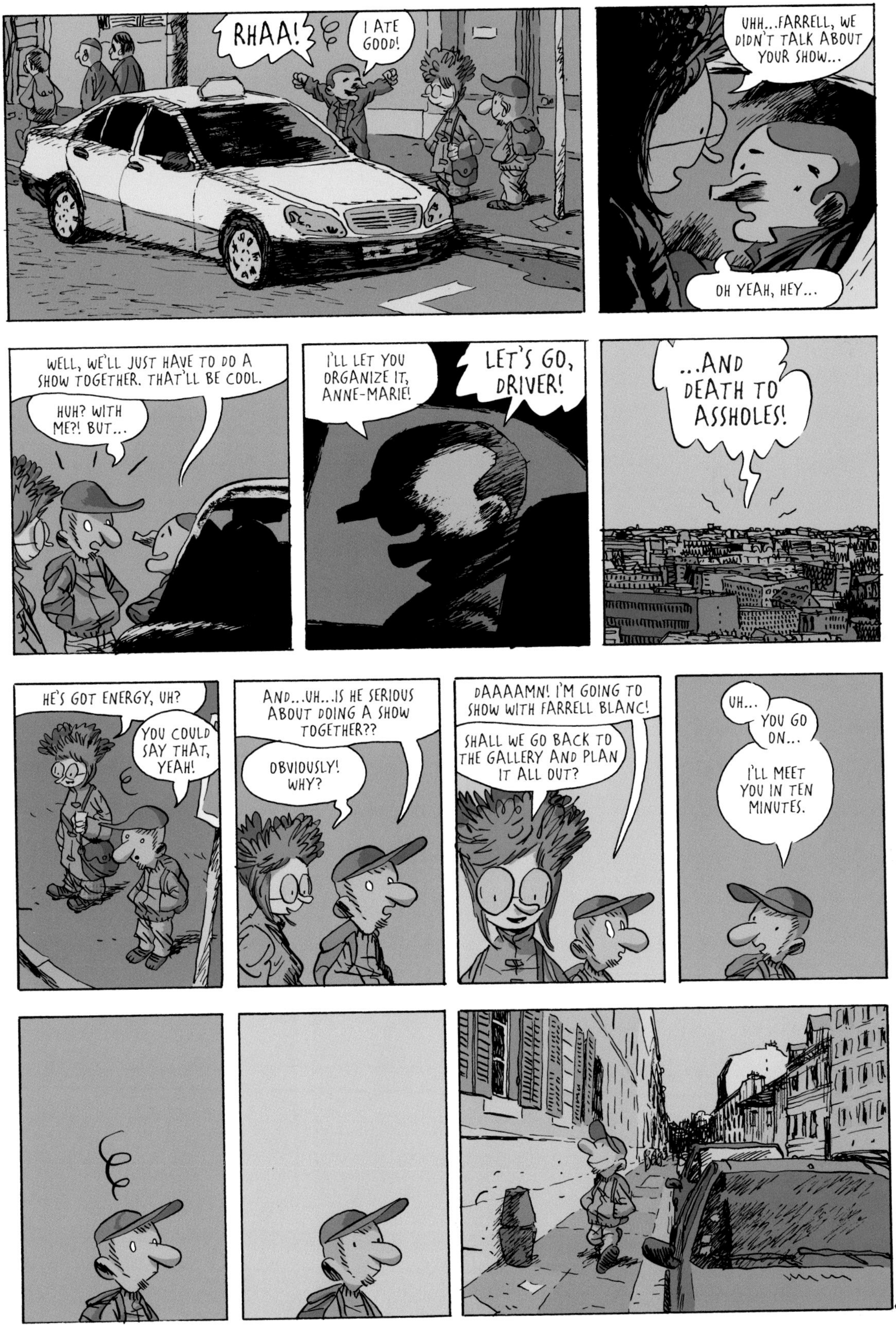
RHAA!
I ATE GOOD!
UHH...FARRELL, WE DIDN'T TALK ABOUT YOUR SHOW...
OH YEAH, HEY...
WELL, WE'LL JUST HAVE TO DO A SHOW TOGETHER. THAT'LL BE COOL.
HUH? WITH ME?! BUT...
I'LL LET YOU ORGANIZE IT, ANNE-MARIE!
LET'S GO, DRIVER!
...AND DEATH TO ASSHOLES!
HE'S GOT ENERGY, UH?
YOU COULD SAY THAT, YEAH!
AND...UH...IS HE SERIOUS ABOUT DOING A SHOW TOGETHER??
OBVIOUSLY! WHY?
DAAAAMN! I'M GOING TO SHOW WITH FARRELL BLANC!
SHALL WE GO BACK TO THE GALLERY AND PLAN IT ALL OUT?
UH...
YOU GO ON...
I'LL MEET YOU IN TEN MINUTES.

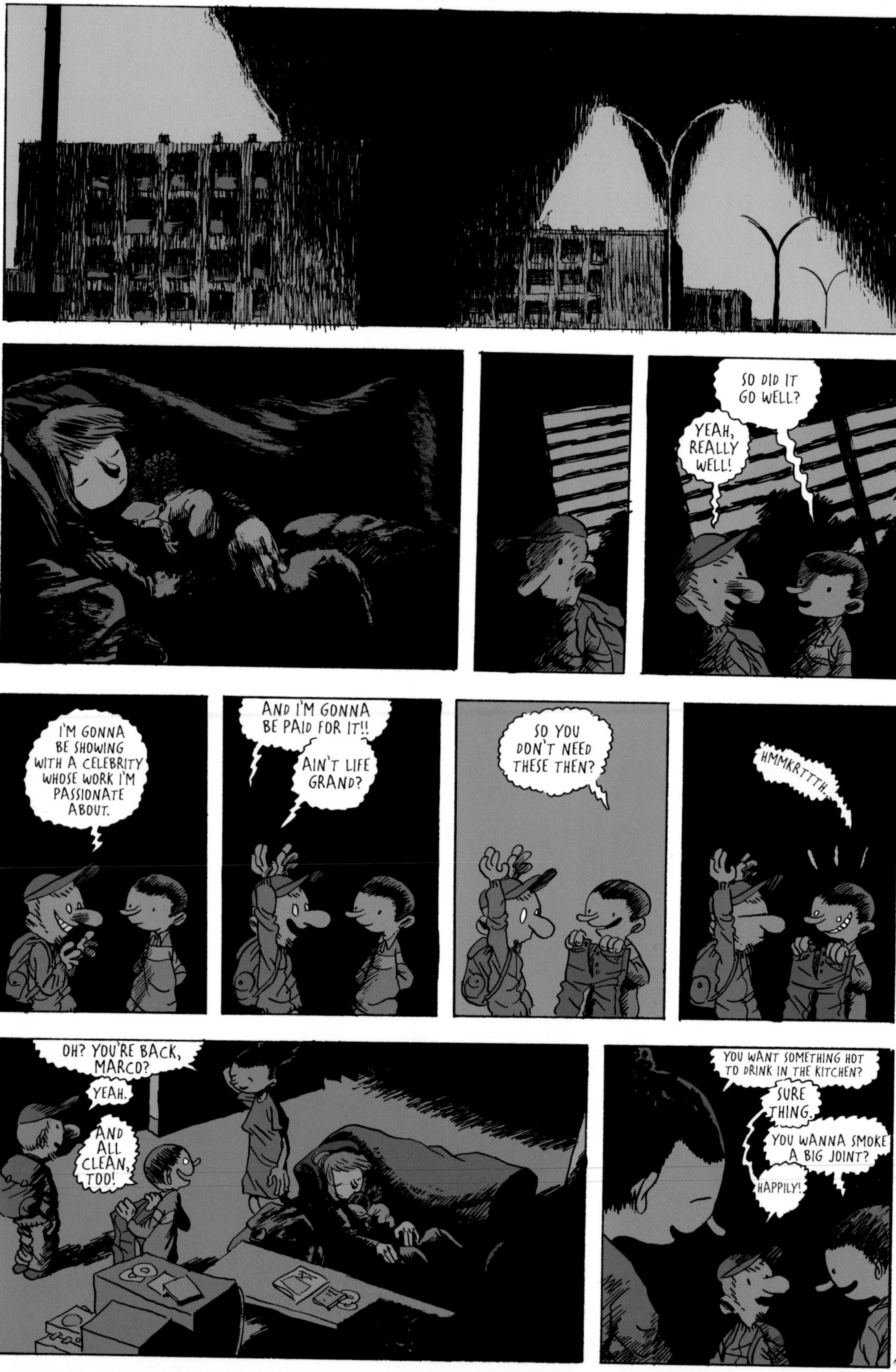
SO DID IT GO WELL?
YEAH, REALLY WELL!
I'M GONNA BE SHOWING WITH A CELEBRITY WHOSE WORK I'M PASSIONATE ABOUT.
AND I'M GONNA BE PAID FOR IT!!
AIN'T LIFE GRAND?
SO YOU DON'T NEED THESE THEN?
HMMKRTTTH.
OH? YOU'RE BACK, MARCO?
YEAH.
AND ALL CLEAN, TOO!
YOU WANT SOMETHING HOT TO DRINK IN THE KITCHEN?
SURE THING.
YOU WANNA SMOKE A BIG JOINT?
HAPPILY!

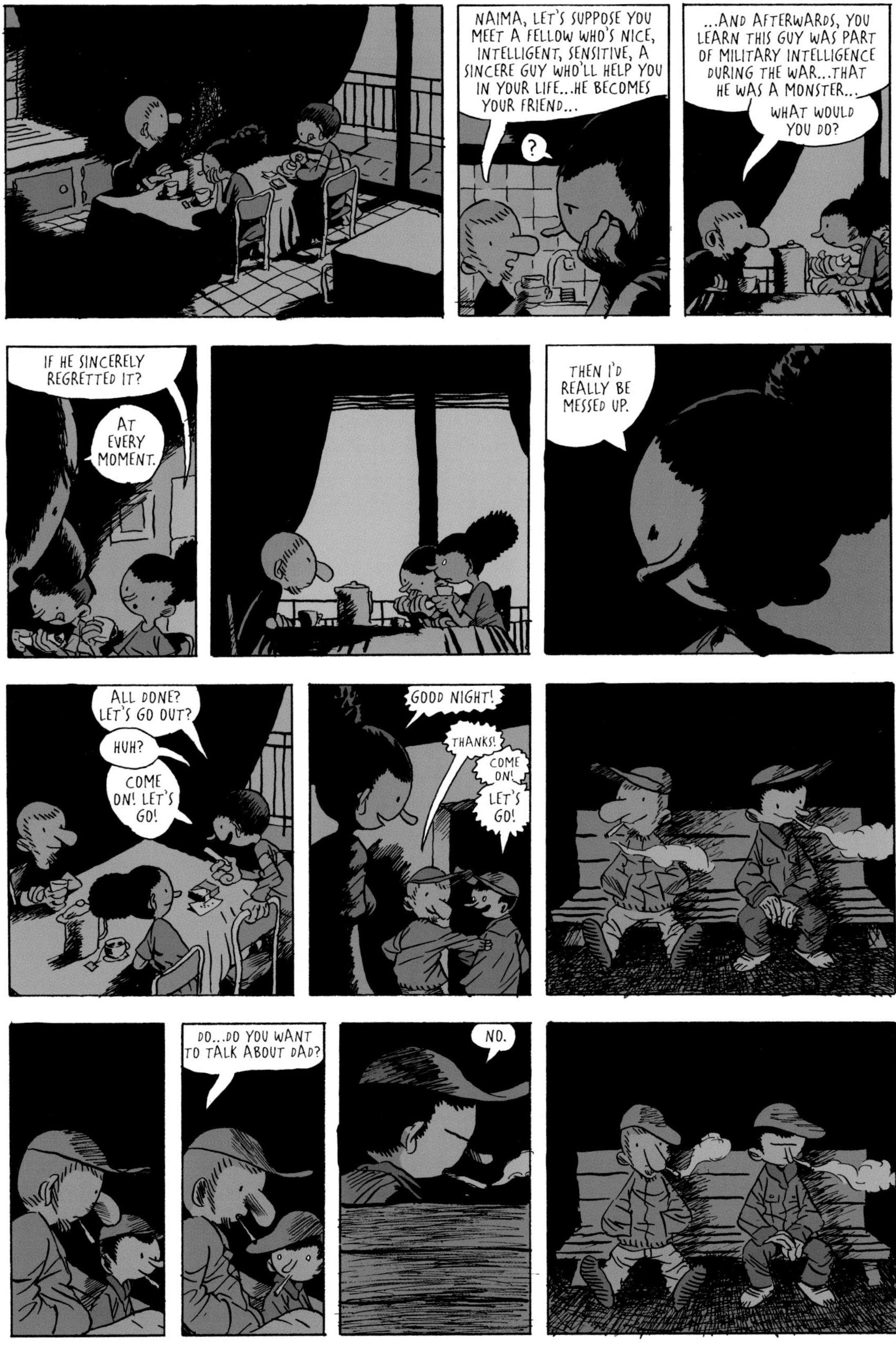
NAIMA, LET'S SUPPOSE YOU MEET A FELLOW WHO'S NICE, INTELLIGENT, SENSITIVE, A SINCERE GUY WHO'LL HELP YOU IN YOUR LIFE...HE BECOMES YOUR FRIEND...
?
...AND AFTERWARDS, YOU LEARN THIS GUY WAS PART OF MILITARY INTELLIGENCE DURING THE WAR...THAT HE WAS A MONSTER...
WHAT WOULD YOU DO?
IF HE SINCERELY REGRETTED IT?
AT EVERY MOMENT.
THEN I'D REALLY BE MESSED UP.
ALL DONE? LET'S GO OUT?
HUH?
COME ON! LET'S GO!
GOOD NIGHT!
THANKS!
COME ON!
LET'S GO!
DO...DO YOU WANT TO TALK ABOUT DAD?
NO.

WE ALL HAVE DIFFERENT WAYS OF REACTING TO GRIEF, TO PAIN, TO SHORTCOMINGS.

SOME PEOPLE TALK, ARGUE, OR STRING TOGETHER THEORIES, AT LENGTH, AS THOUGH TO FILL THE VOID.

OTHERS, ON THE CONTRARY, SILENCE THEMSELVES WITH THE DILIGENCE OF A CHILD CONCENTRATING ON A MATH PROBLEM.

AS FOR ME, INTENSE PAINS ANESTHETIZE ME.

WHETHER I TALK OR KEEP QUIET, I'M DEVOID THEN.

THE SUDDEN ANNIHILATION OF MY EMOTIONS SEEMS TO BE MY PERSONAL SYSTEM OF PROTECTION.

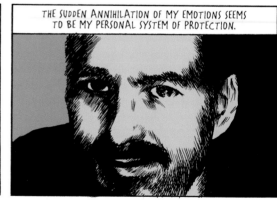

THEN I'M CAPABLE OF GOING ON. PART OF ME WILL ATTEND TO OTHERS, TO RELATIONSHIPS, TO A STEWARDSHIP, YOU MIGHT SAY...

...WHEREAS THE OTHER HALF LIVES IN MY CAREFULLY PRIVATE PATCH OF HELL, SHELTERED FROM ONLOOKERS.

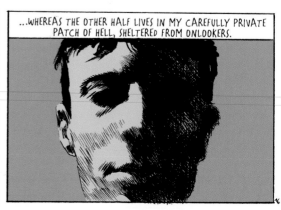

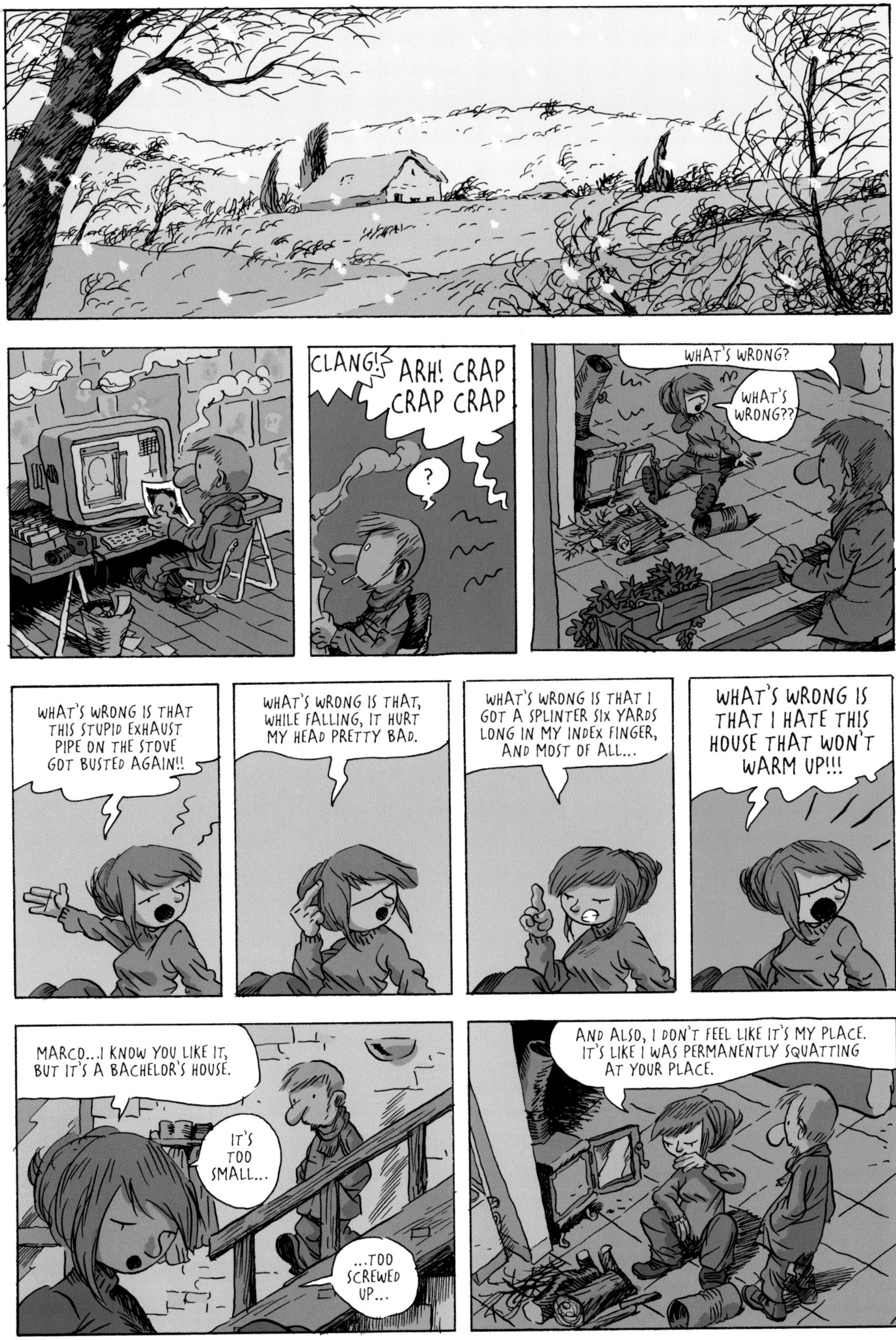
CLANG!
ARH! CRAP CRAP CRAP
?
WHAT'S WRONG?
WHAT'S WRONG??
WHAT'S WRONG IS THAT THIS STUPID EXHAUST PIPE ON THE STOVE GOT BUSTED AGAIN!!
WHAT'S WRONG IS THAT, WHILE FALLING, IT HURT MY HEAD PRETTY BAD.
WHAT'S WRONG IS THAT I GOT A SPLINTER SIX YARDS LONG IN MY INDEX FINGER, AND MOST OF ALL...
WHAT'S WRONG IS THAT I HATE THIS HOUSE THAT WON'T WARM UP!!!
MARCO...I KNOW YOU LIKE IT, BUT IT'S A BACHELOR'S HOUSE.
IT'S TOO SMALL...
...TOO SCREWED UP...
AND ALSO, I DON'T FEEL LIKE IT'S MY PLACE. IT'S LIKE I WAS PERMANENTLY SQUATTING AT YOUR PLACE.

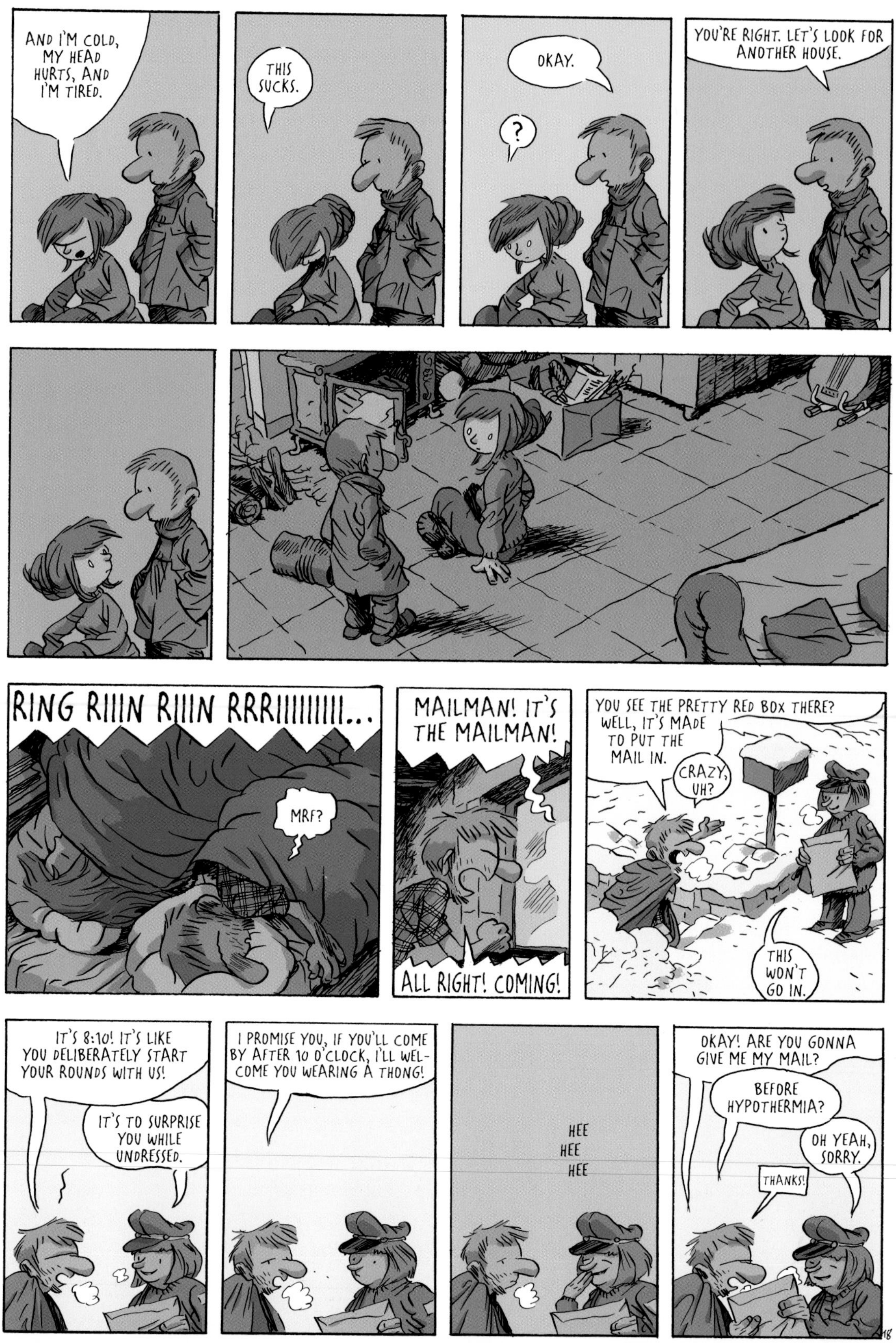
AND I'M COLD, MY HEAD HURTS, AND I'M TIRED.
THIS SUCKS.
OKAY.
?
YOU'RE RIGHT. LET'S LOOK FOR ANOTHER HOUSE.
RING RIIIN RIIIN RRRIIIIIIIIII...
MRF?
MAILMAN! IT'S THE MAILMAN!
ALL RIGHT! COMING!
YOU SEE THE PRETTY RED BOX THERE? WELL, IT'S MADE TO PUT THE MAIL IN.
CRAZY, UH?
THIS WON'T GO IN.
IT'S 8:10! IT'S LIKE YOU DELIBERATELY START YOUR ROUNDS WITH US!
IT'S TO SURPRISE YOU WHILE UNDRESSED.
I PROMISE YOU, IF YOU'LL COME BY AFTER 10 O'CLOCK, I'LL WELCOME YOU WEARING A THONG!
HEE HEE HEE
OKAY! ARE YOU GONNA GIVE ME MY MAIL?
BEFORE HYPOTHERMIA?
OH YEAH, SORRY.
THANKS!

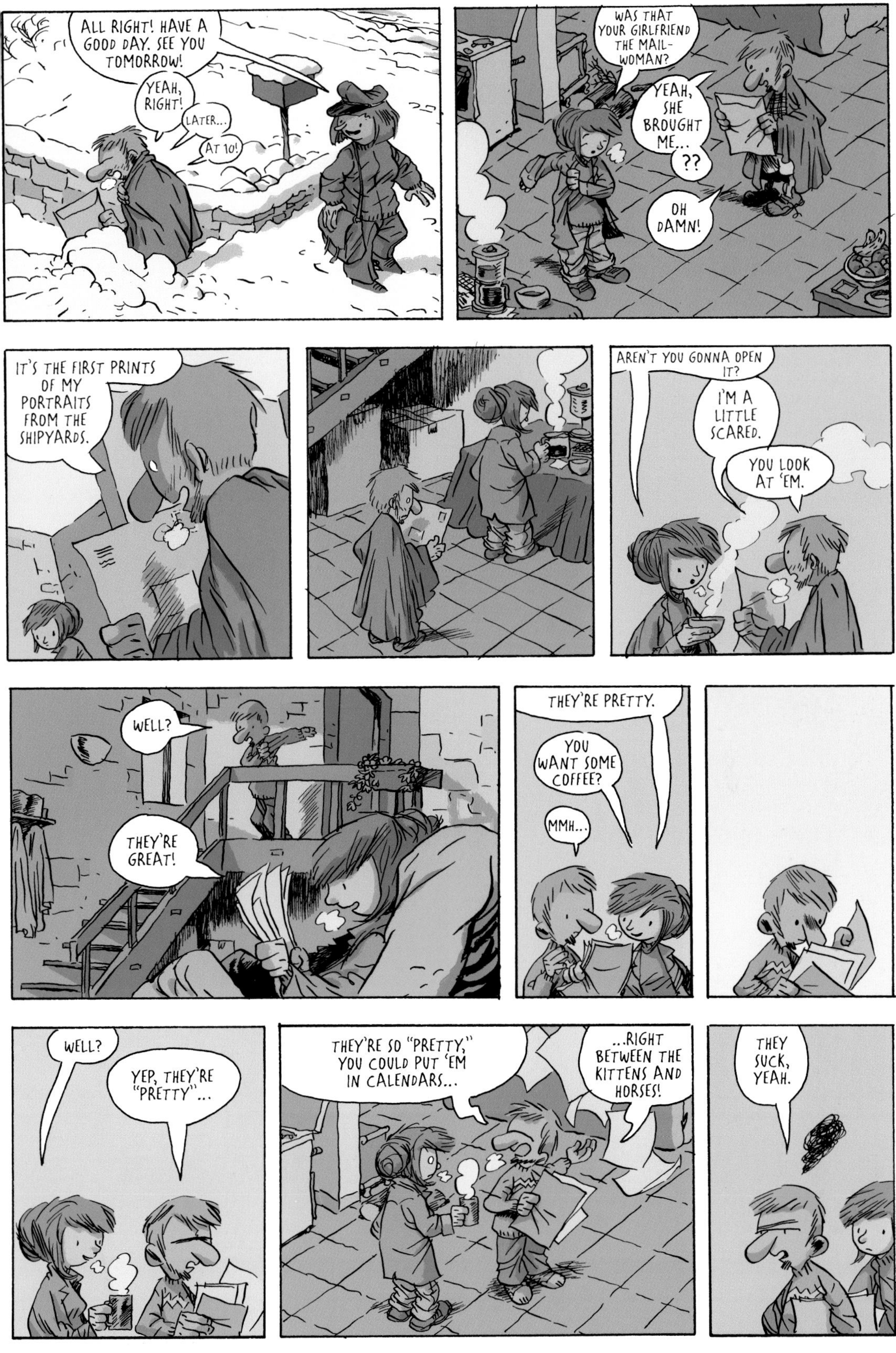
ALL RIGHT! HAVE A GOOD DAY. SEE YOU TOMORROW!
YEAH, RIGHT!
LATER...
AT 10!
WAS THAT YOUR GIRLFRIEND THE MAIL-WOMAN?
YEAH, SHE BROUGHT ME...
??
OH DAMN!
IT'S THE FIRST PRINTS OF MY PORTRAITS FROM THE SHIPYARDS.
AREN'T YOU GONNA OPEN IT?
I'M A LITTLE SCARED.
YOU LOOK AT 'EM.
WELL?
THEY'RE GREAT!
THEY'RE PRETTY.
YOU WANT SOME COFFEE?
MMH...
WELL?
YEP, THEY'RE "PRETTY"...
THEY'RE SO "PRETTY," YOU COULD PUT 'EM IN CALENDARS...
...RIGHT BETWEEN THE KITTENS AND HORSES!
THEY SUCK, YEAH.

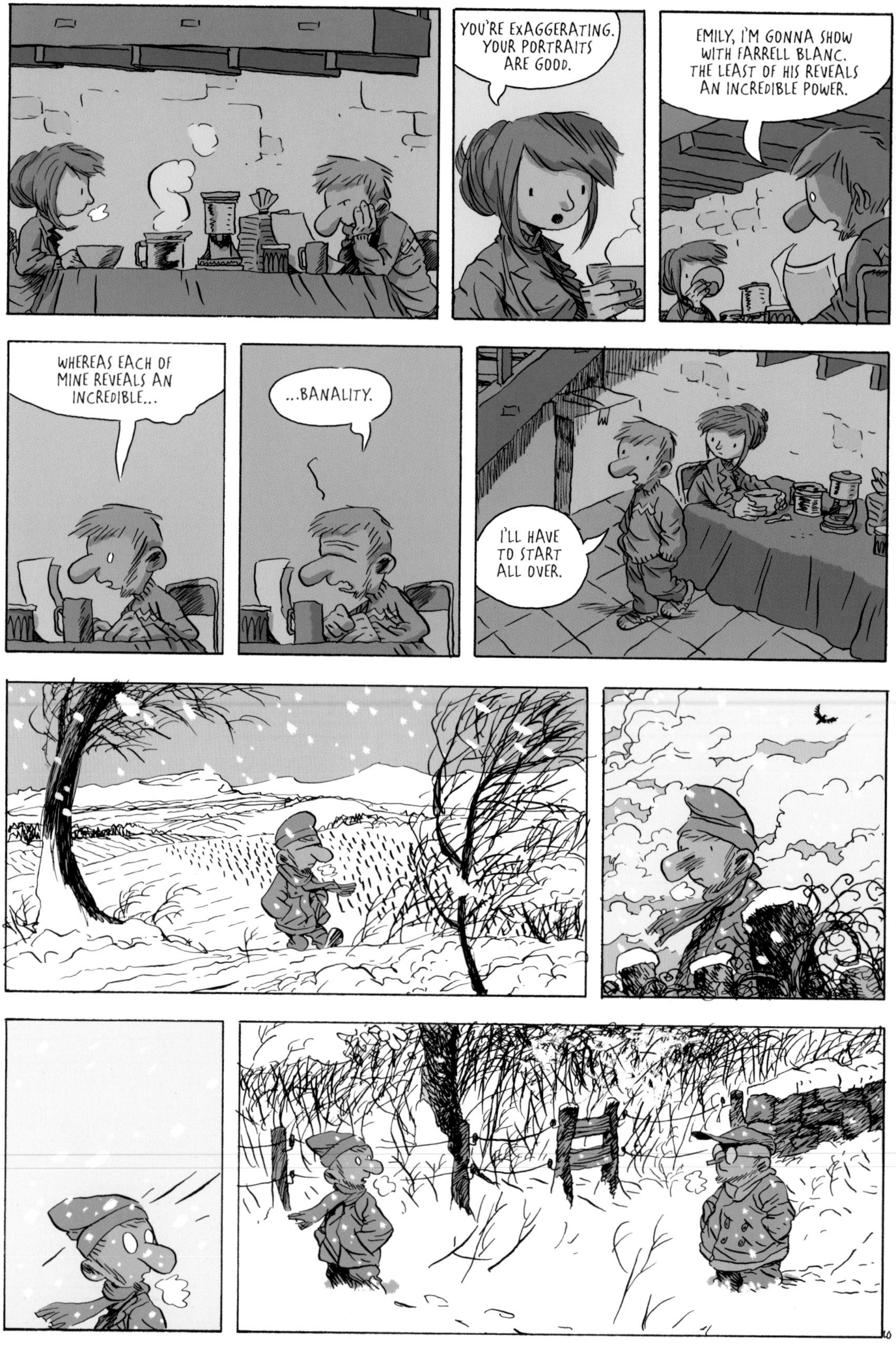
YOU'RE EXAGGERATING. YOUR PORTRAITS ARE GOOD.
EMILY, I'M GONNA SHOW WITH FARRELL BLANC. THE LEAST OF HIS REVEALS AN INCREDIBLE POWER.
WHEREAS EACH OF MINE REVEALS AN INCREDIBLE...
...BANALITY.
I'LL HAVE TO START ALL OVER.

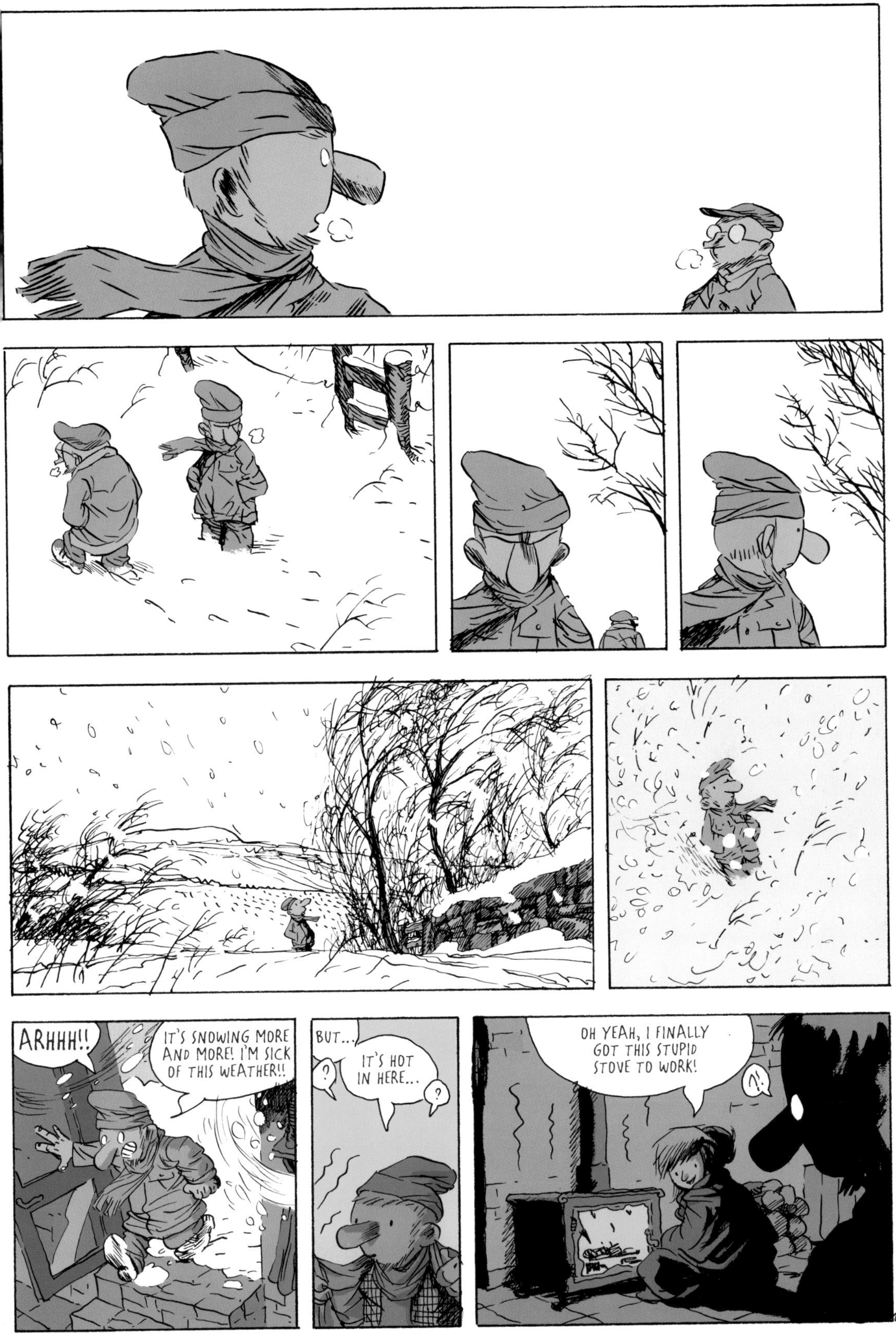
ARHHH!!
IT'S SNOWING MORE AND MORE! I'M SICK OF THIS WEATHER!!
BUT...
?
IT'S HOT IN HERE...
?
OH YEAH, I FINALLY GOT THIS STUPID STOVE TO WORK!
?!

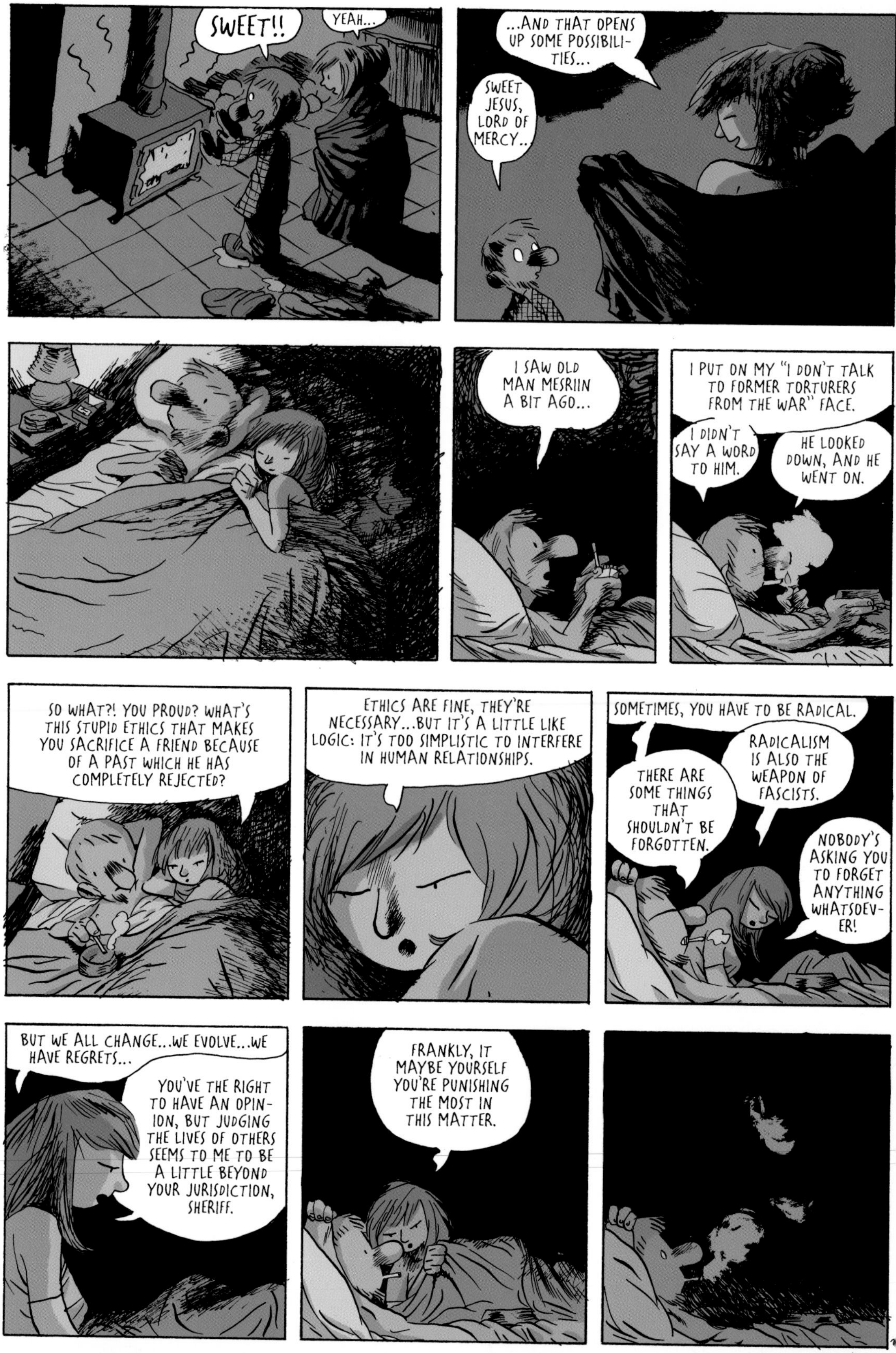
SWEET!!
YEAH...
...AND THAT OPENS UP SOME POSSIBILITIES...
SWEET JESUS, LORD OF MERCY...
I SAW OLD MAN MESRIIN A BIT AGO...
I PUT ON MY "I DON'T TALK TO FORMER TORTURERS FROM THE WAR" FACE.
I DIDN'T SAY A WORD TO HIM.
HE LOOKED DOWN, AND HE WENT ON.
SO WHAT?! YOU PROUD? WHAT'S THIS STUPID ETHICS THAT MAKES YOU SACRIFICE A FRIEND BECAUSE OF A PAST WHICH HE HAS COMPLETELY REJECTED?
ETHICS ARE FINE, THEY'RE NECESSARY...BUT IT'S A LITTLE LIKE LOGIC: IT'S TOO SIMPLISTIC TO INTERFERE IN HUMAN RELATIONSHIPS.
SOMETIMES, YOU HAVE TO BE RADICAL.
THERE ARE SOME THINGS THAT SHOULDN'T BE FORGOTTEN.
RADICALISM IS ALSO THE WEAPON OF FASCISTS.
NOBODY'S ASKING YOU TO FORGET ANYTHING WHATSOEVER!
BUT WE ALL CHANGE...WE EVOLVE...WE HAVE REGRETS...
YOU'VE THE RIGHT TO HAVE AN OPINION, BUT JUDGING THE LIVES OF OTHERS SEEMS TO ME TO BE A LITTLE BEYOND YOUR JURISDICTION, SHERIFF.
FRANKLY, IT MAYBE YOURSELF YOU'RE PUNISHING THE MOST IN THIS MATTER.

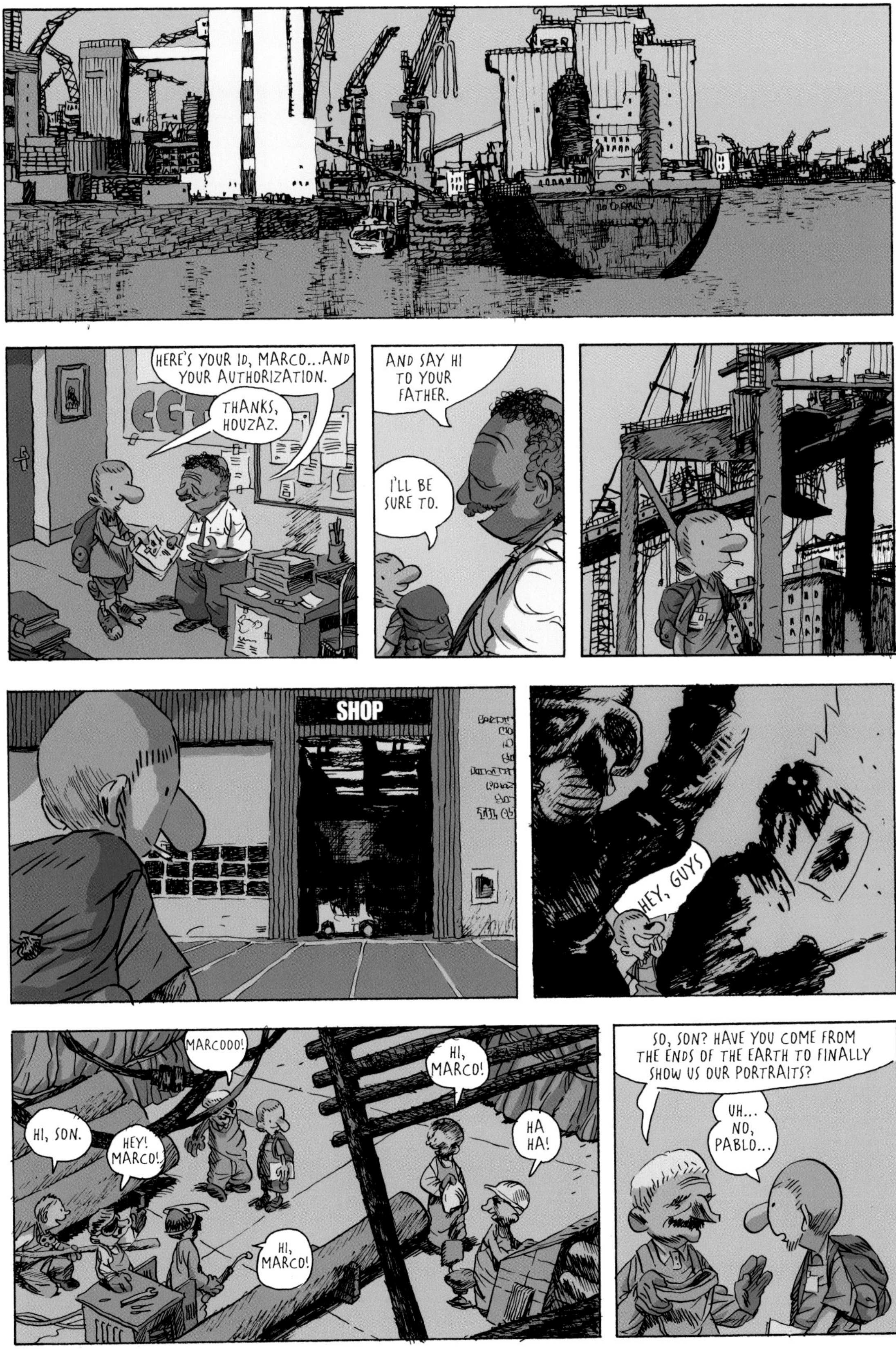

HERE'S YOUR ID, MARCO...AND YOUR AUTHORIZATION.
THANKS, HOUZAZ.
CGT
AND SAY HI TO YOUR FATHER.
I'LL BE SURE TO.
SHOP
HEY, GUYS
MARCOOO!
HI, MARCO!
HI, SON.
HEY! MARCO!
HA HA!
HI, MARCO!
SO, SON? HAVE YOU COME FROM THE ENDS OF THE EARTH TO FINALLY SHOW US OUR PORTRAITS?
UH... NO, PABLO...

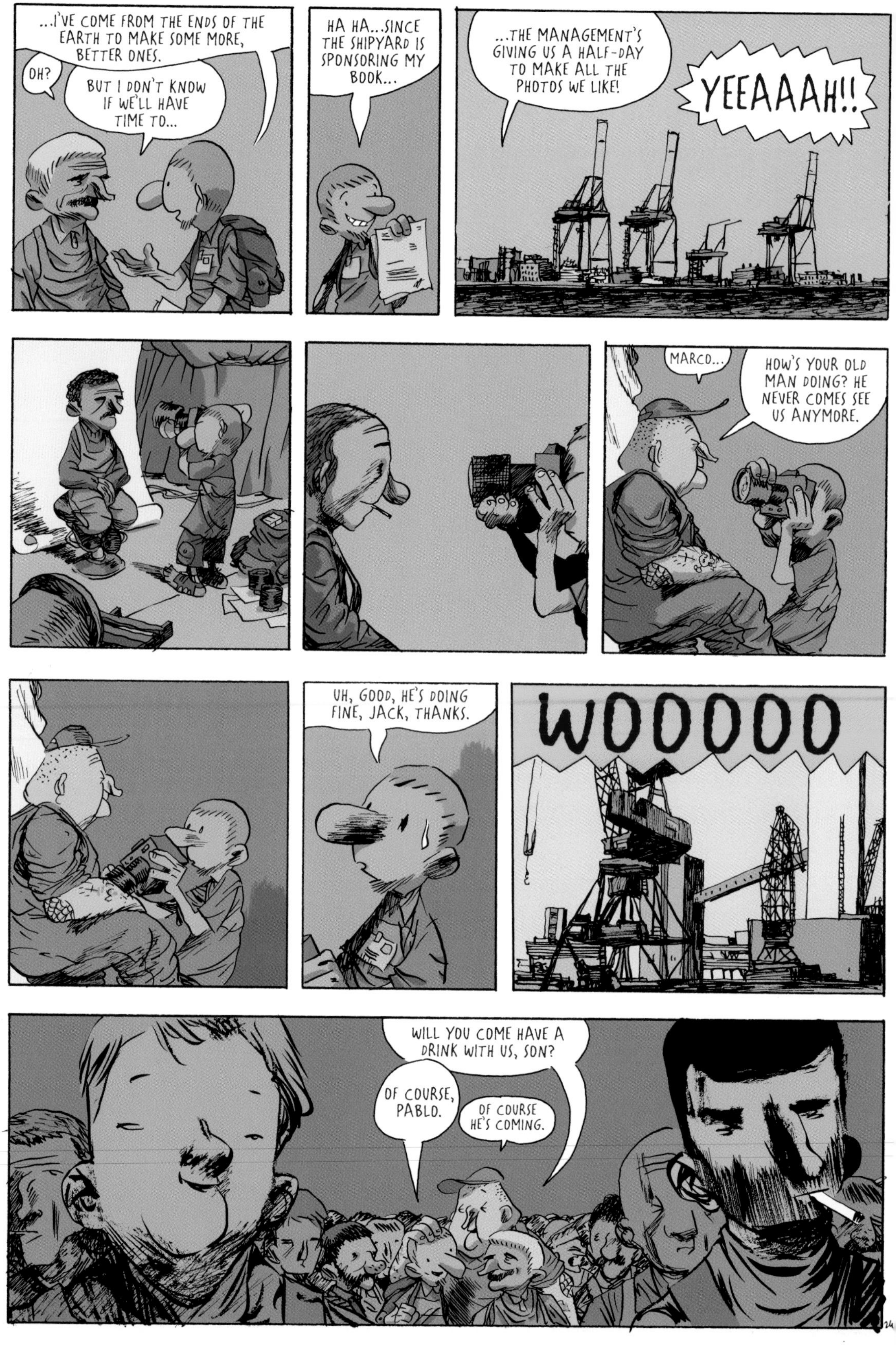
...I'VE COME FROM THE ENDS OF THE EARTH TO MAKE SOME MORE, BETTER ONES.
OH?
BUT I DON'T KNOW IF WE'LL HAVE TIME TO...
HA HA...SINCE THE SHIPYARD IS SPONSORING MY BOOK...
...THE MANAGEMENT'S GIVING US A HALF-DAY TO MAKE ALL THE PHOTOS WE LIKE!
YEEAAAH!!
MARCO...
HOW'S YOUR OLD MAN DOING? HE NEVER COMES SEE US ANYMORE.
UH, GOOD, HE'S DOING FINE, JACK, THANKS.
WOOOOO
WILL YOU COME HAVE A DRINK WITH US, SON?
OF COURSE, PABLO.
OF COURSE HE'S COMING.

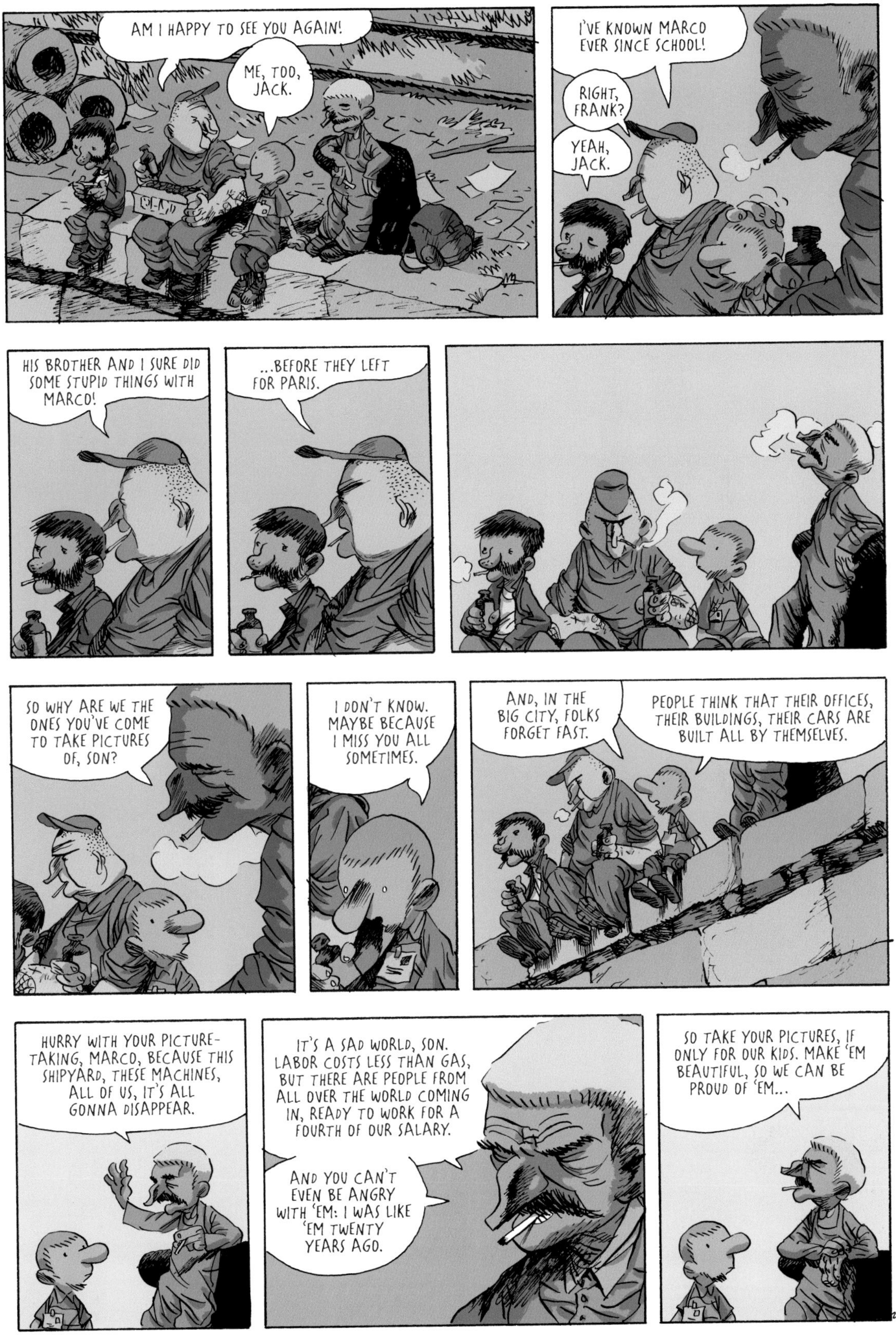

AM I HAPPY TO SEE YOU AGAIN!
ME, TOO, JACK.
I'VE KNOWN MARCO EVER SINCE SCHOOL!
RIGHT, FRANK?
YEAH, JACK.
HIS BROTHER AND I SURE DID SOME STUPID THINGS WITH MARCO!
...BEFORE THEY LEFT FOR PARIS.
SO WHY ARE WE THE ONES YOU'VE COME TO TAKE PICTURES OF, SON?
I DON'T KNOW. MAYBE BECAUSE I MISS YOU ALL SOMETIMES.
AND, IN THE BIG CITY, FOLKS FORGET FAST.
PEOPLE THINK THAT THEIR OFFICES, THEIR BUILDINGS, THEIR CARS ARE BUILT ALL BY THEMSELVES.
HURRY WITH YOUR PICTURE-TAKING, MARCO, BECAUSE THIS SHIPYARD, THESE MACHINES, ALL OF US, IT'S ALL GONNA DISAPPEAR.
IT'S A SAD WORLD, SON. LABOR COSTS LESS THAN GAS, BUT THERE ARE PEOPLE FROM ALL OVER THE WORLD COMING IN, READY TO WORK FOR A FOURTH OF OUR SALARY.
AND YOU CAN'T EVEN BE ANGRY WITH 'EM: I WAS LIKE 'EM TWENTY YEARS AGO.
SO TAKE YOUR PICTURES, IF ONLY FOR OUR KIDS. MAKE 'EM BEAUTIFUL, SO WE CAN BE PROUD OF 'EM...

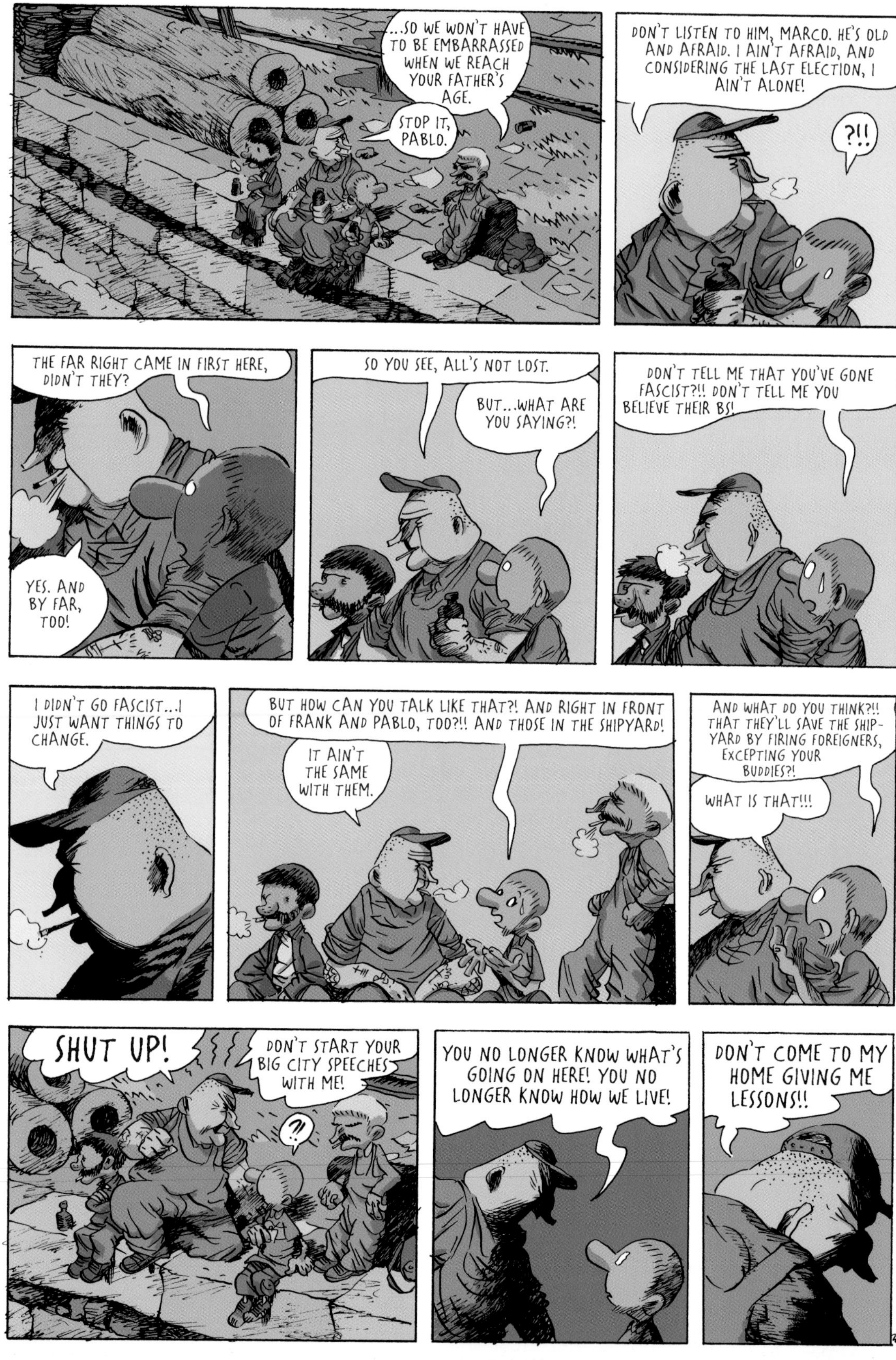
...SO WE WON'T HAVE TO BE EMBARRASSED WHEN WE REACH YOUR FATHER'S AGE.
STOP IT, PABLO.
DON'T LISTEN TO HIM, MARCO. HE'S OLD AND AFRAID. I AIN'T AFRAID, AND CONSIDERING THE LAST ELECTION, I AIN'T ALONE!
?!!
THE FAR RIGHT CAME IN FIRST HERE, DIDN'T THEY?
YES. AND BY FAR, TOO!
SO YOU SEE, ALL'S NOT LOST.
BUT...WHAT ARE YOU SAYING?!
DON'T TELL ME THAT YOU'VE GONE FASCIST?!! DON'T TELL ME YOU BELIEVE THEIR BS!
I DIDN'T GO FASCIST...I JUST WANT THINGS TO CHANGE.
BUT HOW CAN YOU TALK LIKE THAT?! AND RIGHT IN FRONT OF FRANK AND PABLO, TOO?!! AND THOSE IN THE SHIPYARD!
IT AIN'T THE SAME WITH THEM.
AND WHAT DO YOU THINK?!! THAT THEY'LL SAVE THE SHIPYARD BY FIRING FOREIGNERS, EXCEPTING YOUR BUDDIES?!
WHAT IS THAT!!!
SHUT UP!
DON'T START YOUR BIG CITY SPEECHES WITH ME!
?!
YOU NO LONGER KNOW WHAT'S GOING ON HERE! YOU NO LONGER KNOW HOW WE LIVE!
DON'T COME TO MY HOME GIVING ME LESSONS!!

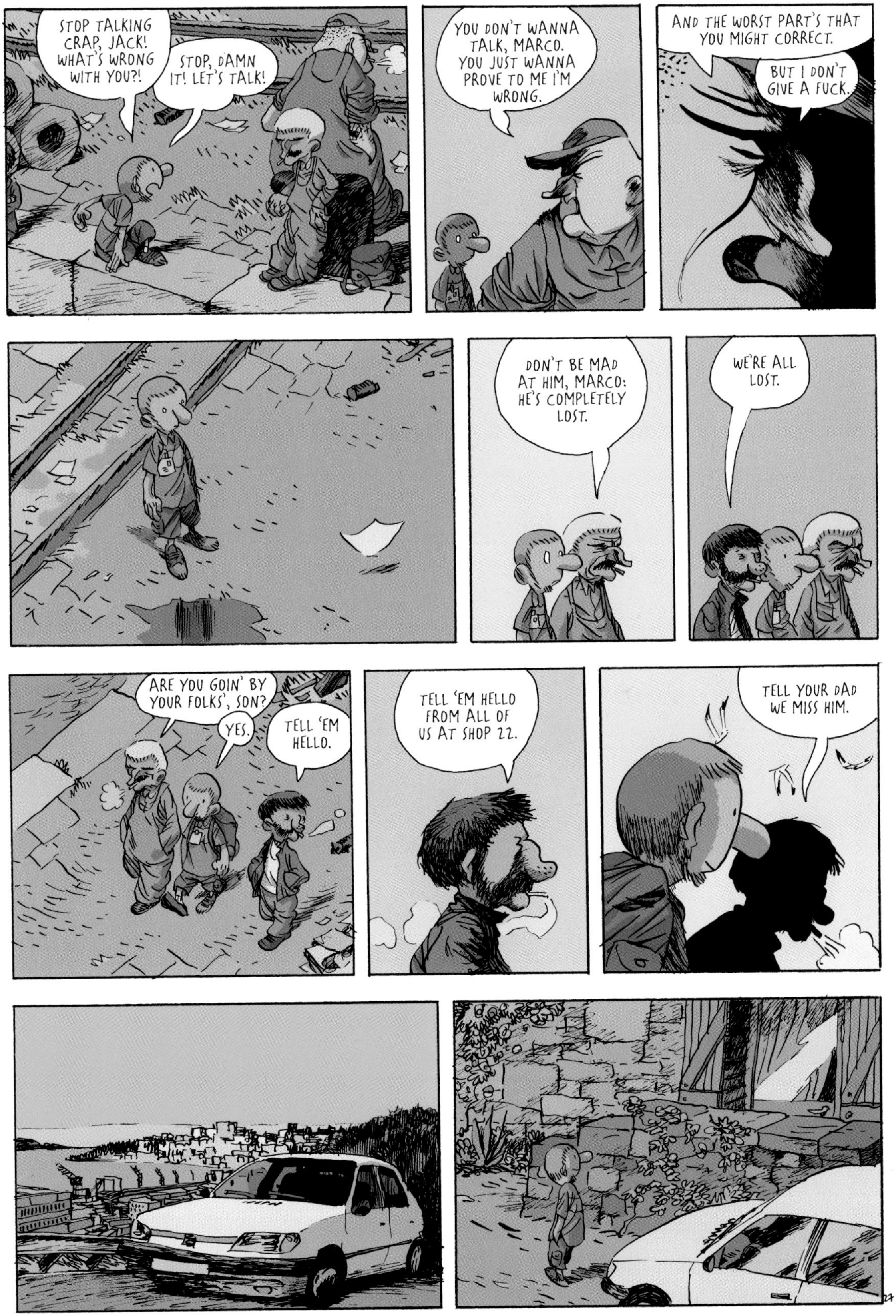
STOP TALKING CRAP, JACK! WHAT'S WRONG WITH YOU?!
STOP, DAMN IT! LET'S TALK!
YOU DON'T WANNA TALK, MARCO. YOU JUST WANNA PROVE TO ME I'M WRONG.
AND THE WORST PART'S THAT YOU MIGHT CORRECT.
BUT I DON'T GIVE A FUCK.
DON'T BE MAD AT HIM, MARCO: HE'S COMPLETELY LOST.
WE'RE ALL LOST.
ARE YOU GOIN' BY YOUR FOLKS', SON?
YES.
TELL 'EM HELLO.
TELL 'EM HELLO FROM ALL OF US AT SHOP 22.
TELL YOUR DAD WE MISS HIM.

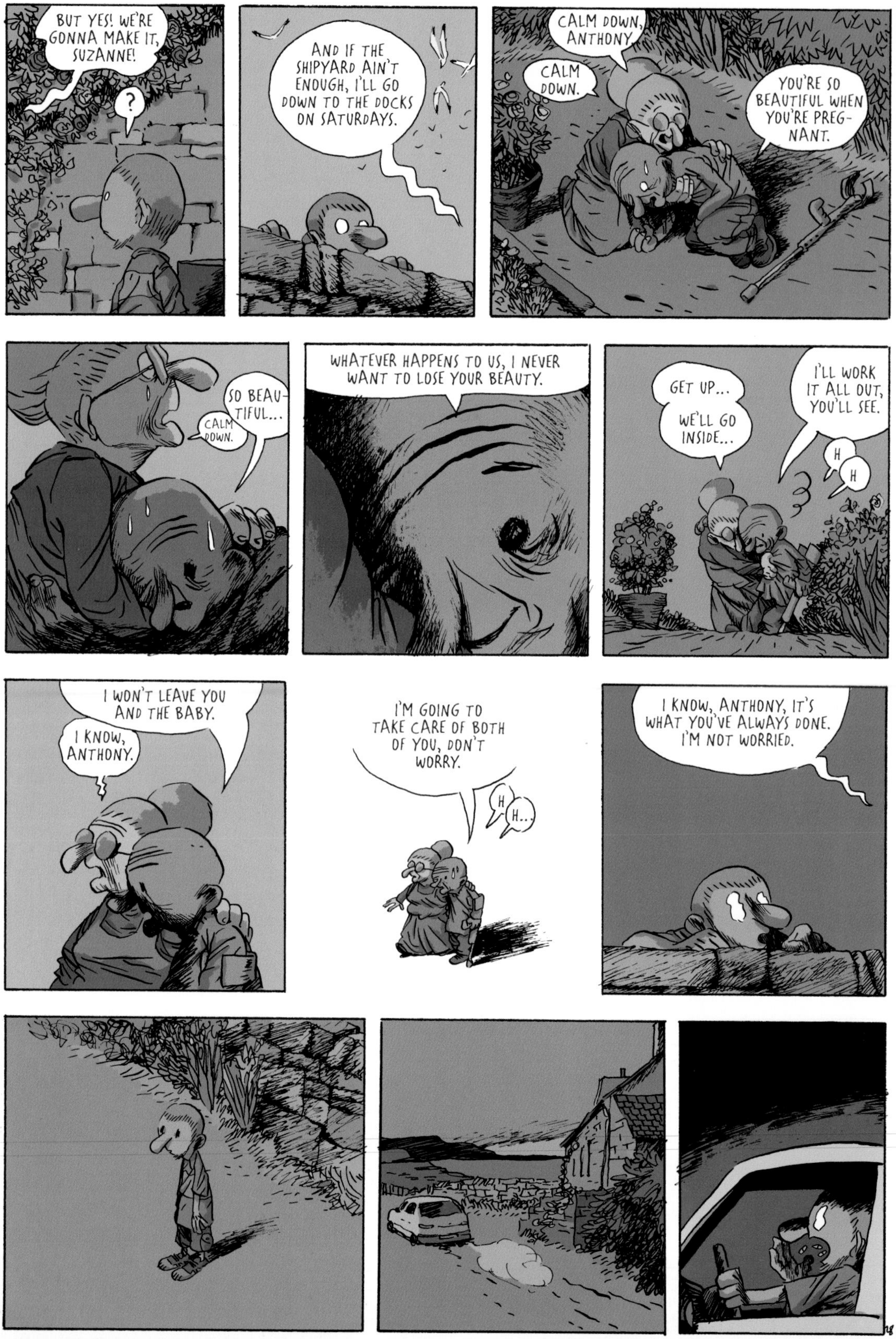

BUT YES! WE'RE GONNA MAKE IT, SUZANNE!
?
AND IF THE SHIPYARD AIN'T ENOUGH, I'LL GO DOWN TO THE DOCKS ON SATURDAYS.
CALM DOWN, ANTHONY.
CALM DOWN.
YOU'RE SO BEAUTIFUL WHEN YOU'RE PREG-NANT.
SO BEAU-TIFUL...
CALM DOWN.
WHATEVER HAPPENS TO US, I NEVER WANT TO LOSE YOUR BEAUTY.
GET UP...
WE'LL GO INSIDE...
I'LL WORK IT ALL OUT, YOU'LL SEE.
H
H
I WON'T LEAVE YOU AND THE BABY.
I KNOW, ANTHONY.
I'M GOING TO TAKE CARE OF BOTH OF YOU, DON'T WORRY.
H
H...
I KNOW, ANTHONY, IT'S WHAT YOU'VE ALWAYS DONE. I'M NOT WORRIED.

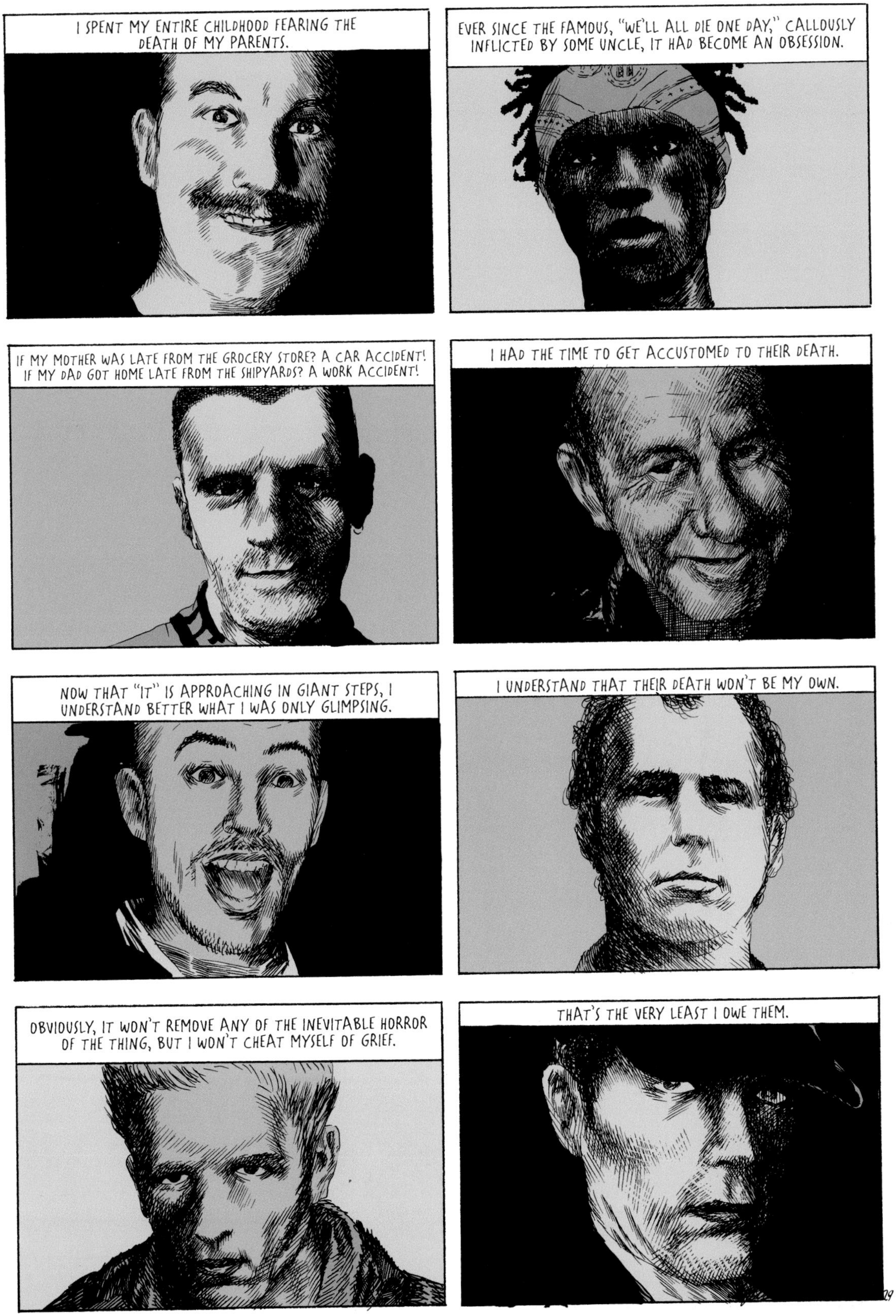
I SPENT MY ENTIRE CHILDHOOD FEARING THE DEATH OF MY PARENTS.
EVER SINCE THE FAMOUS, "WE'LL ALL DIE ONE DAY," CALLOUSLY INFLICTED BY SOME UNCLE, IT HAD BECOME AN OBSESSION.
IF MY MOTHER WAS LATE FROM THE GROCERY STORE? A CAR ACCIDENT! IF MY DAD GOT HOME LATE FROM THE SHIPYARDS? A WORK ACCIDENT!
I HAD THE TIME TO GET ACCUSTOMED TO THEIR DEATH.
NOW THAT "IT" IS APPROACHING IN GIANT STEPS, I UNDERSTAND BETTER WHAT I WAS ONLY GLIMPSING.
I UNDERSTAND THAT THEIR DEATH WON'T BE MY OWN.
OBVIOUSLY, IT WON'T REMOVE ANY OF THE INEVITABLE HORROR OF THE THING, BUT I WON'T CHEAT MYSELF OF GRIEF.
THAT'S THE VERY LEAST I OWE THEM.

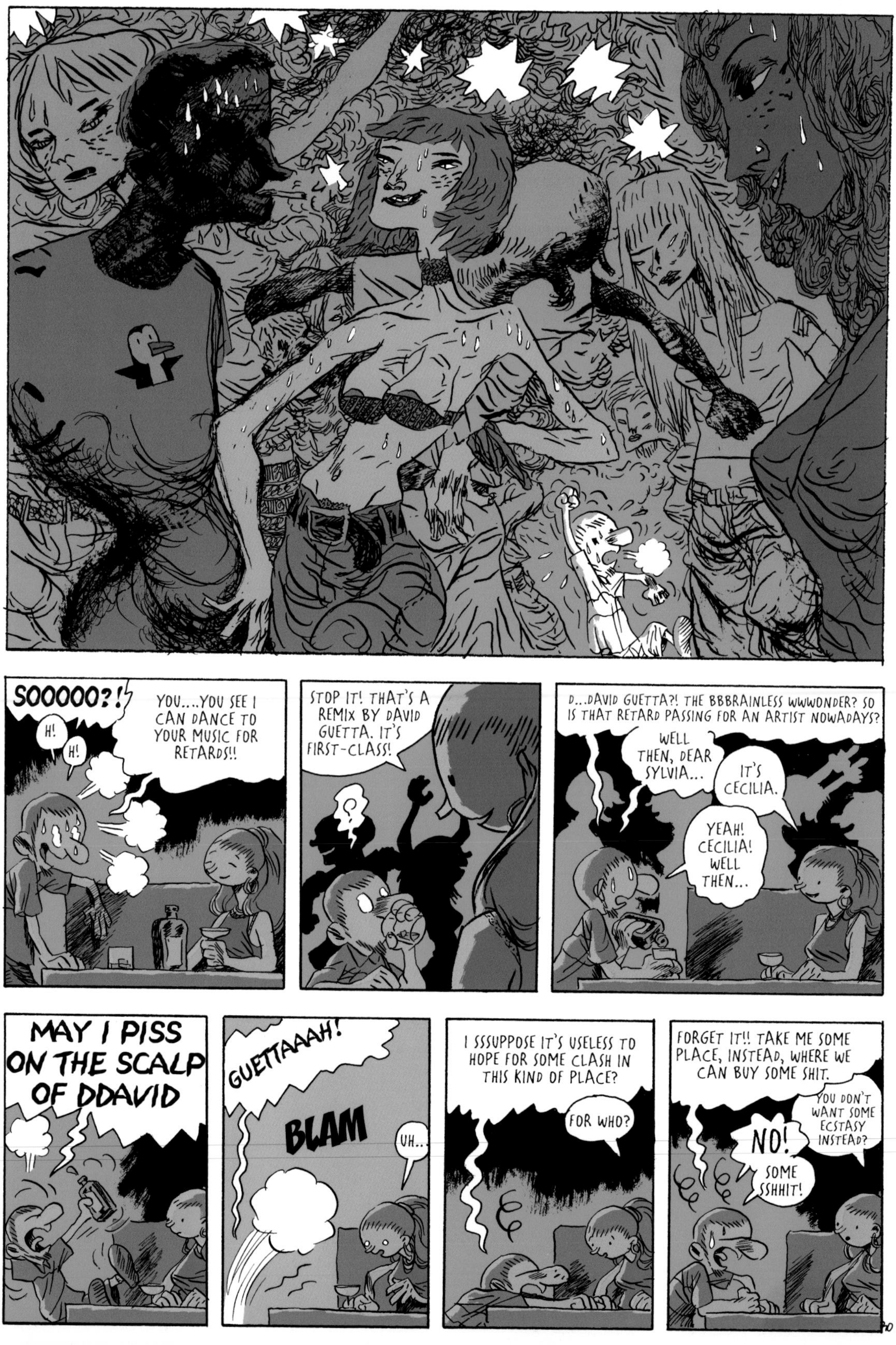
SOOOOO?!
H!
H!
YOU....YOU SEE I CAN DANCE TO YOUR MUSIC FOR RETARDS!!
STOP IT! THAT'S A REMIX BY DAVID GUETTA. IT'S FIRST-CLASS!
?
D...DAVID GUETTA?! THE BBBRAINLESS WWWONDER? SO IS THAT RETARD PASSING FOR AN ARTIST NOWADAYS?
WELL THEN, DEAR SYLVIA...
IT'S CECILIA.
YEAH! CECILIA! WELL THEN...
MAY I PISS ON THE SCALP OF DDAVID
GUETTAAAH!
BLAM
UH...
I SSSUPPOSE IT'S USELESS TO HOPE FOR SOME CLASH IN THIS KIND OF PLACE?
FOR WHO?
FORGET IT!! TAKE ME SOME PLACE, INSTEAD, WHERE WE CAN BUY SOME SHIT.
YOU DON'T WANT SOME ECSTASY INSTEAD?
NO!
SOME SSHHIT!

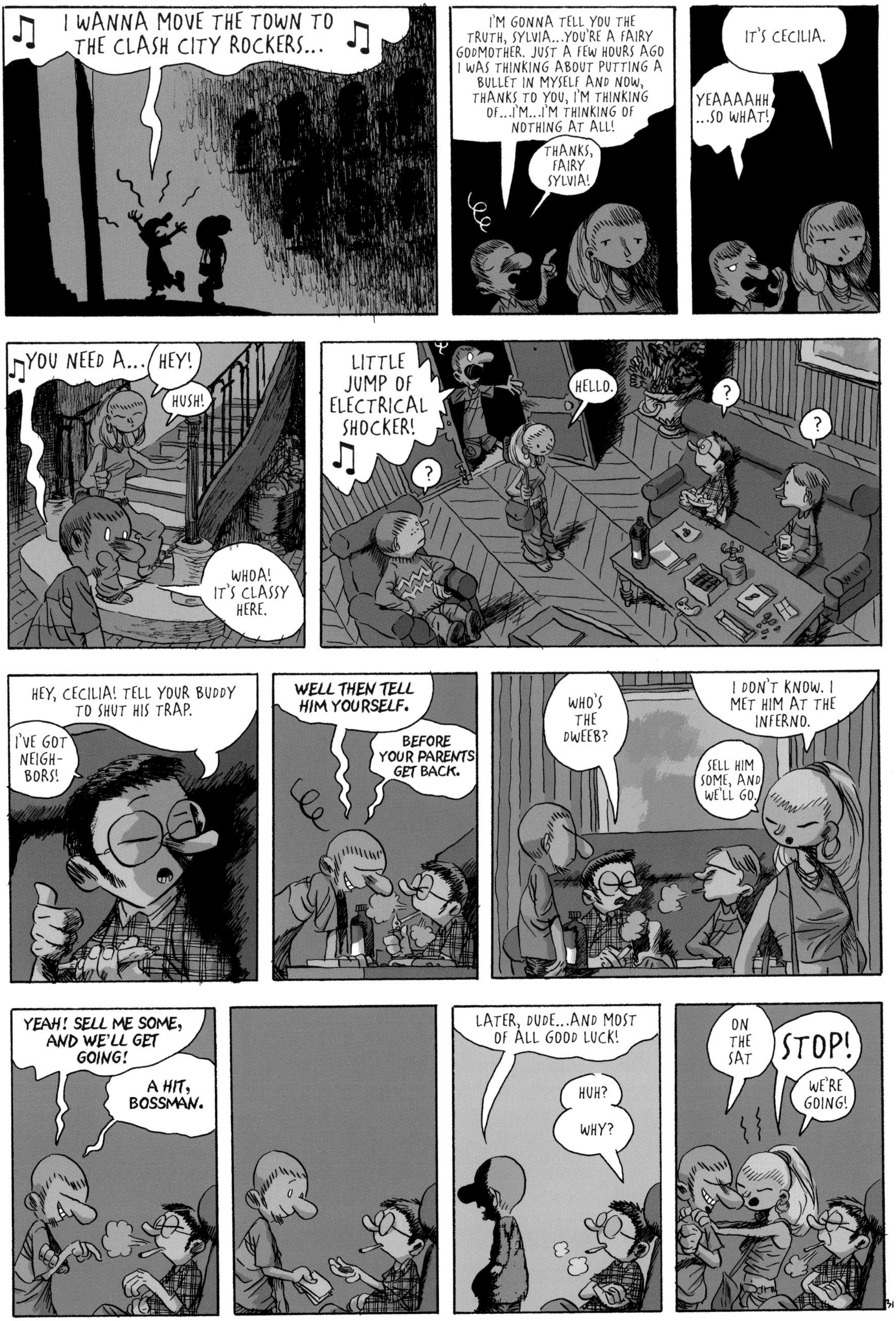
♫ I WANNA MOVE THE TOWN TO THE CLASH CITY ROCKERS... ♫
I'M GONNA TELL YOU THE TRUTH, SYLVIA...YOU'RE A FAIRY GODMOTHER. JUST A FEW HOURS AGO I WAS THINKING ABOUT PUTTING A BULLET IN MYSELF AND NOW, THANKS TO YOU, I'M THINKING OF...I'M...I'M THINKING OF NOTHING AT ALL!
THANKS, FAIRY SYLVIA!
IT'S CECILIA.
YEAAAAHH ...SO WHAT!
♫ YOU NEED A...
HEY!
HUSH!
WHOA! IT'S CLASSY HERE.
LITTLE JUMP OF ELECTRICAL SHOCKER! ♫
HELLO.
?
?
?
HEY, CECILIA! TELL YOUR BUDDY TO SHUT HIS TRAP.
I'VE GOT NEIGH-BORS!
WELL THEN TELL HIM YOURSELF.
BEFORE YOUR PARENTS GET BACK.
WHO'S THE DWEEB?
I DON'T KNOW. I MET HIM AT THE INFERNO.
SELL HIM SOME, AND WE'LL GO.
YEAH! SELL ME SOME, AND WE'LL GET GOING!
A HIT, BOSSMAN.
LATER, DUDE...AND MOST OF ALL GOOD LUCK!
HUH?
WHY?
ON THE SAT
STOP!
WE'RE GOING!

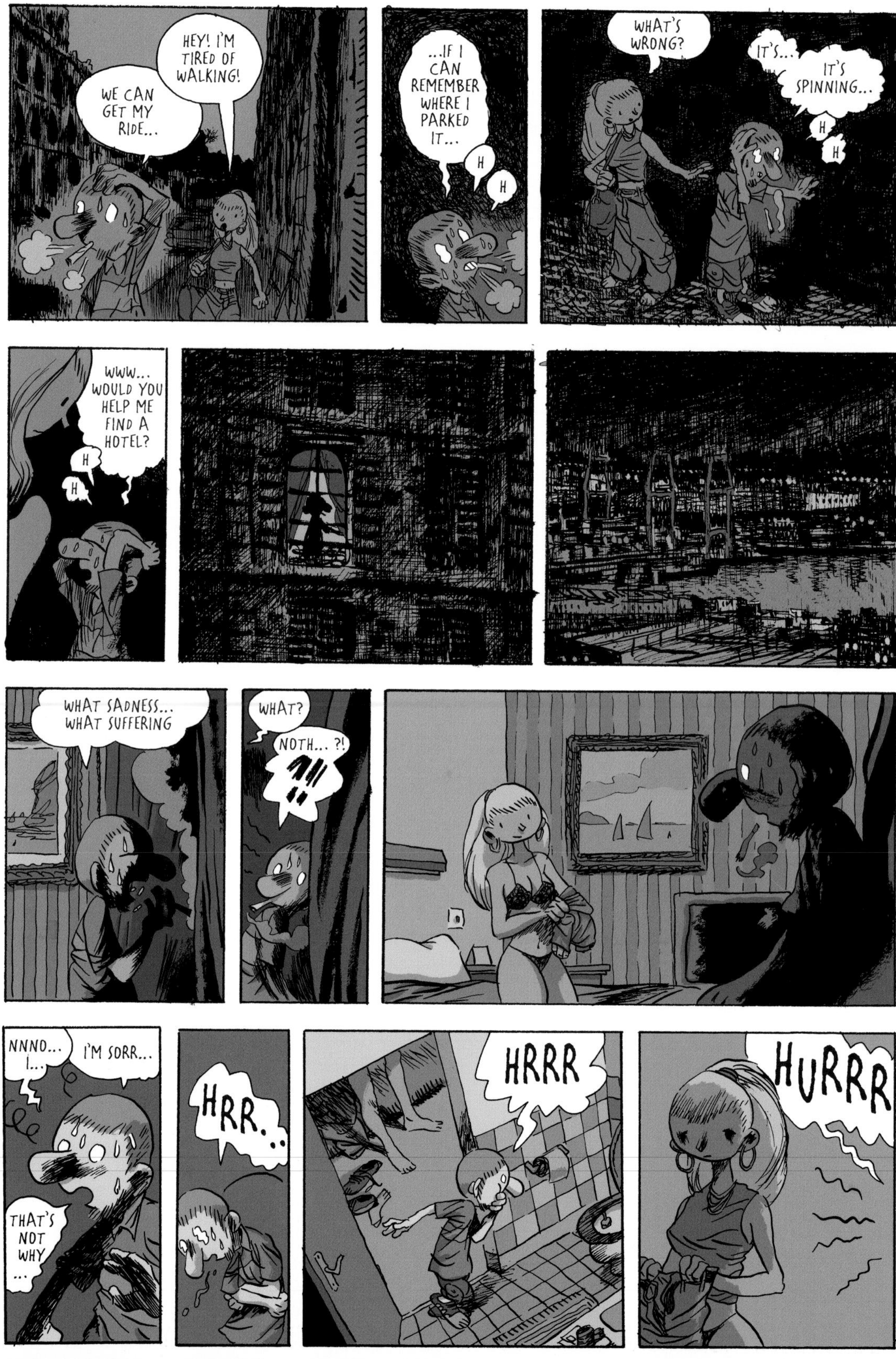
WE CAN GET MY RIDE...
HEY! I'M TIRED OF WALKING!
...IF I CAN REMEMBER WHERE I PARKED IT...
H
H
WHAT'S WRONG?
IT'S...
IT'S SPINNING...
H
H
WWW... WOULD YOU HELP ME FIND A HOTEL?
H
H
WHAT SADNESS... WHAT SUFFERING
WHAT?
NOTH... ?!
NNNO... I...
I'M SORR...
THAT'S NOT WHY ...
HRR...
HRRR
HURRR

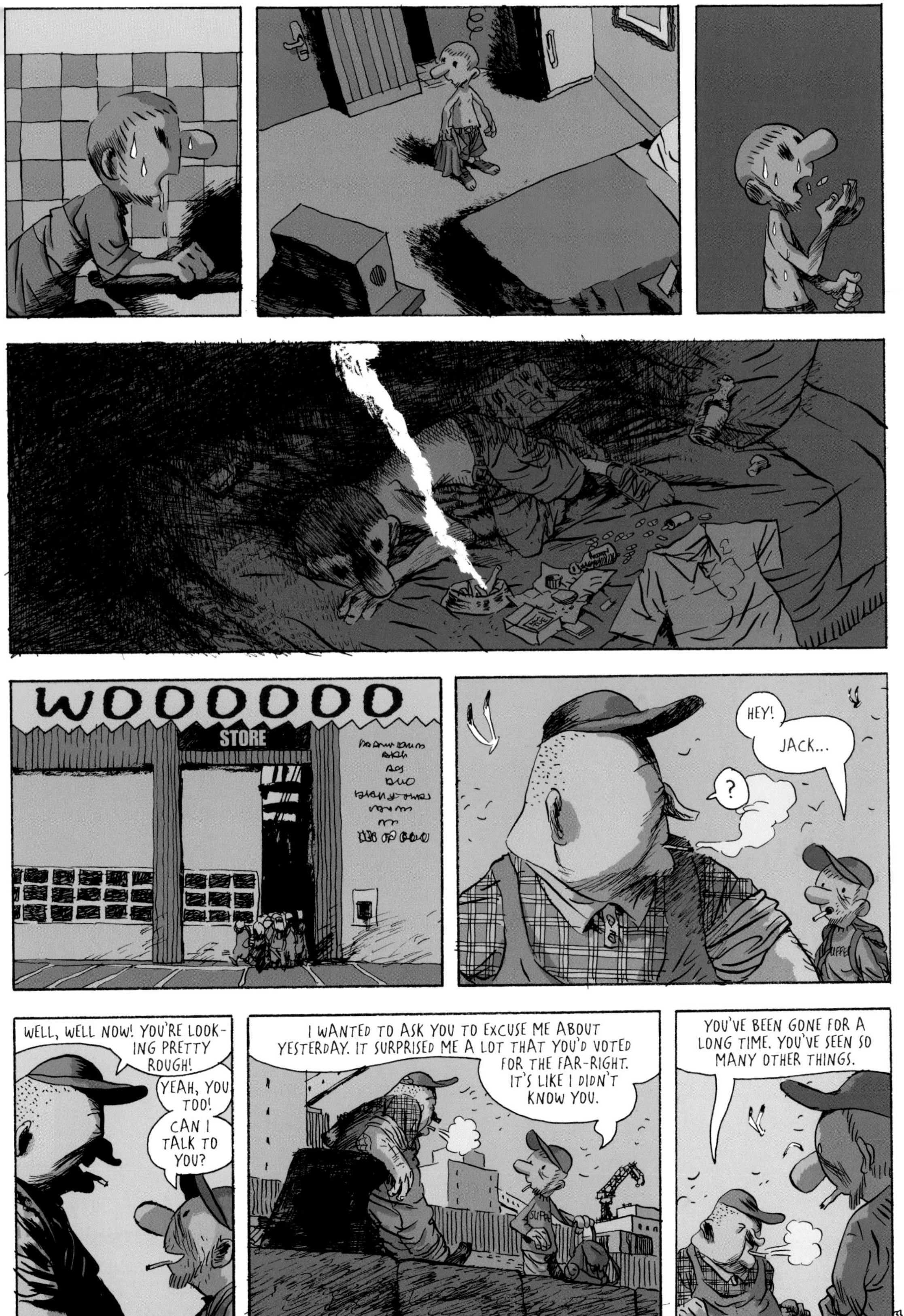
WOOOOOO
STORE
HEY!
JACK...
?
WELL, WELL NOW! YOU'RE LOOKING PRETTY ROUGH!
YEAH, YOU TOO!
CAN I TALK TO YOU?
I WANTED TO ASK YOU TO EXCUSE ME ABOUT YESTERDAY. IT SURPRISED ME A LOT THAT YOU'D VOTED FOR THE FAR-RIGHT. IT'S LIKE I DIDN'T KNOW YOU.
YOU'VE BEEN GONE FOR A LONG TIME. YOU'VE SEEN SO MANY OTHER THINGS.

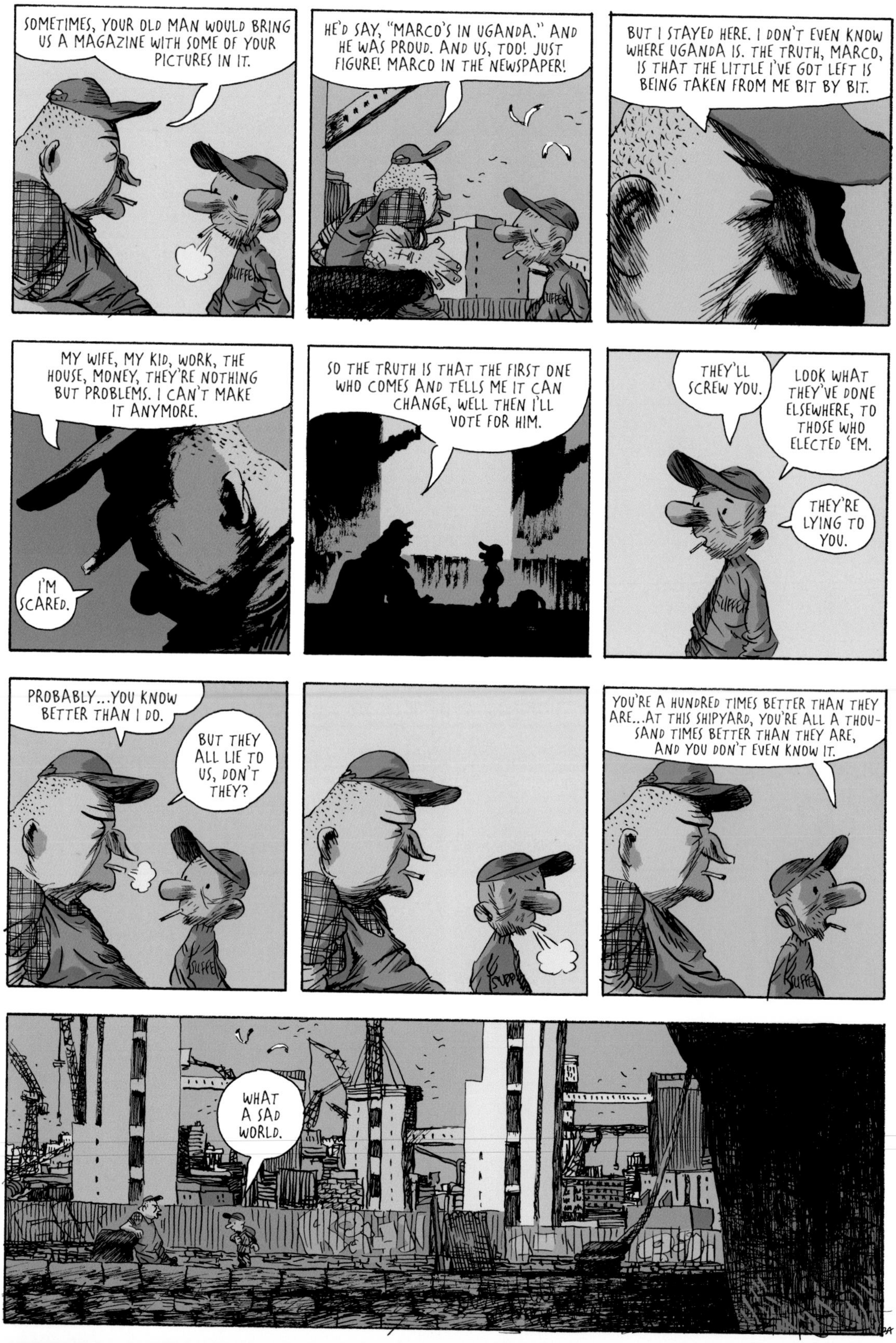
SOMETIMES, YOUR OLD MAN WOULD BRING US A MAGAZINE WITH SOME OF YOUR PICTURES IN IT.
HE'D SAY, "MARCO'S IN UGANDA." AND HE WAS PROUD. AND US, TOO! JUST FIGURE! MARCO IN THE NEWSPAPER!
BUT I STAYED HERE. I DON'T EVEN KNOW WHERE UGANDA IS. THE TRUTH, MARCO, IS THAT THE LITTLE I'VE GOT LEFT IS BEING TAKEN FROM ME BIT BY BIT.
MY WIFE, MY KID, WORK, THE HOUSE, MONEY, THEY'RE NOTHING BUT PROBLEMS. I CAN'T MAKE IT ANYMORE.
I'M SCARED.
SO THE TRUTH IS THAT THE FIRST ONE WHO COMES AND TELLS ME IT CAN CHANGE, WELL THEN I'LL VOTE FOR HIM.
THEY'LL SCREW YOU.
LOOK WHAT THEY'VE DONE ELSEWHERE, TO THOSE WHO ELECTED 'EM.
THEY'RE LYING TO YOU.
PROBABLY...YOU KNOW BETTER THAN I DO.
BUT THEY ALL LIE TO US, DON'T THEY?
YOU'RE A HUNDRED TIMES BETTER THAN THEY ARE...AT THIS SHIPYARD, YOU'RE ALL A THOU-SAND TIMES BETTER THAN THEY ARE, AND YOU DON'T EVEN KNOW IT.
WHAT A SAD WORLD.

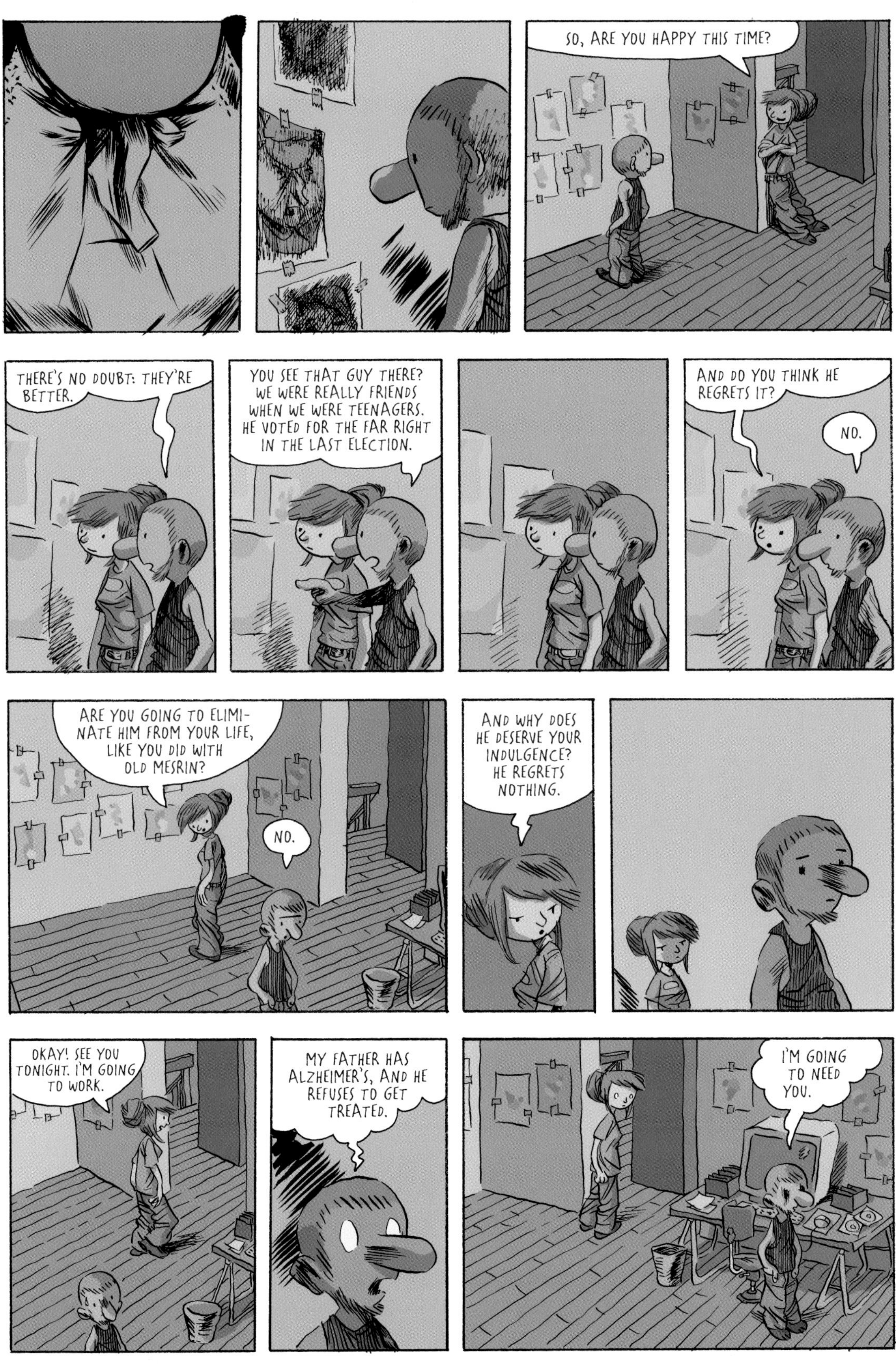
SO, ARE YOU HAPPY THIS TIME?
THERE'S NO DOUBT: THEY'RE BETTER.
YOU SEE THAT GUY THERE? WE WERE REALLY FRIENDS WHEN WE WERE TEENAGERS. HE VOTED FOR THE FAR RIGHT IN THE LAST ELECTION.
AND DO YOU THINK HE REGRETS IT?
NO.
ARE YOU GOING TO ELIMI-NATE HIM FROM YOUR LIFE, LIKE YOU DID WITH OLD MESRIN?
NO.
AND WHY DOES HE DESERVE YOUR INDULGENCE? HE REGRETS NOTHING.
OKAY! SEE YOU TONIGHT. I'M GOING TO WORK.
MY FATHER HAS ALZHEIMER'S, AND HE REFUSES TO GET TREATED.
I'M GOING TO NEED YOU.

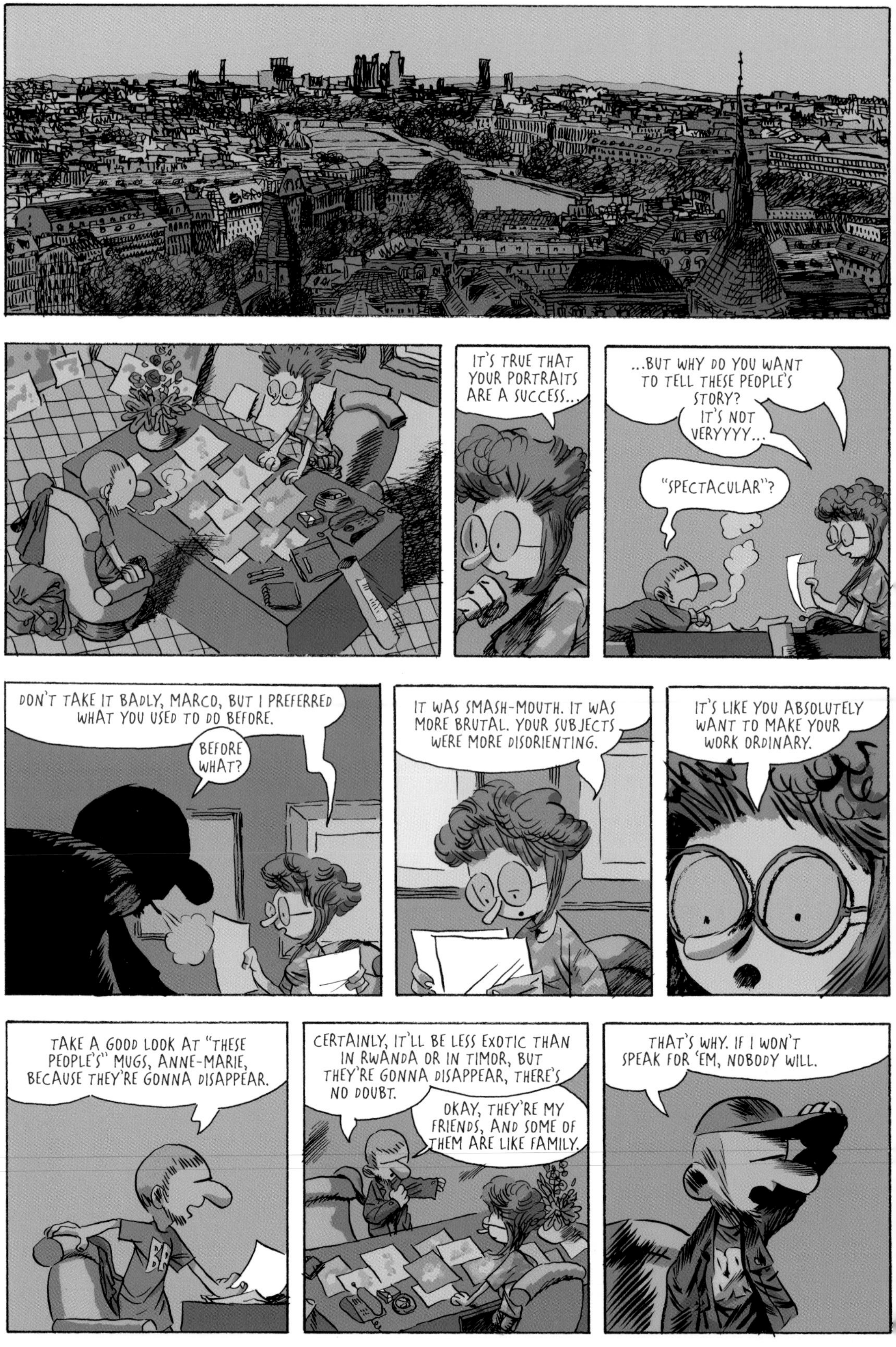
IT'S TRUE THAT YOUR PORTRAITS ARE A SUCCESS...
...BUT WHY DO YOU WANT TO TELL THESE PEOPLE'S STORY? IT'S NOT VERYYYY...
"SPECTACULAR"?
DON'T TAKE IT BADLY, MARCO, BUT I PREFERRED WHAT YOU USED TO DO BEFORE.
BEFORE WHAT?
IT WAS SMASH-MOUTH. IT WAS MORE BRUTAL. YOUR SUBJECTS WERE MORE DISORIENTING.
IT'S LIKE YOU ABSOLUTELY WANT TO MAKE YOUR WORK ORDINARY.
TAKE A GOOD LOOK AT "THESE PEOPLE'S" MUGS, ANNE-MARIE, BECAUSE THEY'RE GONNA DISAPPEAR.
CERTAINLY, IT'LL BE LESS EXOTIC THAN IN RWANDA OR IN TIMOR, BUT THEY'RE GONNA DISAPPEAR, THERE'S NO DOUBT.
OKAY, THEY'RE MY FRIENDS, AND SOME OF THEM ARE LIKE FAMILY.
THAT'S WHY. IF I WON'T SPEAK FOR 'EM, NOBODY WILL.

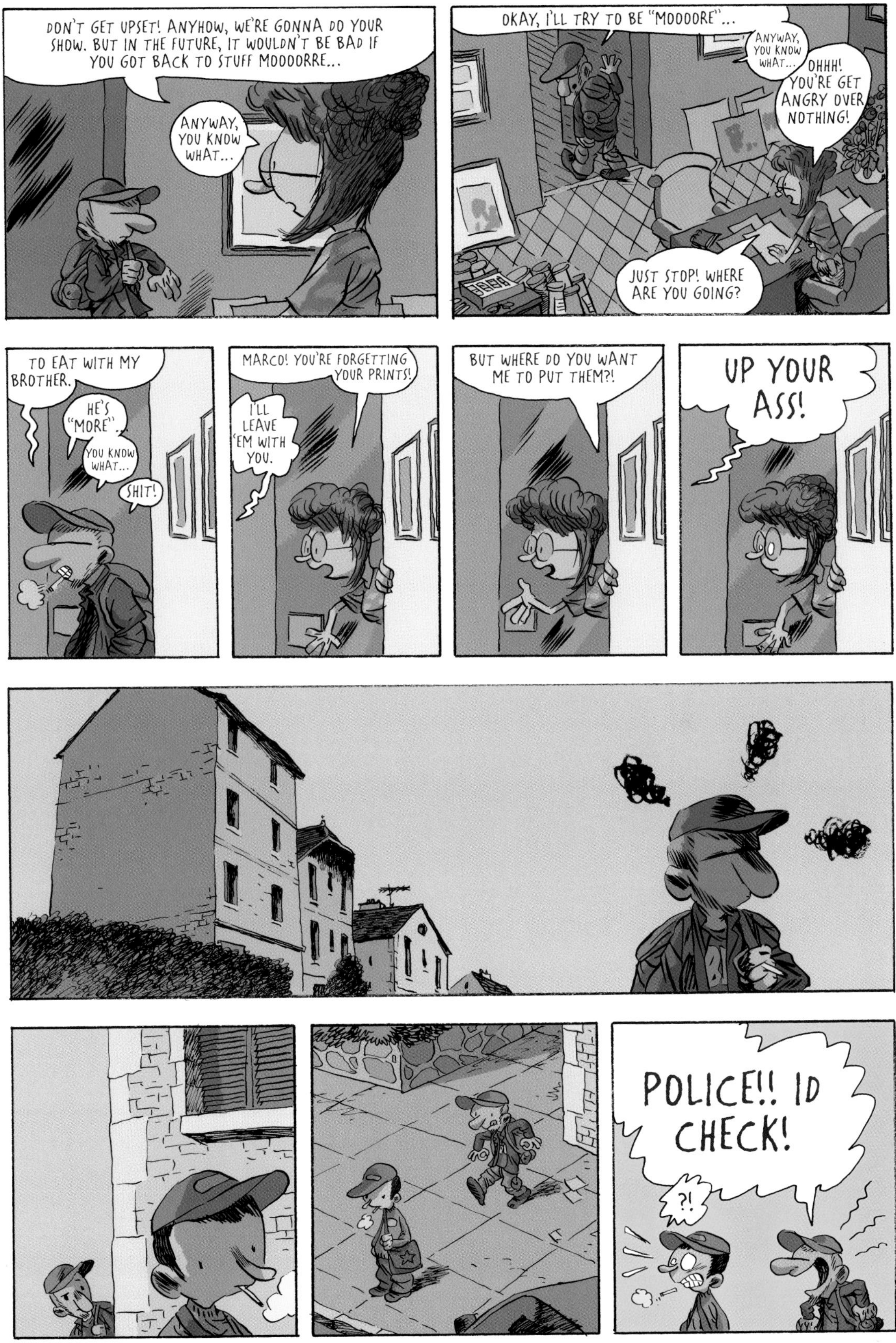
DON'T GET UPSET! ANYHOW, WE'RE GONNA DO YOUR SHOW. BUT IN THE FUTURE, IT WOULDN'T BE BAD IF YOU GOT BACK TO STUFF MOOOORRE...
ANYWAY, YOU KNOW WHAT...
OKAY, I'LL TRY TO BE "MOOOORE"...
ANYWAY, YOU KNOW WHAT...
OHHH! YOU'RE GET ANGRY OVER NOTHING!
JUST STOP! WHERE ARE YOU GOING?
TO EAT WITH MY BROTHER.
HE'S "MORE"...
YOU KNOW WHAT...
SHIT!
MARCO! YOU'RE FORGETTING YOUR PRINTS!
I'LL LEAVE 'EM WITH YOU.
BUT WHERE DO YOU WANT ME TO PUT THEM?!
UP YOUR ASS!
POLICE!! ID CHECK!
?!

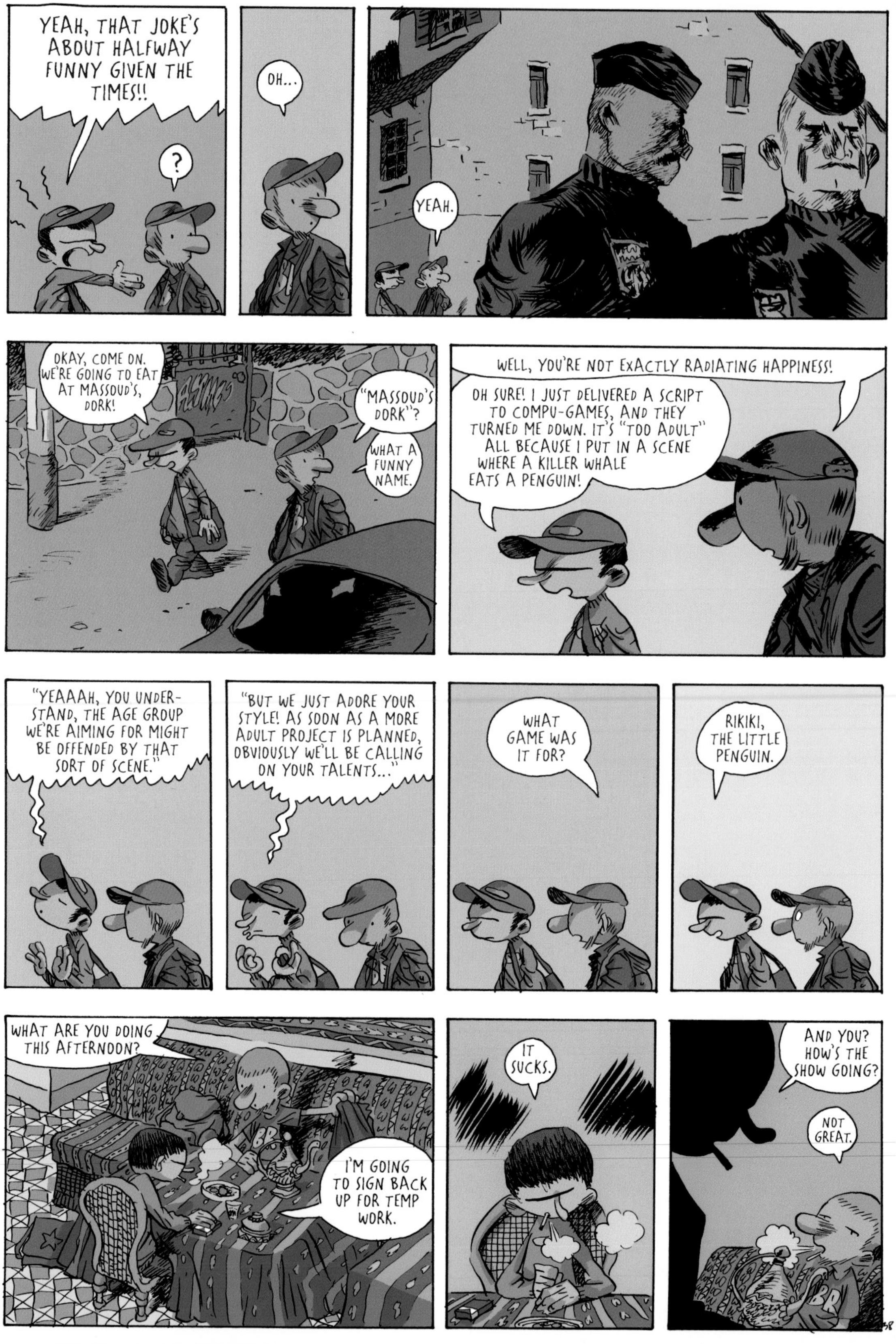
YEAH, THAT JOKE'S ABOUT HALFWAY FUNNY GIVEN THE TIMES!!
?
OH...
YEAH.
OKAY, COME ON. WE'RE GOING TO EAT AT MASSOUD'S, DORK!
"MASSOUD'S DORK"?
WHAT A FUNNY NAME.
WELL, YOU'RE NOT EXACTLY RADIATING HAPPINESS!
OH SURE! I JUST DELIVERED A SCRIPT TO COMPU-GAMES, AND THEY TURNED ME DOWN. IT'S "TOO ADULT" ALL BECAUSE I PUT IN A SCENE WHERE A KILLER WHALE EATS A PENGUIN!
"YEAAAH, YOU UNDER-STAND, THE AGE GROUP WE'RE AIMING FOR MIGHT BE OFFENDED BY THAT SORT OF SCENE."
"BUT WE JUST ADORE YOUR STYLE! AS SOON AS A MORE ADULT PROJECT IS PLANNED, OBVIOUSLY WE'LL BE CALLING ON YOUR TALENTS..."
WHAT GAME WAS IT FOR?
RIKIKI, THE LITTLE PENGUIN.
WHAT ARE YOU DOING THIS AFTERNOON?
I'M GOING TO SIGN BACK UP FOR TEMP WORK.
IT SUCKS.
AND YOU? HOW'S THE SHOW GOING?
NOT GREAT.

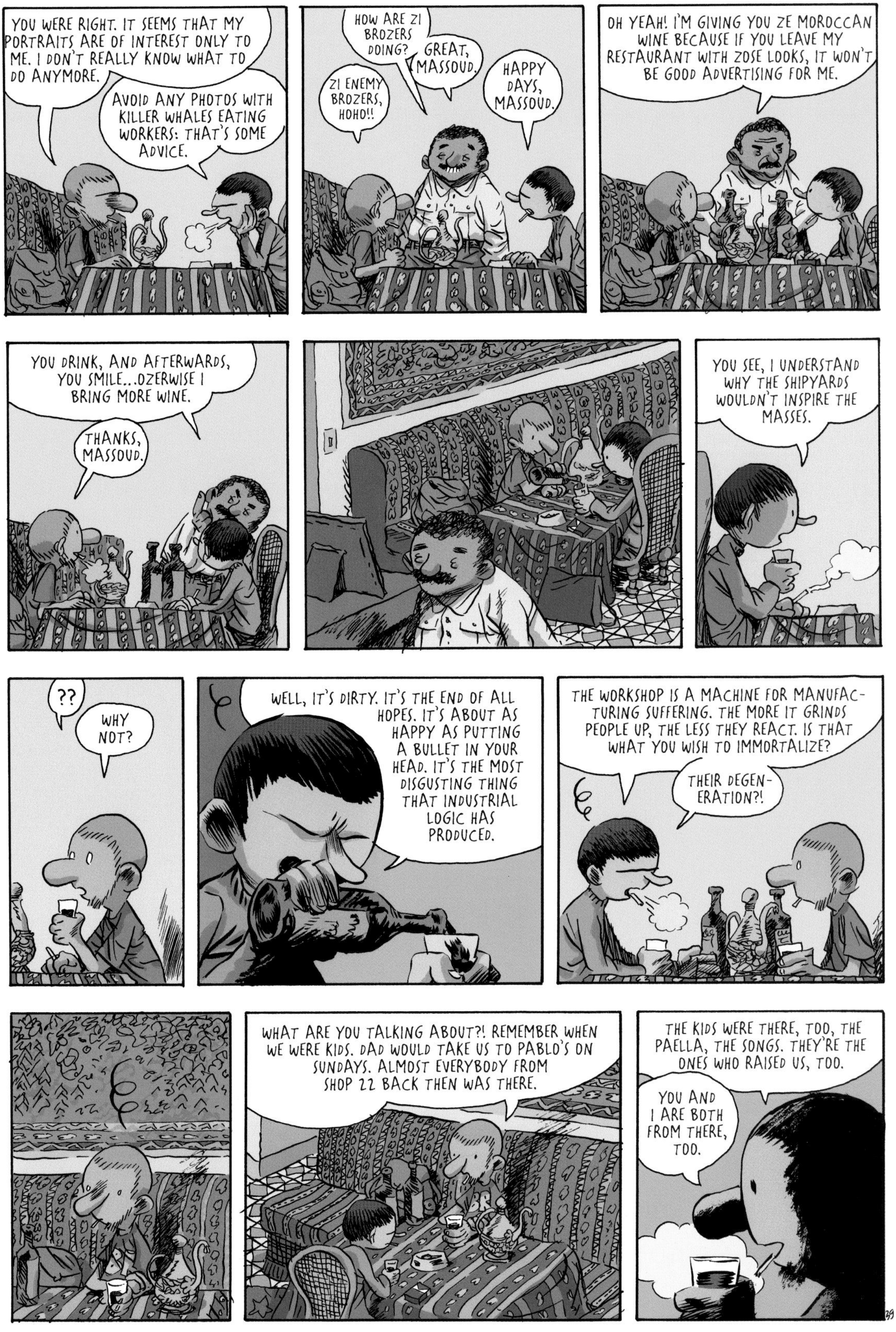
YOU WERE RIGHT. IT SEEMS THAT MY PORTRAITS ARE OF INTEREST ONLY TO ME. I DON'T REALLY KNOW WHAT TO DO ANYMORE.
AVOID ANY PHOTOS WITH KILLER WHALES EATING WORKERS: THAT'S SOME ADVICE.
HOW ARE ZI BROZERS DOING?
ZI ENEMY BROZERS, HOHO!!
GREAT, MASSOUD.
HAPPY DAYS, MASSOUD.
OH YEAH! I'M GIVING YOU ZE MOROCCAN WINE BECAUSE IF YOU LEAVE MY RESTAURANT WITH ZOSE LOOKS, IT WON'T BE GOOD ADVERTISING FOR ME.
YOU DRINK, AND AFTERWARDS, YOU SMILE...OZERWISE I BRING MORE WINE.
THANKS, MASSOUD.
YOU SEE, I UNDERSTAND WHY THE SHIPYARDS WOULDN'T INSPIRE THE MASSES.
??
WHY NOT?
WELL, IT'S DIRTY. IT'S THE END OF ALL HOPES. IT'S ABOUT AS HAPPY AS PUTTING A BULLET IN YOUR HEAD. IT'S THE MOST DISGUSTING THING THAT INDUSTRIAL LOGIC HAS PRODUCED.
THE WORKSHOP IS A MACHINE FOR MANUFAC-TURING SUFFERING. THE MORE IT GRINDS PEOPLE UP, THE LESS THEY REACT. IS THAT WHAT YOU WISH TO IMMORTALIZE?
THEIR DEGEN-ERATION?!
WHAT ARE YOU TALKING ABOUT?! REMEMBER WHEN WE WERE KIDS. DAD WOULD TAKE US TO PABLO'S ON SUNDAYS. ALMOST EVERYBODY FROM SHOP 22 BACK THEN WAS THERE.
THE KIDS WERE THERE, TOO, THE PAELLA, THE SONGS. THEY'RE THE ONES WHO RAISED US, TOO.
YOU AND I ARE BOTH FROM THERE, TOO.

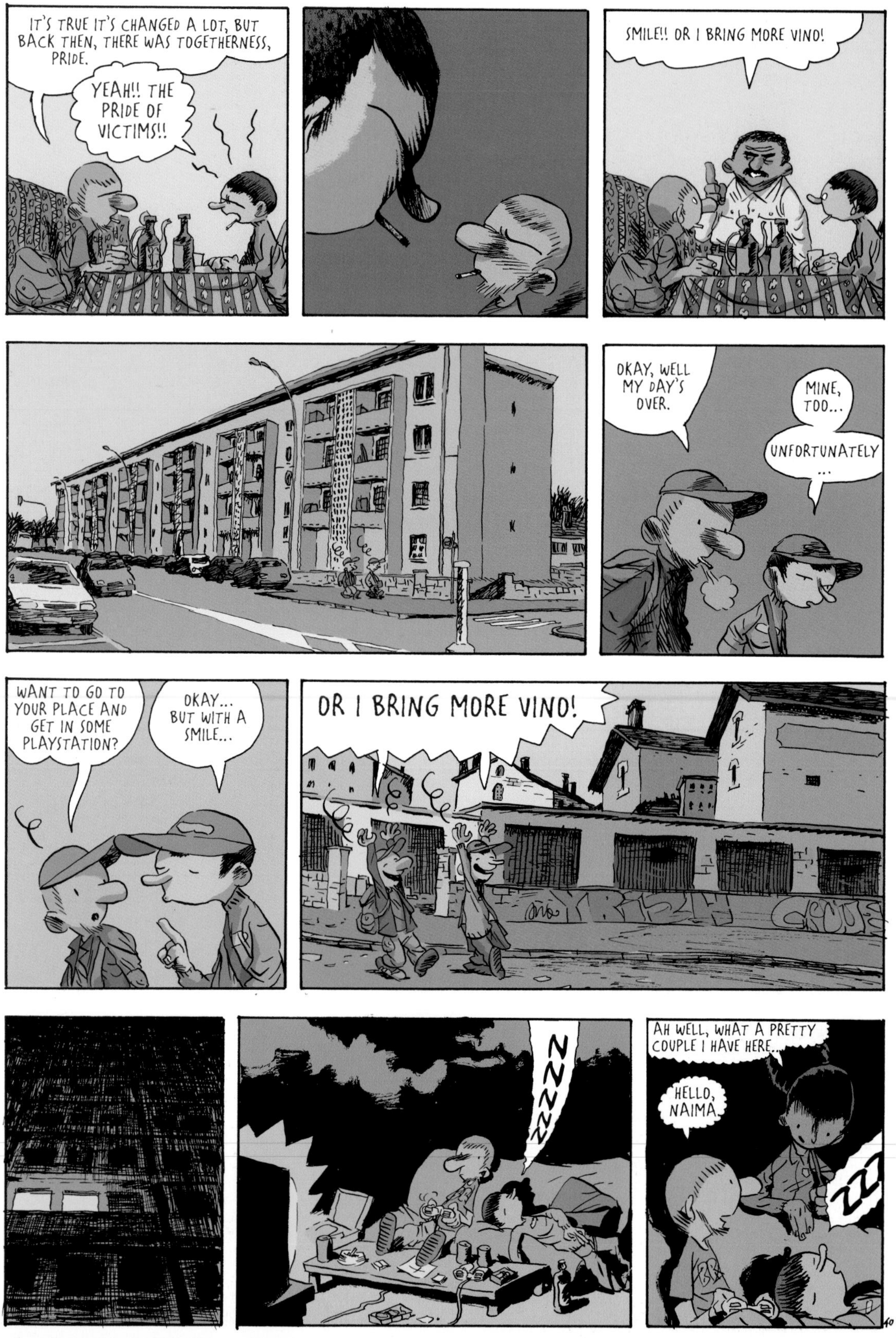
IT'S TRUE IT'S CHANGED A LOT, BUT BACK THEN, THERE WAS TOGETHERNESS, PRIDE.
YEAH!! THE PRIDE OF VICTIMS!!
SMILE!! OR I BRING MORE VINO!
OKAY, WELL MY DAY'S OVER.
MINE, TOO...
UNFORTUNATELY ...
WANT TO GO TO YOUR PLACE AND GET IN SOME PLAYSTATION?
OKAY... BUT WITH A SMILE...
OR I BRING MORE VINO!
NNNNZ
AH WELL, WHAT A PRETTY COUPLE I HAVE HERE...
HELLO, NAIMA.
ZZZ

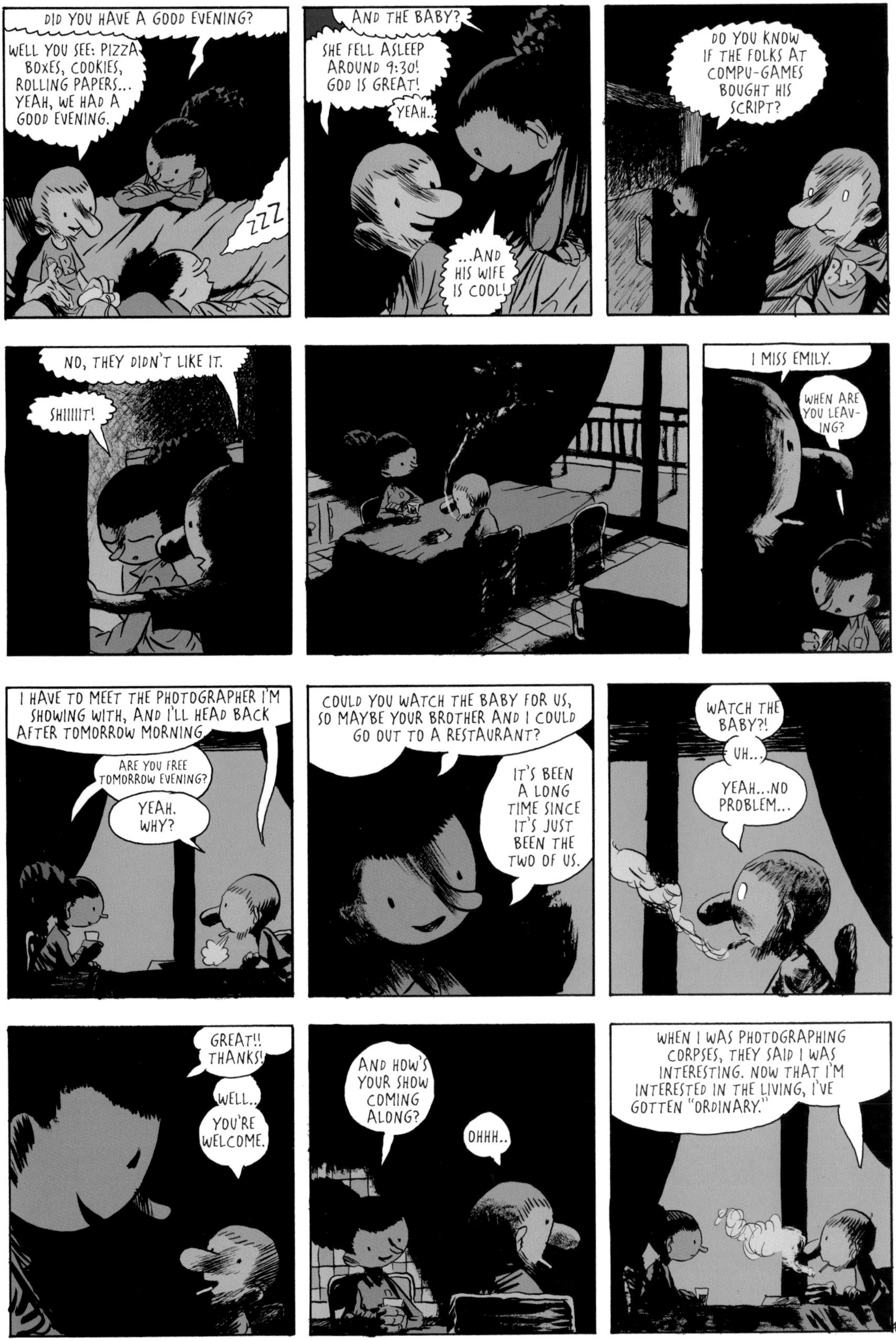
DID YOU HAVE A GOOD EVENING?
WELL YOU SEE: PIZZA BOXES, COOKIES, ROLLING PAPERS... YEAH, WE HAD A GOOD EVENING.
ZZZ
AND THE BABY?
SHE FELL ASLEEP AROUND 9:30! GOD IS GREAT!
YEAH..
...AND HIS WIFE IS COOL!
DO YOU KNOW IF THE FOLKS AT COMPU-GAMES BOUGHT HIS SCRIPT?
NO, THEY DIDN'T LIKE IT.
SHIIIIIT!
I MISS EMILY.
WHEN ARE YOU LEAVING?
I HAVE TO MEET THE PHOTOGRAPHER I'M SHOWING WITH, AND I'LL HEAD BACK AFTER TOMORROW MORNING.
ARE YOU FREE TOMORROW EVENING?
YEAH. WHY?
COULD YOU WATCH THE BABY FOR US, SO MAYBE YOUR BROTHER AND I COULD GO OUT TO A RESTAURANT?
IT'S BEEN A LONG TIME SINCE IT'S JUST BEEN THE TWO OF US.
WATCH THE BABY?!
UH...
YEAH...NO PROBLEM...
GREAT!! THANKS!
WELL.. YOU'RE WELCOME.
AND HOW'S YOUR SHOW COMING ALONG?
OHHH..
WHEN I WAS PHOTOGRAPHING CORPSES, THEY SAID I WAS INTERESTING. NOW THAT I'M INTERESTED IN THE LIVING, I'VE GOTTEN "ORDINARY."

MY MOTHER SAYS, "IT'S NOT THE ROAD THAT'S DIFFICULT, IT'S THE DIFFICULTY THAT'S THE ROAD."

ALL THE SAME, MY MOTHER SAYS A LOT OF STUPID THINGS!

wAAAAHHHHHHHHHHHHHHHHH

OH SHIT!

wwwAAAAAAAHHHHHHHH

YEAH, YEAH! ALL RIGHT, I'M COMING!

wwwAAAAAAAHHHHHHHH

wwwAAAAAAAHHHHHHHH

WHAT TIME DOES THE ADOPTION AGENCY OFFICE OPEN?

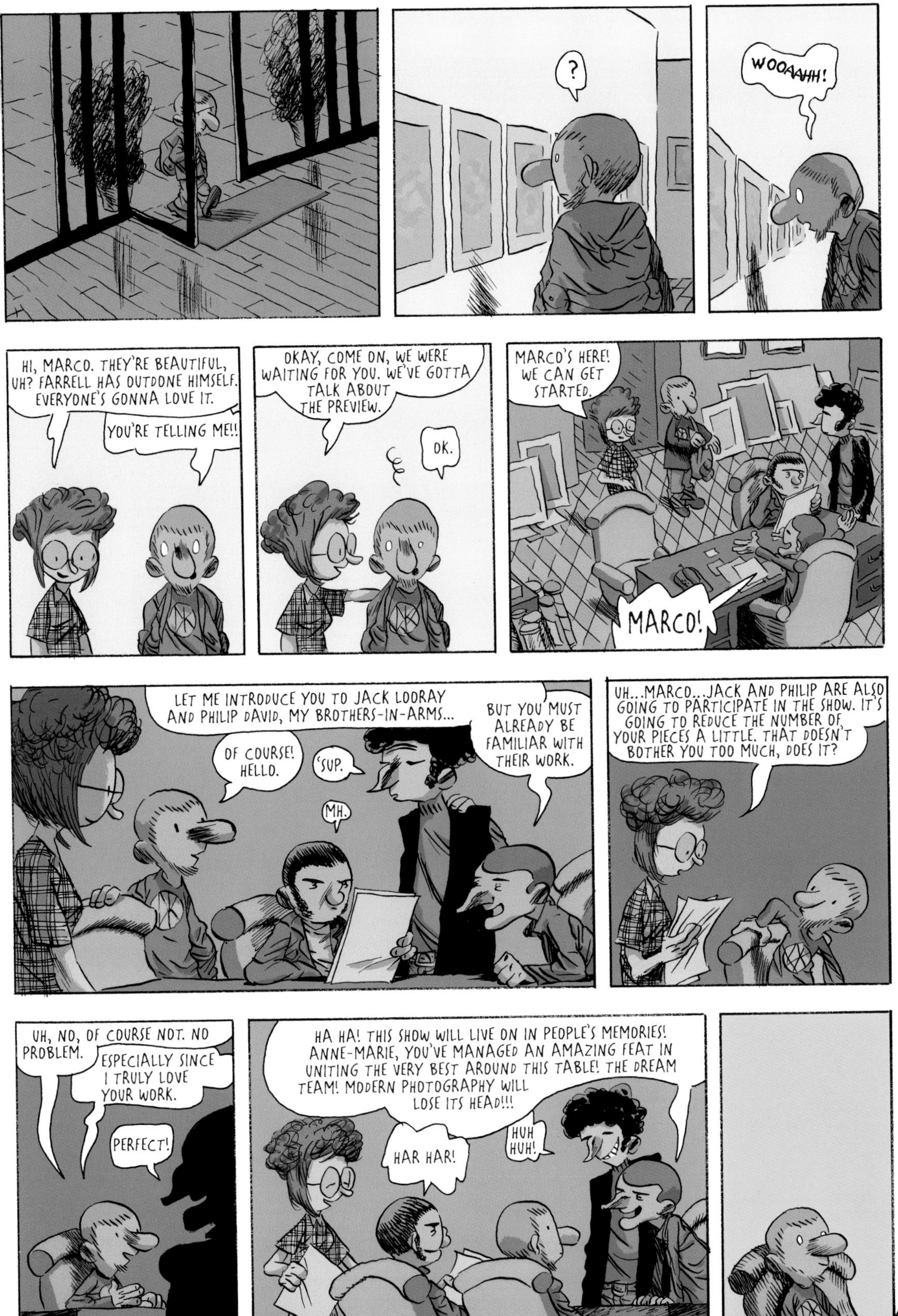
?
WOOAAHH!
HI, MARCO. THEY'RE BEAUTIFUL, UH? FARRELL HAS OUTDONE HIMSELF. EVERYONE'S GONNA LOVE IT.
YOU'RE TELLING ME!!
OKAY, COME ON, WE WERE WAITING FOR YOU. WE'VE GOTTA TALK ABOUT THE PREVIEW.
OK.
MARCO'S HERE! WE CAN GET STARTED.
MARCO!
LET ME INTRODUCE YOU TO JACK LOORAY AND PHILIP DAVID, MY BROTHERS-IN-ARMS...
BUT YOU MUST ALREADY BE FAMILIAR WITH THEIR WORK.
OF COURSE! HELLO.
'SUP.
MH.
UH...MARCO...JACK AND PHILIP ARE ALSO GOING TO PARTICIPATE IN THE SHOW. IT'S GOING TO REDUCE THE NUMBER OF YOUR PIECES A LITTLE. THAT DOESN'T BOTHER YOU TOO MUCH, DOES IT?
UH, NO, OF COURSE NOT. NO PROBLEM.
ESPECIALLY SINCE I TRULY LOVE YOUR WORK.
PERFECT!
HA HA! THIS SHOW WILL LIVE ON IN PEOPLE'S MEMORIES! ANNE-MARIE, YOU'VE MANAGED AN AMAZING FEAT IN UNITING THE VERY BEST AROUND THIS TABLE! THE DREAM TEAM! MODERN PHOTOGRAPHY WILL LOSE ITS HEAD!!!
HAR HAR!
HUH HUH!

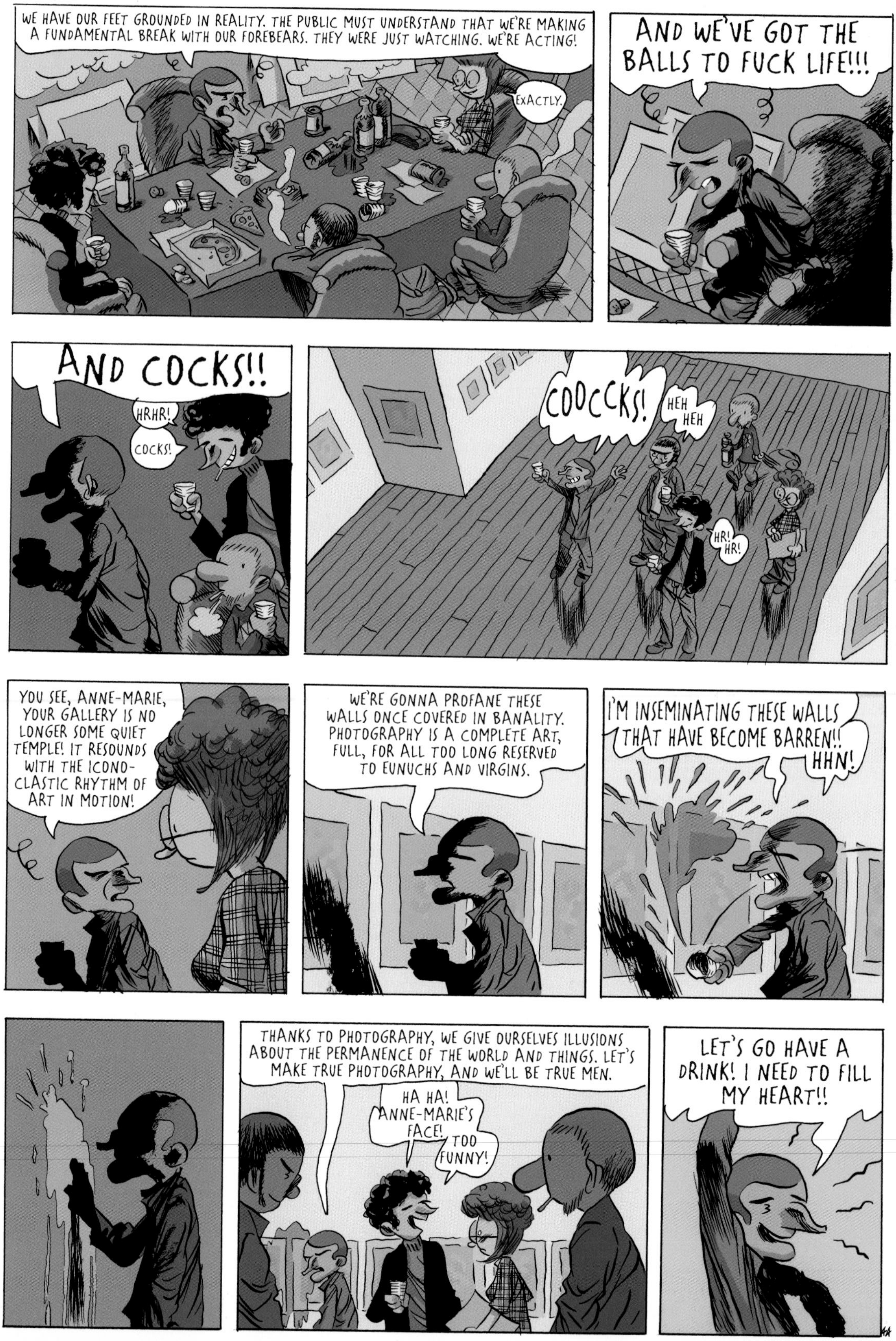
WE HAVE OUR FEET GROUNDED IN REALITY. THE PUBLIC MUST UNDERSTAND THAT WE'RE MAKING A FUNDAMENTAL BREAK WITH OUR FOREBEARS. THEY WERE JUST WATCHING. WE'RE ACTING!
EXACTLY.
AND WE'VE GOT THE BALLS TO FUCK LIFE!!!
AND COCKS!!
HRHR!
COCKS!
COOCCKS!
HEH HEH
HR! HR!
YOU SEE, ANNE-MARIE, YOUR GALLERY IS NO LONGER SOME QUIET TEMPLE! IT RESOUNDS WITH THE ICONO-CLASTIC RHYTHM OF ART IN MOTION!
WE'RE GONNA PROFANE THESE WALLS ONCE COVERED IN BANALITY. PHOTOGRAPHY IS A COMPLETE ART, FULL, FOR ALL TOO LONG RESERVED TO EUNUCHS AND VIRGINS.
I'M INSEMINATING THESE WALLS THAT HAVE BECOME BARREN!!
HHN!
THANKS TO PHOTOGRAPHY, WE GIVE OURSELVES ILLUSIONS ABOUT THE PERMANENCE OF THE WORLD AND THINGS. LET'S MAKE TRUE PHOTOGRAPHY, AND WE'LL BE TRUE MEN.
HA HA! ANNE-MARIE'S FACE!
TOO FUNNY!
LET'S GO HAVE A DRINK! I NEED TO FILL MY HEART!!

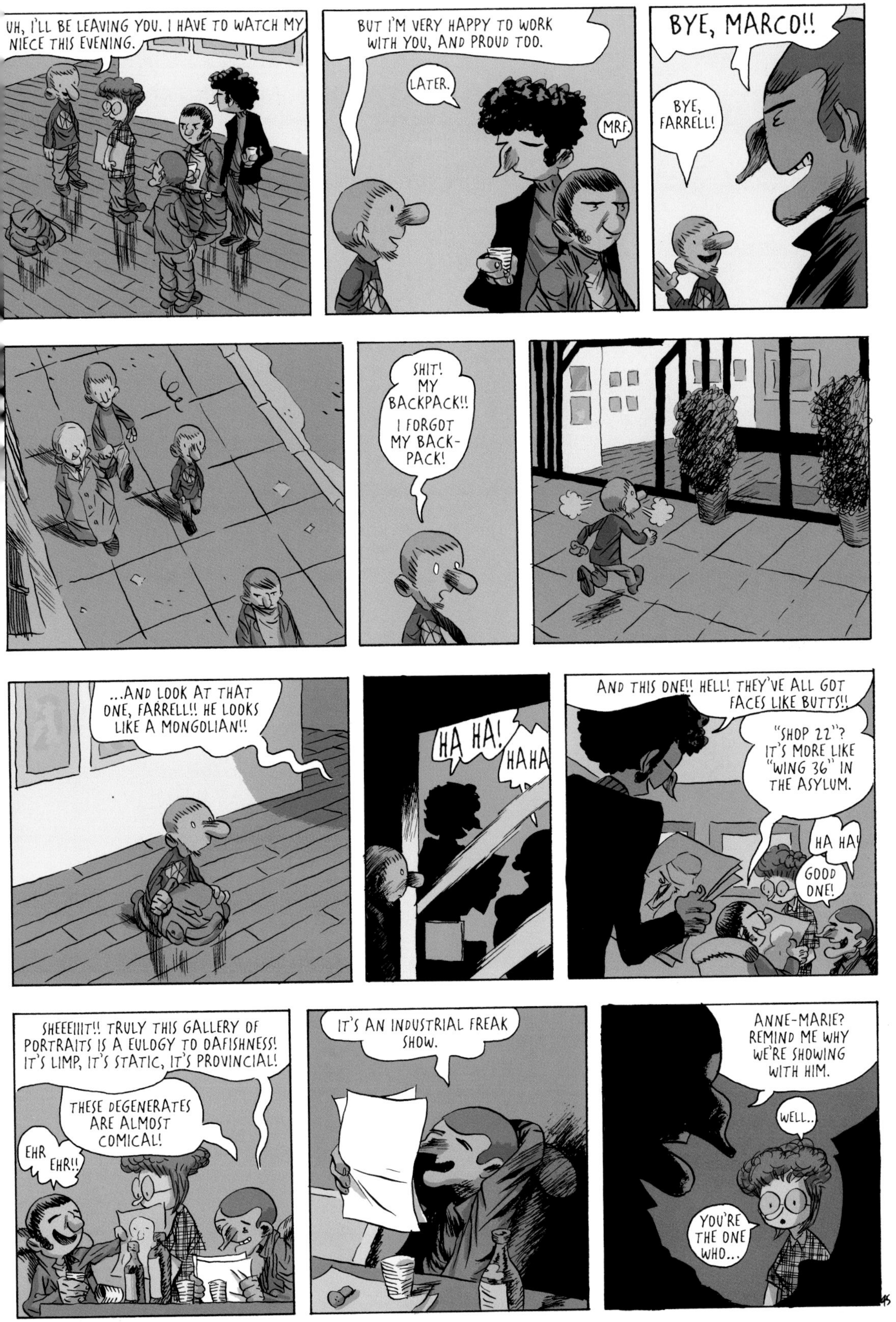
UH, I'LL BE LEAVING YOU. I HAVE TO WATCH MY NIECE THIS EVENING.
BUT I'M VERY HAPPY TO WORK WITH YOU, AND PROUD TOO.
LATER.
MRF.
BYE, MARCO!!
BYE, FARRELL!
SHIT! MY BACKPACK!! I FORGOT MY BACK-PACK!
...AND LOOK AT THAT ONE, FARRELL!! HE LOOKS LIKE A MONGOLIAN!!
HA HA!
HAHA
AND THIS ONE!! HELL! THEY'VE ALL GOT FACES LIKE BUTTS!!
"SHOP 22"? IT'S MORE LIKE "WING 36" IN THE ASYLUM.
HA HA!
GOOD ONE!
SHEEEIIIT!! TRULY THIS GALLERY OF PORTRAITS IS A EULOGY TO DAFISHNESS! IT'S LIMP, IT'S STATIC, IT'S PROVINCIAL!
THESE DEGENERATES ARE ALMOST COMICAL!
EHR
EHR!!
IT'S AN INDUSTRIAL FREAK SHOW.
ANNE-MARIE? REMIND ME WHY WE'RE SHOWING WITH HIM.
WELL..
YOU'RE THE ONE WHO...

I LONG CONFUSED THE ARTIST WITH HIS WORK.

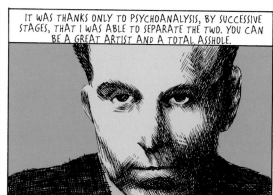

IT WAS THANKS ONLY TO PSYCHOANALYSIS, BY SUCCESSIVE STAGES, THAT I WAS ABLE TO SEPARATE THE TWO. YOU CAN BE A GREAT ARTIST AND A TOTAL ASSHOLE.

YOU CAN DO VERY BEAUTIFUL THINGS, WHILE BEING RATHER UGLY YOURSELF. YOU CAN CAPTURE ALL THE BEAUTY OF THE WORLD ON PAPER, YET NEVER BE PART OF IT.

IT'S STRANGE: HOW CAN ONE BE SO SURPASSED BY WHAT ONE CREATES?

BUT IF THE WORK IS BETTER THAN THE ARTIST, WHY DOESN'T IT IMPROVE HIM?

THE HAND REACHES FOR THE DIVINE, WHILE THE FEET FLOUNDER IN MEDIOCRITY.

WHETHER YOU PREFER ONE OR THE OTHER, THE MESSENGER AND THE MESSAGE MAY NEVER MERGE TOGETHER.

MY BUTCHER IS AN ABOMINABLE FELLOW, BUT HIS DRIED HAM IS A PURE MOMENT OF HAPPINESS...ART AND THE DELI.

46

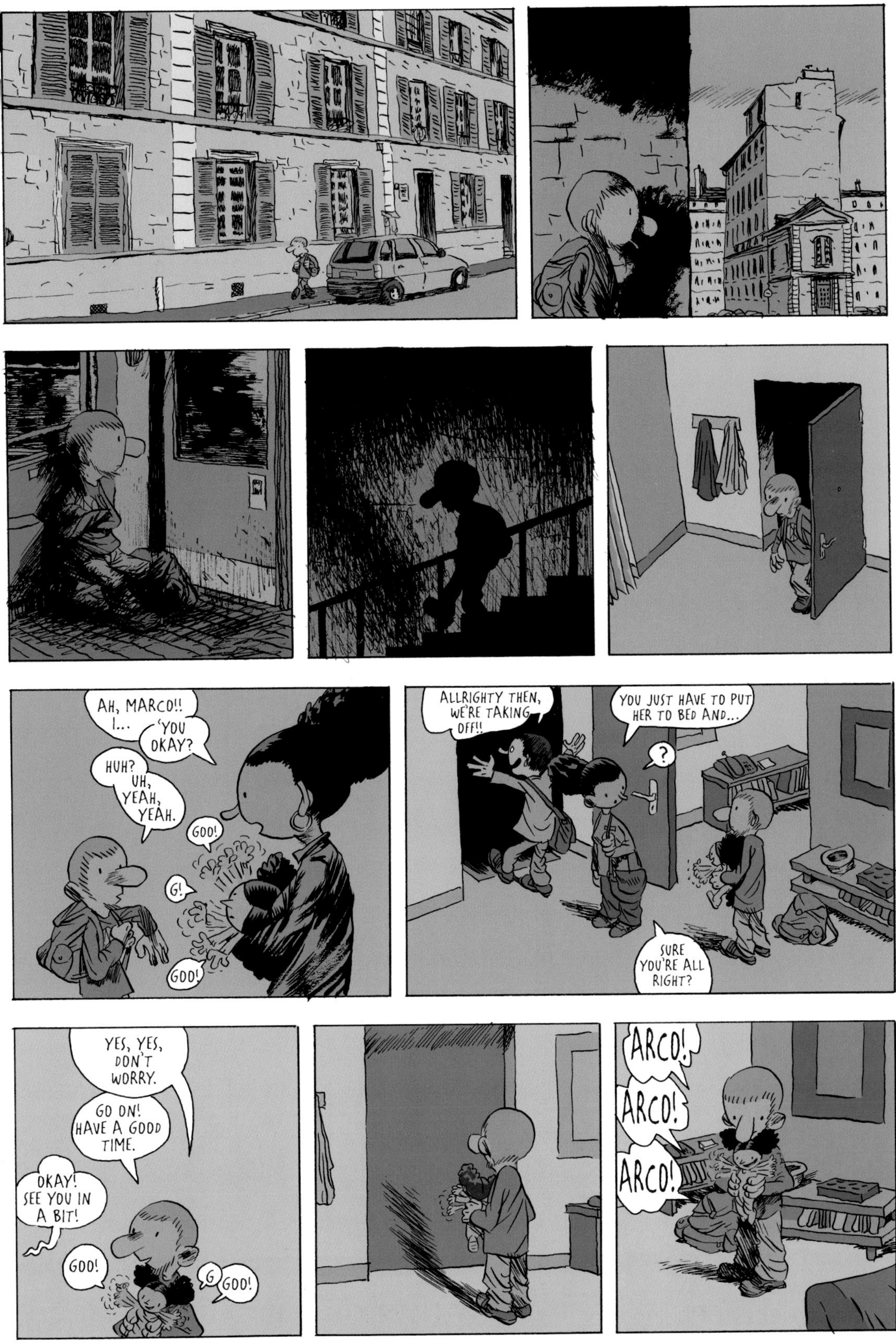
AH, MARCO!! I...
'YOU OKAY?
HUH? UH, YEAH, YEAH.
GOO!
G!
GOO!
ALLRIGHTY THEN, WE'RE TAKING OFF!!
YOU JUST HAVE TO PUT HER TO BED AND...
?
SURE YOU'RE ALL RIGHT?
YES, YES, DON'T WORRY.
GO ON! HAVE A GOOD TIME.
OKAY! SEE YOU IN A BIT!
GOO!
G
GOO!
ARCO!
ARCO!
ARCO!

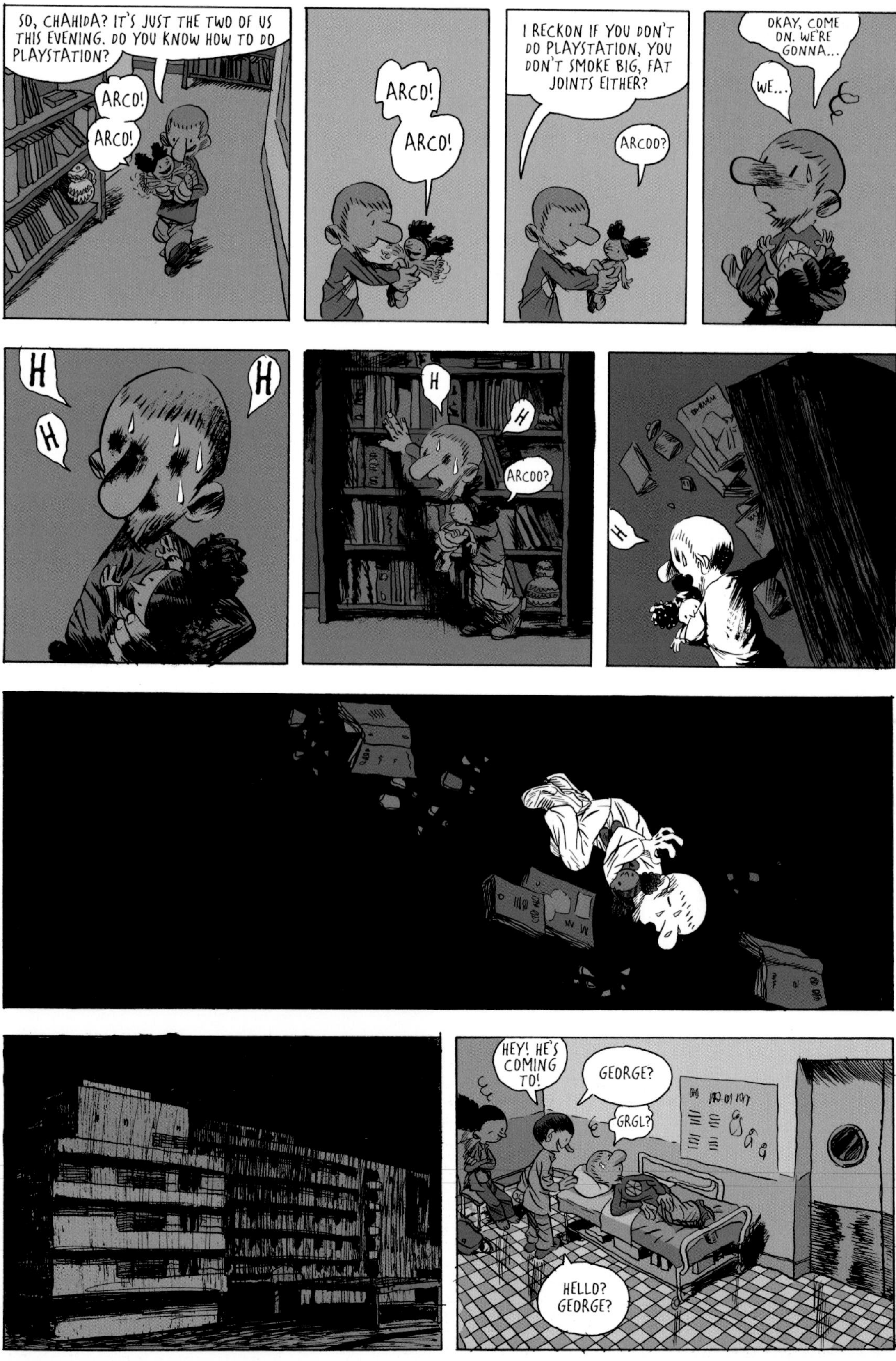
SO, CHAHIDA? IT'S JUST THE TWO OF US THIS EVENING. DO YOU KNOW HOW TO DO PLAYSTATION?
ARCO!
ARCO!
ARCO!
ARCO!
I RECKON IF YOU DON'T DO PLAYSTATION, YOU DON'T SMOKE BIG, FAT JOINTS EITHER?
ARCOO?
OKAY, COME ON. WE'RE GONNA...
WE...
H
H
H
H
H
ARCOO?
H
HEY! HE'S COMING TO!
GEORGE?
GRGL?
HELLO? GEORGE?

HELLO HELLO? GEORGE, THIS IS THE CONTROL TOWER... DO YOU READ ME?

KRSHHH

STOP YOUR SILLINESS!

HOW'S IT GOING, MARCO?

I'M TIRED...WHAT HAPPENED...

THE BABY?!!

CALM DOWN! WE FOUND YOU PASSED OUT WHEN WE GOT BACK, AND WE BROUGHT YOU HERE.

KRSHH 800 FEET COMING

AND THE BABY?!!

SHE'S JUST FINE! SHE'S AT A FRIEND'S HOME. IN FACT, WHEN WE FOUND YOU, SHE WAS SLEEPING IN YOUR ARMS.

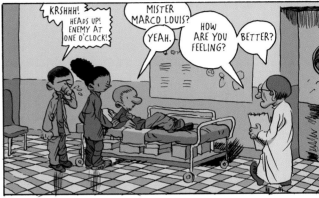

KRSHHH! HEADS UP! ENEMY AT ONE O'CLOCK!

MISTER MARCO LOUIS?

YEAH.

HOW ARE YOU FEELING?

BETTER?

I'M VERY TIRED.

YOUR BROTHER TOLD ME THAT YOU'VE HAD A PSYCHIATRIC HISTORY.

NO. I HAD PSYCHO-ANALYSIS FOR EIGHT YEARS, WHICH HAS NOTHING TO DO WITH PSYCHIA-TRY.

DO YOU REMEMBER WHAT HAPPENED TO YOU LAST NIGHT?

I HAD A STRONG PANIC ATTACK AND I FAINTED. IT HAPPENS TO ME SOMETIMES. I'M USED TO IT.

BUT YOU WERE WATCHING OVER A VERY YOUNG CHILD, WEREN'T YOU?

YES.

YOUR BROTHER TELLS ME THAT YOU'RE ON AN ANXIOLYTIC DRUG THERAPY?

I DIDN'T HAVE TIME TO TAKE THEM.

49

OKAY. I WON'T BOTHER YOU ANY MORE, MISTER LOUIS. STILL, WE'LL KEEP YOU OVERNIGHT.

AND I'LL ASK A PSYCHIATRIST TO COME SEE YOU.

KRSHHH! READY FOR LIFT OFF?

?

READY!

W... WAIT.

MAYBE IT'D BE BETTER IF WE WAITED A LITTLE, NO?

IF WE WAIT, THEY'RE GONNA SEND HIM OFF TO THE LOONY BIN FOR THE NIGHT.

THEY DON'T HAVE ANY PSYCHIATRIC WARD HERE, SO THEY DUMP THEIR DOUBTFUL CASES ON THE PSYCH-HOSPITAL IN SAINTE-ANNE. IT'S ALREADY HAPPENED TO ME.

I JUST NEED SOME SLEEP.

PFSHHRRT! IMMEDIATE LIFT-OFF!

I'M SORRY ABOUT CHAHIDA.

NOTHING'S WRONG WITH HER, WHICH IS THE IMPORTANT THING. AND ALSO, IT'S NOT YOUR FAULT.

ON THE OTHER HAND, YOU OWE US A MING VASE!

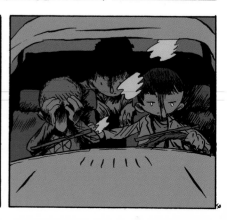

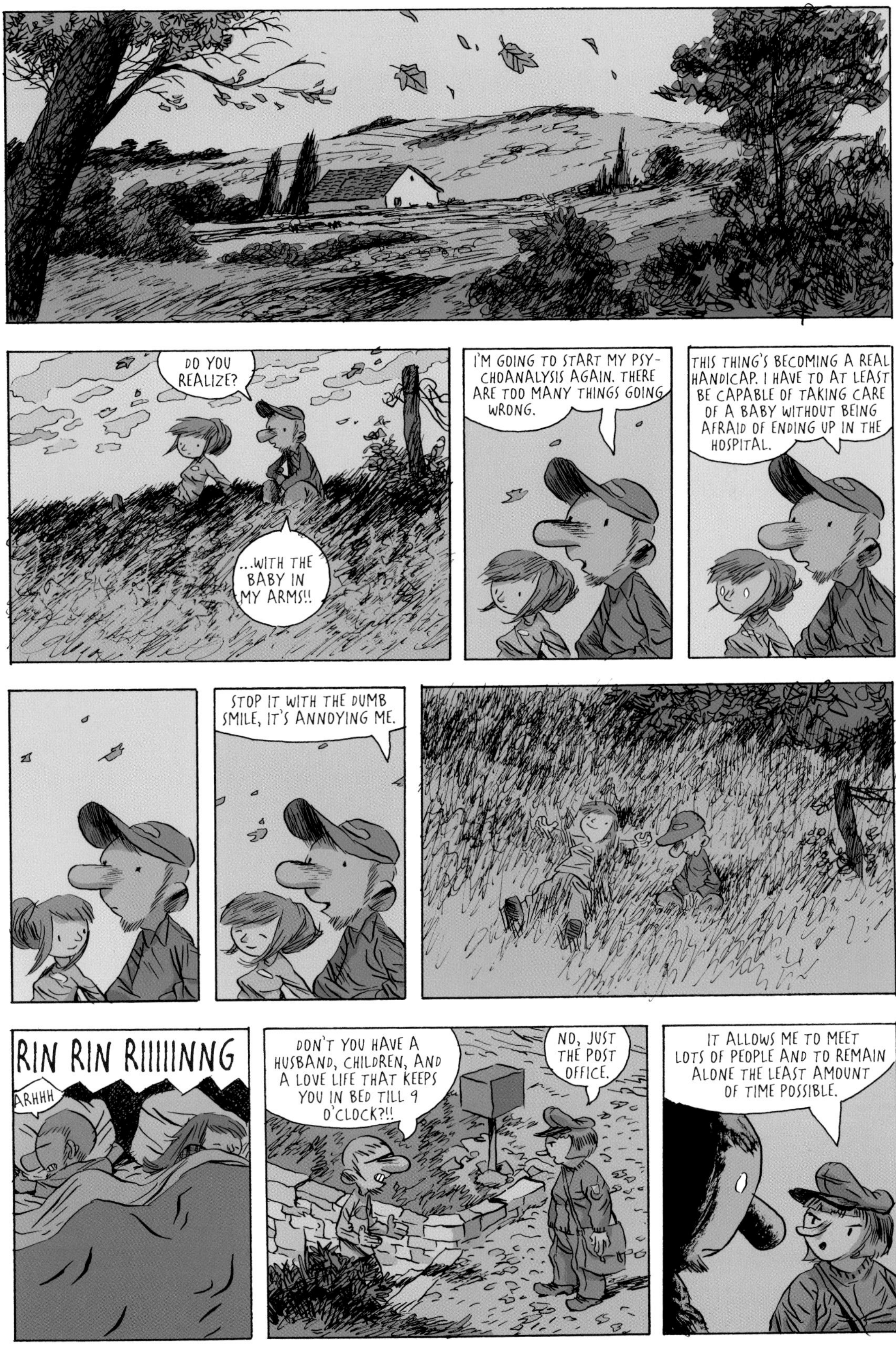

DO YOU REALIZE?
...WITH THE BABY IN MY ARMS!!
I'M GOING TO START MY PSYCHOANALYSIS AGAIN. THERE ARE TOO MANY THINGS GOING WRONG.
THIS THING'S BECOMING A REAL HANDICAP. I HAVE TO AT LEAST BE CAPABLE OF TAKING CARE OF A BABY WITHOUT BEING AFRAID OF ENDING UP IN THE HOSPITAL.
STOP IT WITH THE DUMB SMILE, IT'S ANNOYING ME.
RIN RIN RIIIIINNG
ARHHH
DON'T YOU HAVE A HUSBAND, CHILDREN, AND A LOVE LIFE THAT KEEPS YOU IN BED TILL 9 O'CLOCK?!!
NO, JUST THE POST OFFICE.
IT ALLOWS ME TO MEET LOTS OF PEOPLE AND TO REMAIN ALONE THE LEAST AMOUNT OF TIME POSSIBLE.

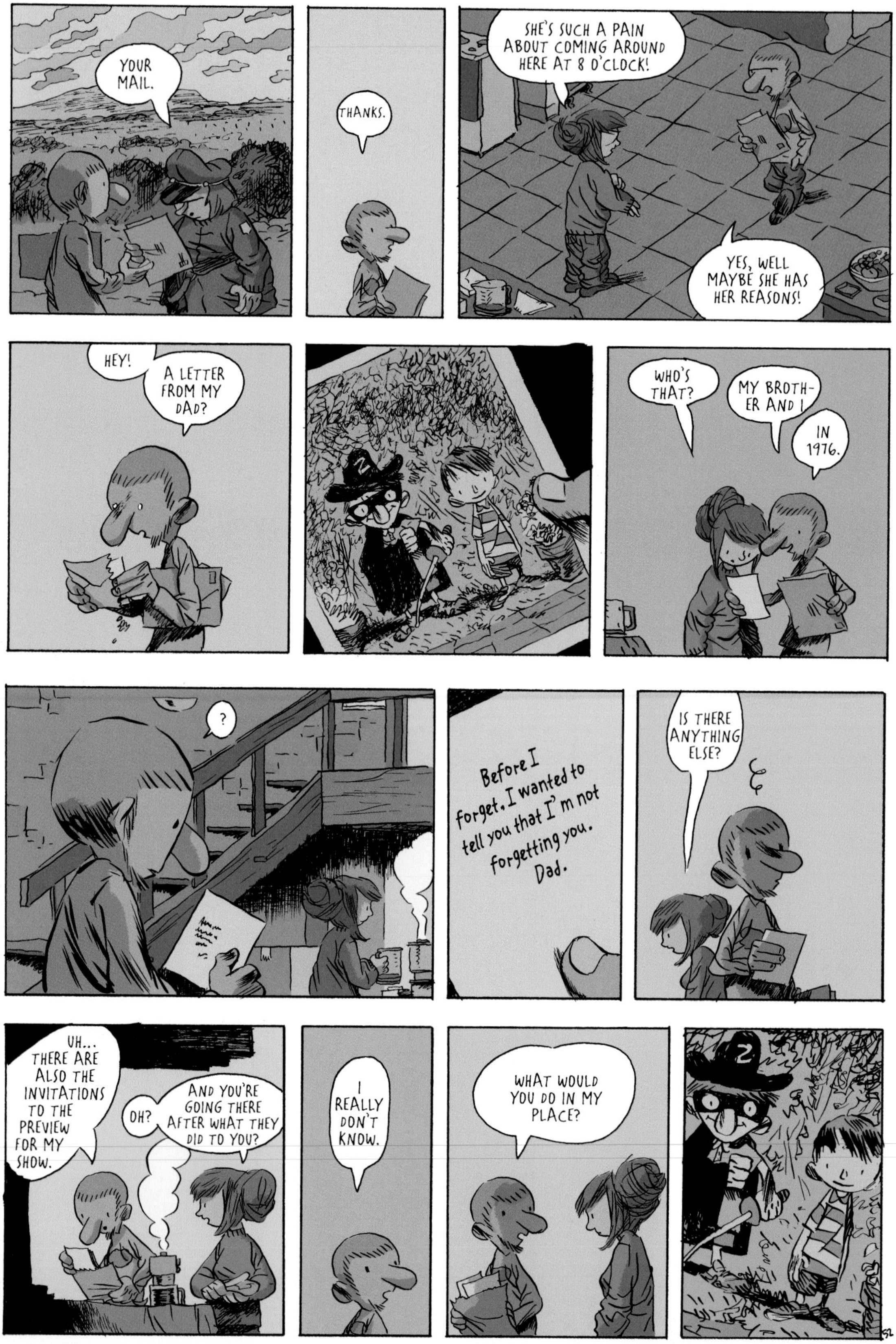
YOUR MAIL.
THANKS.
SHE'S SUCH A PAIN ABOUT COMING AROUND HERE AT 8 O'CLOCK!
YES, WELL MAYBE SHE HAS HER REASONS!
HEY!
A LETTER FROM MY DAD?
WHO'S THAT?
MY BROTHER AND I.
IN 1976.
?
Before I forget, I wanted to tell you that I'm not forgetting you. Dad.
IS THERE ANYTHING ELSE?
UH... THERE ARE ALSO THE INVITATIONS TO THE PREVIEW FOR MY SHOW.
OH?
AND YOU'RE GOING THERE AFTER WHAT THEY DID TO YOU?
I REALLY DON'T KNOW.
WHAT WOULD YOU DO IN MY PLACE?

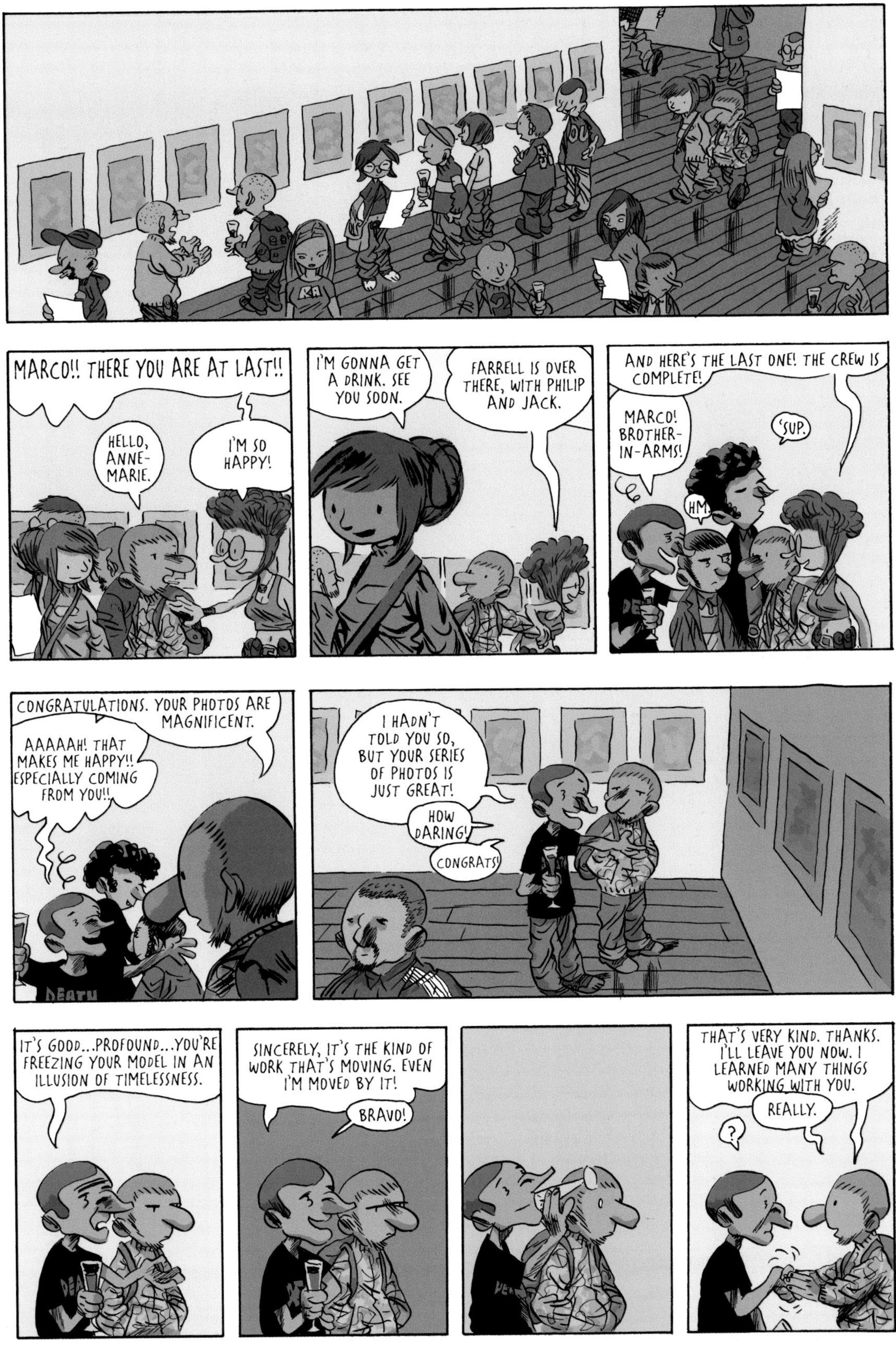
MARCO!! THERE YOU ARE AT LAST!!
HELLO, ANNE-MARIE.
I'M SO HAPPY!
I'M GONNA GET A DRINK. SEE YOU SOON.
FARRELL IS OVER THERE, WITH PHILIP AND JACK.
AND HERE'S THE LAST ONE! THE CREW IS COMPLETE!
MARCO! BROTHER-IN-ARMS!
'SUP.
HM.
CONGRATULATIONS. YOUR PHOTOS ARE MAGNIFICENT.
AAAAAH! THAT MAKES ME HAPPY!! ESPECIALLY COMING FROM YOU!!
I HADN'T TOLD YOU SO, BUT YOUR SERIES OF PHOTOS IS JUST GREAT!
HOW DARING!
CONGRATS!
IT'S GOOD...PROFOUND...YOU'RE FREEZING YOUR MODEL IN AN ILLUSION OF TIMELESSNESS.
SINCERELY, IT'S THE KIND OF WORK THAT'S MOVING. EVEN I'M MOVED BY IT!
BRAVO!
THAT'S VERY KIND. THANKS. I'LL LEAVE YOU NOW. I LEARNED MANY THINGS WORKING WITH YOU.
REALLY.
?

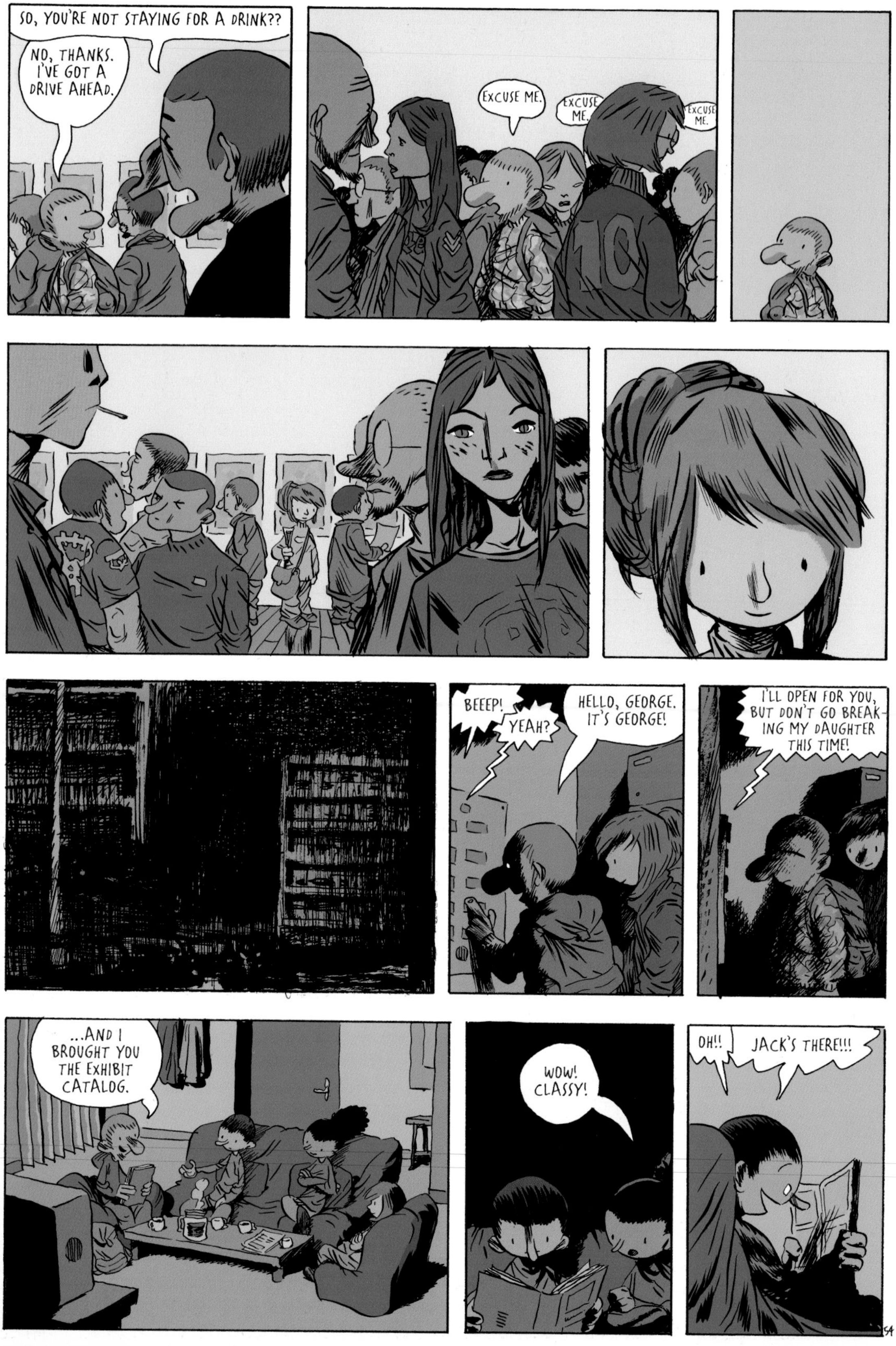
SO, YOU'RE NOT STAYING FOR A DRINK??
NO, THANKS. I'VE GOT A DRIVE AHEAD.
EXCUSE ME.
EXCUSE ME.
EXCUSE ME.
BEEEP!
YEAH?
HELLO, GEORGE. IT'S GEORGE!
I'LL OPEN FOR YOU, BUT DON'T GO BREAKING MY DAUGHTER THIS TIME!
...AND I BROUGHT YOU THE EXHIBIT CATALOG.
WOW! CLASSY!
OH!!
JACK'S THERE!!!

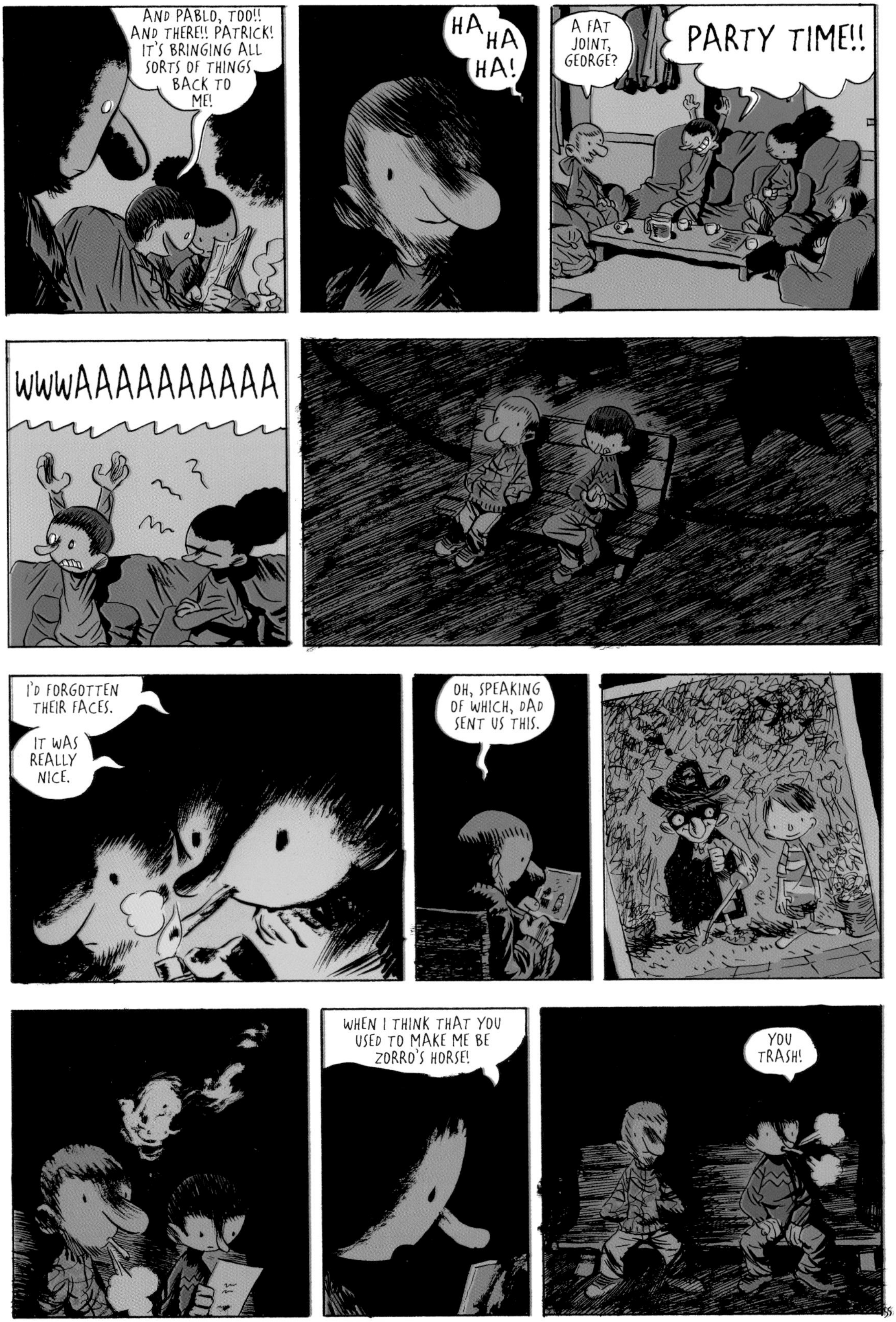

AND PABLO, TOO!! AND THERE!! PATRICK! IT'S BRINGING ALL SORTS OF THINGS BACK TO ME!
HA HA HA!
A FAT JOINT, GEORGE?
PARTY TIME!!
WWWAAAAAAAAAA
I'D FORGOTTEN THEIR FACES.
IT WAS REALLY NICE.
OH, SPEAKING OF WHICH, DAD SENT US THIS.
WHEN I THINK THAT YOU USED TO MAKE ME BE ZORRO'S HORSE!
YOU TRASH!

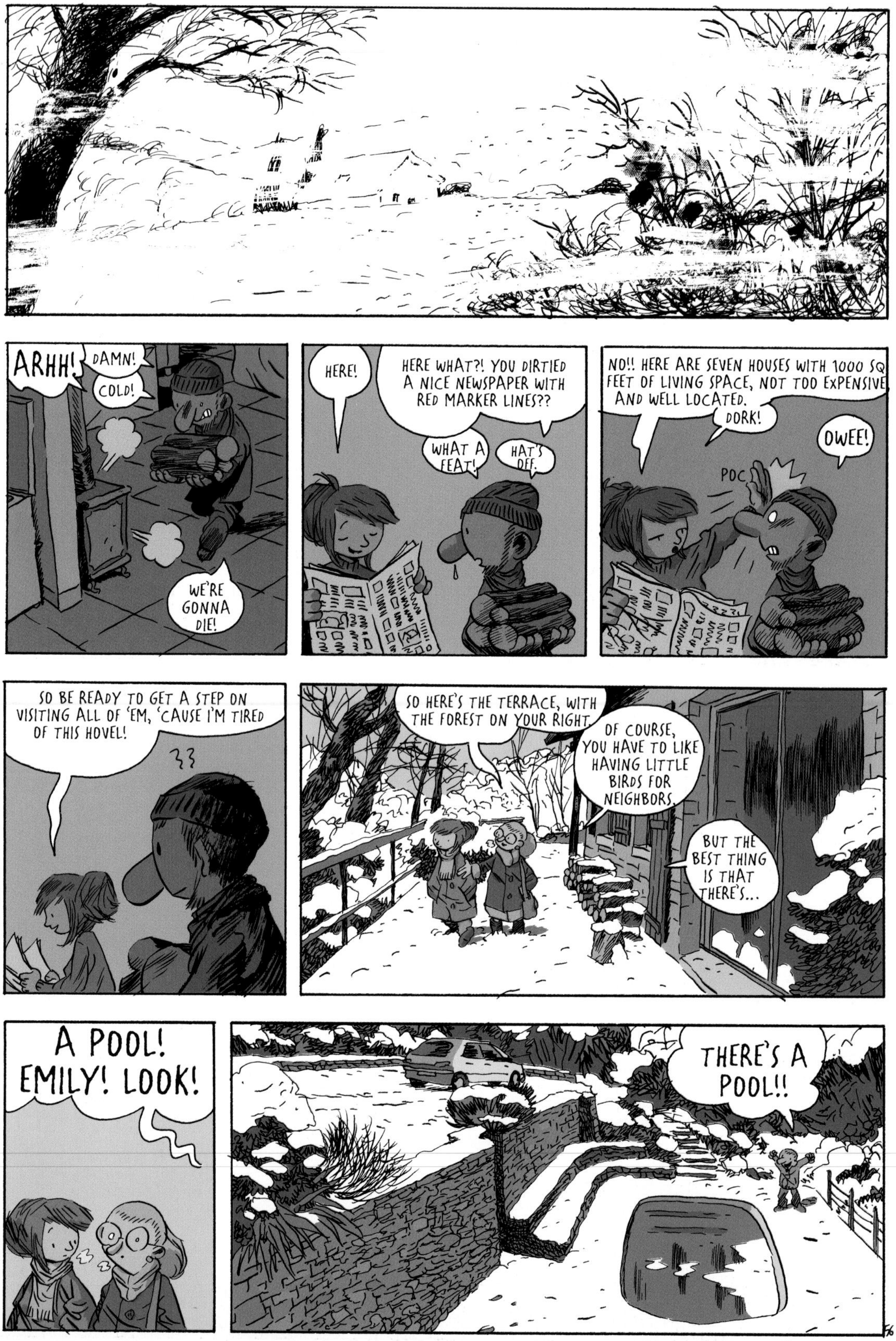
ARHH!
DAMN!
COLD!
WE'RE GONNA DIE!
HERE!
HERE WHAT?! YOU DIRTIED A NICE NEWSPAPER WITH RED MARKER LINES??
WHAT A FEAT!
HAT'S OFF.
NO!! HERE ARE SEVEN HOUSES WITH 1000 SQ FEET OF LIVING SPACE, NOT TOO EXPENSIVE, AND WELL LOCATED.
DORK!
POC
OWEE!
SO BE READY TO GET A STEP ON VISITING ALL OF 'EM, 'CAUSE I'M TIRED OF THIS HOVEL!
SO HERE'S THE TERRACE, WITH THE FOREST ON YOUR RIGHT.
OF COURSE, YOU HAVE TO LIKE HAVING LITTLE BIRDS FOR NEIGHBORS.
BUT THE BEST THING IS THAT THERE'S...
A POOL! EMILY! LOOK!
THERE'S A POOL!!

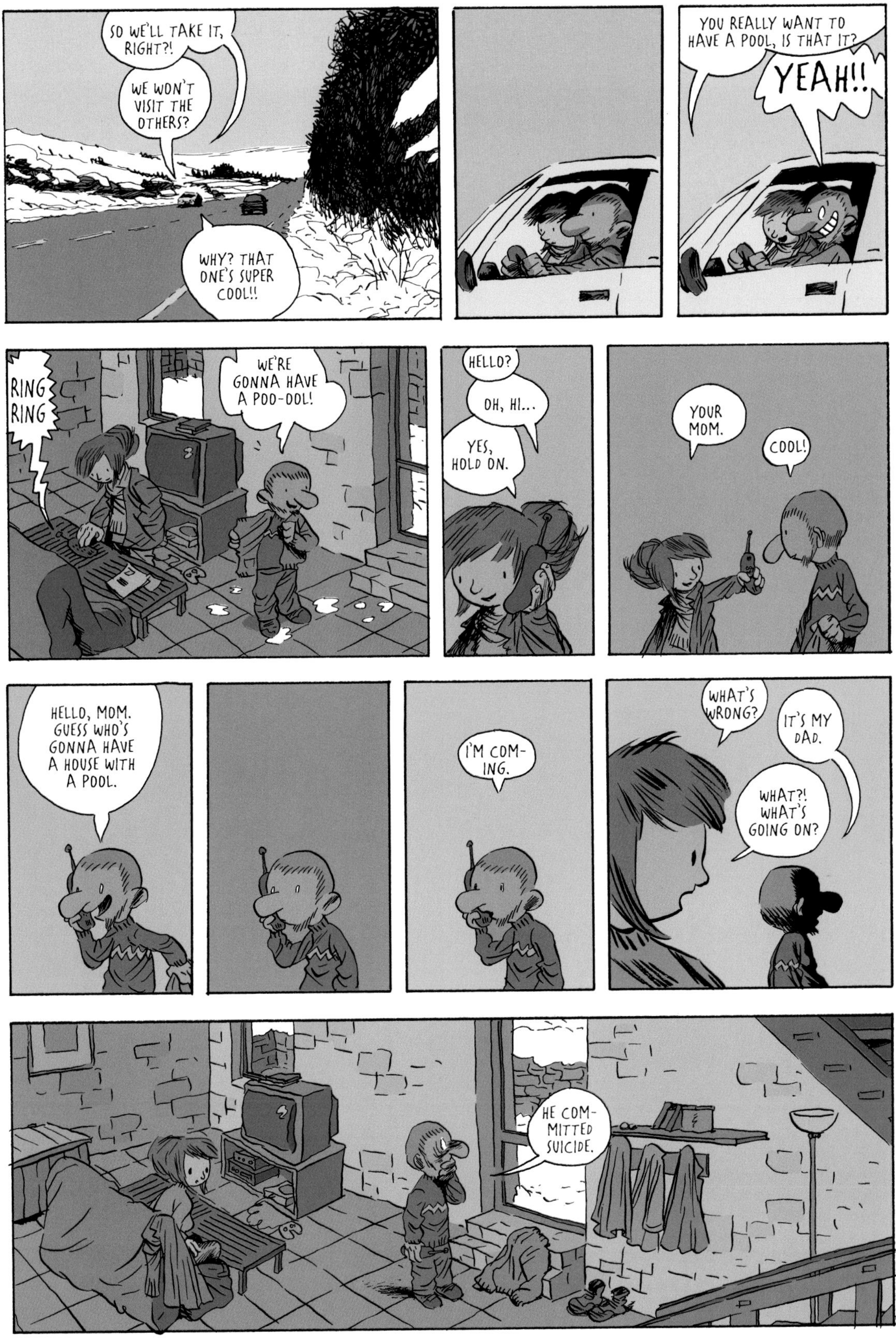
SO WE'LL TAKE IT, RIGHT?!
WE WON'T VISIT THE OTHERS?
WHY? THAT ONE'S SUPER COOL!!
YOU REALLY WANT TO HAVE A POOL, IS THAT IT?
YEAH!!
RING RING
WE'RE GONNA HAVE A POO-OOL!
HELLO?
OH, HI...
YES, HOLD ON.
YOUR MOM.
COOL!
HELLO, MOM. GUESS WHO'S GONNA HAVE A HOUSE WITH A POOL.
I'M COM-ING.
WHAT'S WRONG?
IT'S MY DAD.
WHAT?! WHAT'S GOING ON?
HE COM-MITTED SUICIDE.

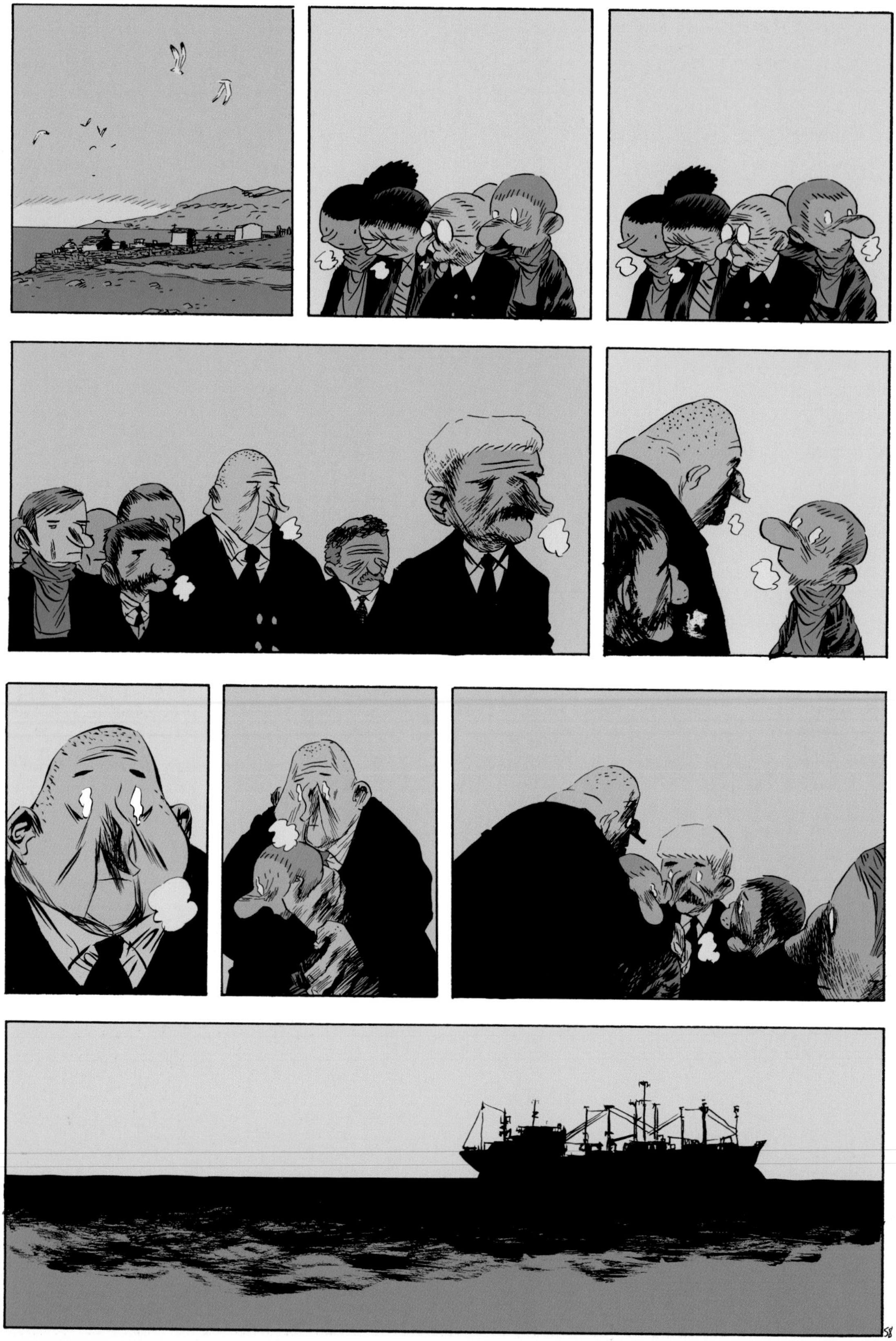

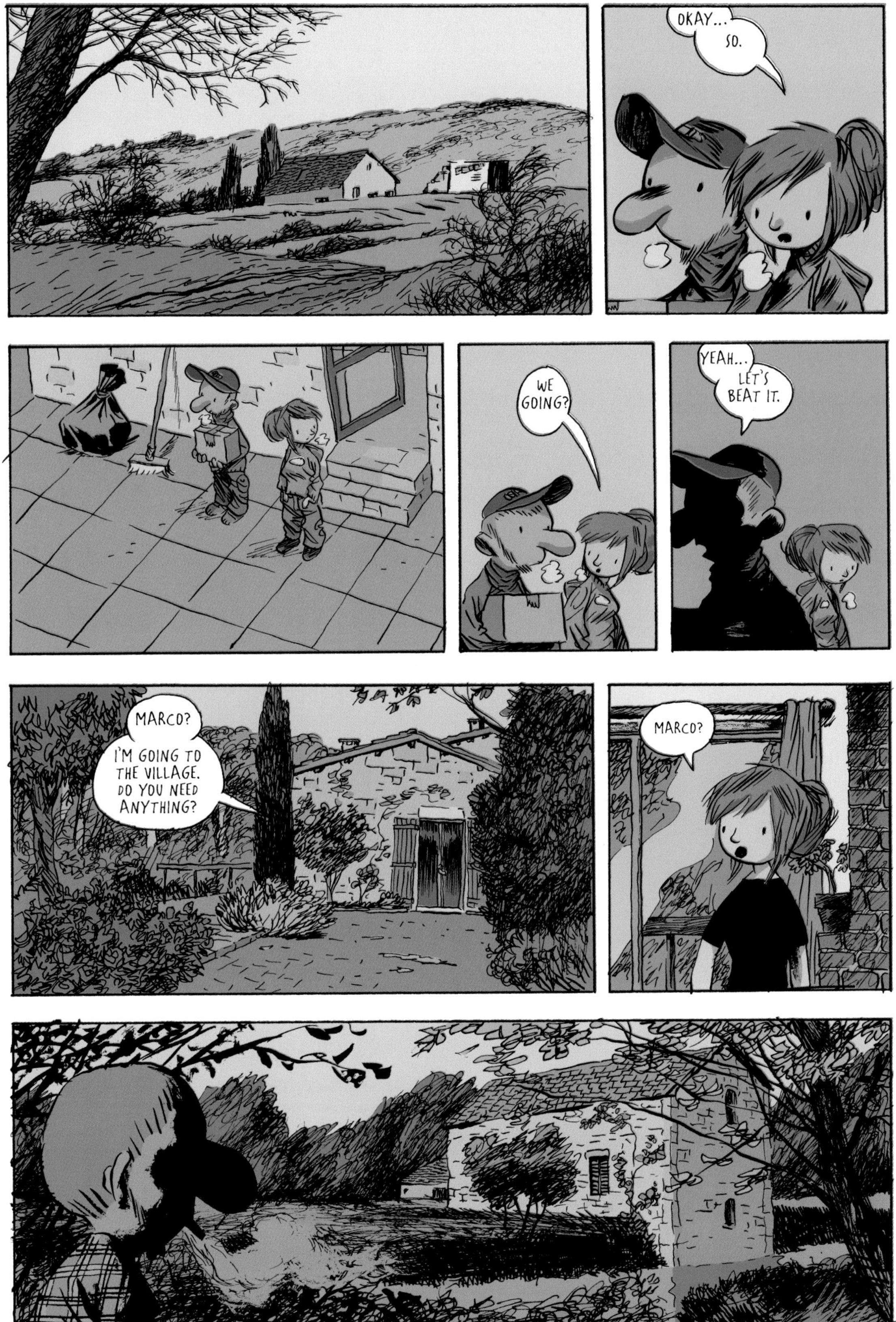
OKAY... SO.
WE GOING?
YEAH... LET'S BEAT IT.
MARCO?
I'M GOING TO THE VILLAGE. DO YOU NEED ANYTHING?
MARCO?

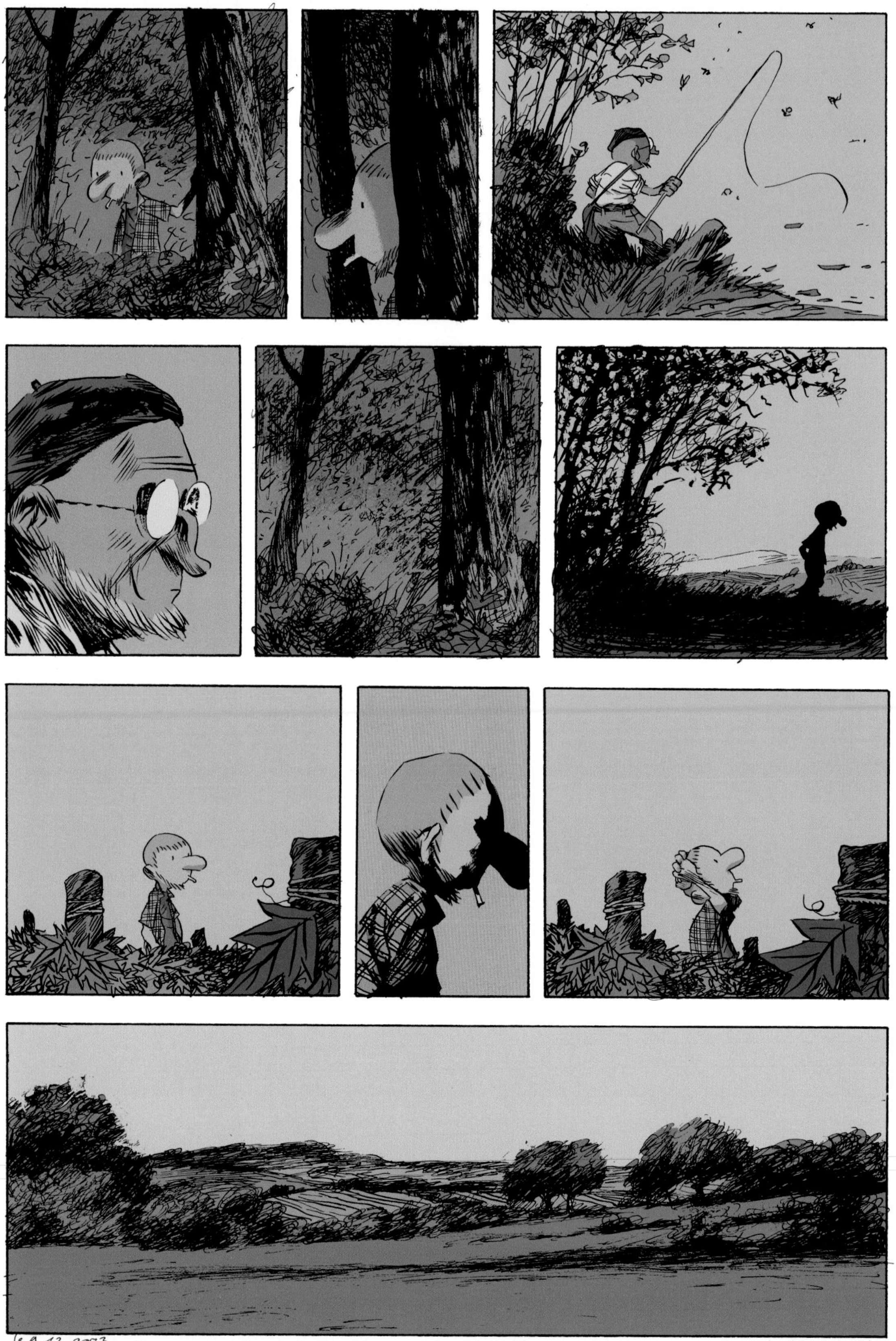

le 9 12 2003

manu larcenet

Also available by Larcenet
With Lewis Trondheim:
Astronauts of the Future, $14.95
From ComicsLit:
Isaac the Pirate, vols 1,2, $14.95 each

($3 P&H 1st item, $1 each addt'l)

We have over 200 graphic novels in
stock, ask for our color catalog:
NBM
555 8th Ave., Suite 1202
New York, NY 10018
www.nbmpublishing.com

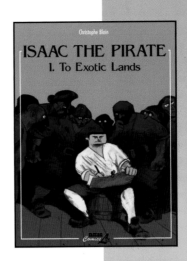